# Latin American
# Spanish

phrase book & dictionary

KU-538-512

**Berlitz Publishing**
**New York   London   Singapore**

**Contacting the Editors**
Every effort has been made to provide accurate information in this publication, but changes are inevitable. The publisher cannot be responsible for any resulting loss, inconvenience or injury. We would appreciate it if readers would call our attention to any errors or outdated information. We also welcome your suggestions; if you come across a relevant expression not in our phrase book, please contact us at: **comments@berlitzpublishing.com**

All Rights Reserved
© 2007 Berlitz Publishing/APA Publications (UK) Ltd.
Berlitz Trademark Reg. U.S. Patent Office and other countries. Marca Registrada. Used under license from Berlitz Investment Corporation.

**Eleventh Printing:** March 2012
Printed in China

**Publishing Director:** Mina Patria
**Commissioning Editor:** Kate Drynan
**Editorial Assistant:** Sophie Cooper
**Translation:** updated by Wordbank
**Cover Design:** Beverley Speight
**Interior Design:** Beverley Speight
**Production Manager:** Raj Trivedi
**Picture Researcher:** Beverley Speight
**Cover Photo:** All shots Team Nowitz/APA except 'currency' image iStockphoto.

**Interior Photos:** Alex Havret/APA 16, 41, 80, 130, 142; iStockphoto 141, 151, 152, 155, 159; Britta Jaschinski/APA 45, 148, 162; Lucy Johnston/APA 178; Mockford & Bonetti/APA 32, 55, 57, 127, 128; Abraham Nowitz/APA 93, 110, 113, 119, 122, 147; Richard Nowitz/APA 1, 18, 23, 26, 29, 49, 96, 109, 114, 145; Corrie Wingate/APA 12, 100, 103, 134.

# Contents

## Food & Drink

## People

## Leisure Time

## Special Requirements

## In an Emergency

## Dictionary

# Pronunciation

This section is designed to make you familiar with the sounds of Spanish using our simplified phonetic transcription. You'll find the pronunciation of the Spanish letters and sounds explained below, together with their 'imitated' equivalents. This system is used throughout the phrase book; simply read the pronunciation as if it were English, noting any special rules below.

Underlined letters indicate that that syllable should be stressed. The acute accent ´ indicates stress, e.g. **río**, _ree_-oh. Some Spanish words have more than one meaning. In these instances, the accent mark is also used to distinguish between them, e.g.: **él** (he) and **el** (the); **sí** (yes) and **si** (if).

There are some differences in vocabulary and pronunciation between the Spanish spoken in Spain and that in the Americas—although each is easily understood by the other. This phrase book and dictionary is specifically geared to travelers in Latin America.

## Consonants

| Letter | Approximate Pronunciation | Symbol | Example | Pronunciation |
|--------|---------------------------|--------|---------|---------------|
| **b** | 1. as in English | **b** | **bueno** | _bweh_•noh |
| | 2. between vowels as in English, | **b** | **bebida** | beh•_bee_•dah |
| **c** | 1. before e and i like s in same | **s** | **centro** | _sehn_•troh |
| | 2. otherwise like k in kit | **k** | **como** | _koh_•moh |
| **ch** | as in English | **ch** | **mucho** | _moo_•choh |

| Letter | Pronunciation | Symbol | Example | Pronunciation |
|---|---|---|---|---|
| **d** | 1. as in English | **d** | **donde** | _dohn_·deh |
| **g** | 1. before e and i, like ch in Scottish loch | **kh** | **urgente** | oor·_khehn_·teh |
| | 2. otherwise, like g in get | **g** | **ninguno** | neen·_goo_·noh |
| **h** | always silent | | **hombre** | _ohm_·breh |
| **j** | like ch in Scottish loch | **kh** | **bajo** | _bah_·khoh |
| **ll** | like y in yellow | **y** | **lleno** | _yeh_·noh |
| **ñ** | like ni in onion | **ny** | **señor** | seh·_nyohr_ |
| **q** | like k in kick | **k** | **quince** | _keen_·seh |
| **r** | trilled, especially at the beginning of a word | **r** | **río** | _ree_·oh |
| **rr** | strongly trilled | **rr** | **arriba** | ah·_rree_·bah |
| **s** | 1. like s in same | **s** | **sus** | soos |
| | 2. before b, d, g, l, m, n, like s in rose | **z** | **mismo** | _meez_·moh |
| **v** | like b in bad, but softer | **b** | **viejo** | _beeyeh_·khoh |
| **z** | like s in same | **s** | **brazo** | _brah_·soh |

Letters f, k, l, m, n, p, t, w, x and y are pronounced as in English.

## Vowels

| Letter | Approximate Pronunciation | Symbol | Example | Pronunciation |
|---|---|---|---|---|
| **a** | like the a in father | ah | **gracias** | _grah·seeyahs_ |
| **e** | like e in get | eh | **esta** | _ehs·tah_ |
| **i** | like ee in meet | ee | **sí** | _see_ |
| **o** | like o in rope | oh | **dos** | _dohs_ |
| **u** | 1. like oo in food | oo | **uno** | _oo·noh_ |
| | 2. silent after g and q | | **que** | _keh_ |
| | 3. when marked ü, like we in well | w | **antigüedad** | _ahn·tee·gweh·dahd_ |
| **y** | 1. like y in yellow | y | **hoy** | _oy_ |
| | 2. when alone, like ee in meet | ee | **y** | _ee_ |
| | 3. when preceded by an a, sounds like y + ee, with ee faintly pronounced | aye | **hay** | _aye_ |

With nearly 400 million Spanish speakers worldwide, Spanish is the third most widely spoken language in the world and the official language of 21 different nations. Over 17 million people in the United States speak Spanish as their native language, and it is one of the official languages of the United Nations. Spanish is the fourth most popular language on the internet, behind English, Japanese and German. Below are estimated numbers of Spanish speakers around the globe.

Central America: 55 million
North America: 112 million
South America: 190 million
Spain: 40 million

# How to use this Book

Sometimes you see two alternatives separated by a slash. Choose the one that's right for your situation.

## ESSENTIAL

I'm on vacation [holiday]/ business.

**Estoy aquí de vacaciones/en viaje de negocios.** ehs·<u>toy</u> ah·<u>kee</u> deh bah·kah·<u>seeyohn</u>·ehs/ehn <u>beeyah</u>·kheh deh neh·<u>goh</u>·seeyohs

I'm going to...
I'm staying at the...
Hotel.

**Voy a...** boy ah...
**Me alojo en el Hotel...** meh ah·<u>loh</u>·khoh ehn ehl oh·<u>tehl</u>...

Words you may see are shown in YOU MAY SEE boxes.

## YOU MAY SEE...

| | |
|---|---|
| **ADUANAS** | customs |
| **ARTÍCULOS LIBRES DE IMPUESTOS** | duty-free goods |
| **ARTÍCULOS QUE DECLARAR** | goods to declare |

Any of the words or phrases listed can be plugged into the sentence below.

## Tickets

I'd like to rent [hire]...
    a bicycle
    a moped
    a motorcycle
How much per day/week?

**Quiero alquilar...** keeyeh·roh ahl·kee·<u>lahr</u>...
**una bicicleta** <u>oo</u>·nah bee·see·<u>kleh</u>·tah
**un ciclomotor** oon see·kloh·moh·<u>tohr</u>
**una motocicleta** <u>oo</u>·nah moh·toh·see·<u>kleh</u>·tah
**¿Cuánto cuesta por día/semana?** <u>kwahn</u>·toh <u>kwehs</u>·tah pohr <u>dee</u>·ah/seh·<u>mah</u>·nah

Spanish phrases appear in purple.

Read the simplified pronunciation as if it were English. For more on pronunciation, see page 7.

## The Dating Game

Can I join you?

**¿Puedo acompañarle _m_/acompañarla _f_?**
_pweh•doh ah•kohm•pah•nyahr•loh /
ah•kohm•pah•nyahr•lah_

You're very
attractive.

**Eres muy guapo _m_/guapa _f_.**
_eh•rehs mooy gwah•poh / gwah•pah_

For Grammar, see page 166.

Related phrases can be found by going to the page number indicated.

When different gender forms apply, the masculine form is followed by _m_; feminine by _f_

When addressing strangers, always use the more formal usted (singular) as opposed to a more familiar **tú** (singular) until told otherwise. **Usted** (plural) is used for addressing people in formal or familiar way. If you know someone's title, it's polite to use it, e.g., **doctor** (male doctor), **doctora** (female doctor). You can also simply say **Señor** (Mr.), **Señora** (Mrs.) or **Señorita** (Miss).

Information boxes contain relevant country, culture and language tips.

Expressions you may hear are shown in You May Hear boxes.

## YOU MAY HEAR...

**Hablo muy poco inglés.**
_ah•bloh mooy poh•koh een•glehs_

I only speak a little English.

Color-coded side bars identify each section of the book.

# Survival

## ESSENTIAL

| | |
|---|---|
| I'm here on vacation [holiday]/business. | **Estoy aquí de vacaciones/en viaje de negocios.** ehs•toy ah•kee deh bah•kah•seeyohn•ehs/ehn beeyah•kheh deh neh•goh•seeyohs |
| I'm going to… | **Voy a…** boy ah… |
| I'm staying at the… Hotel. | **Me alojo en el Hotel…** meh ah•loh•khoh ehn ehl oh•tehl… |

## YOU MAY HEAR…

**Su pasaporte, por favor.**
soo pah•sah•pohr•teh pohr fah•bohr

Your passport, please.

**¿Cuál es el propósito de su visita?**
kwahl ehs ehl proh•poh•see•toh deh
soo bee•see•tah

What's the purpose of your visit?

**¿Dónde se aloja?**
dohn•deh seh ah•loh•khah

Where are you staying?

**¿Cuánto tiempo piensa quedarse?**
kwahn•toh teeyehm•poh peeyehn•sah
keh•dar•seh

How long are you staying?

**¿Con quién viaja?**
kohn keeyehn beeyah•khah

Who are you here with?

## Border Control

| | |
|---|---|
| I'm Just passing through. | **Estoy de paso.** |
| | *ehs-toy deh pah-soh* |
| I'd like to declare… | **Quiero declarar…** *keeyeh-roh deh-klah-rahr…* |
| I have nothing to declare. | **No tengo nada que declarar.** |
| | *noh tehn-goh nah-dah keh deh-klah-rahr* |

### YOU MAY HEAR…

**¿Tiene algo que declarar?**
*teeyeh-neh ahl-goh keh deh-klah-rahr*

Anything to declare?

**Tiene que pagar impuestos por esto.**
*teeyeh-neh keh pah-gahr eem-pwehs-tohs pohr ehs-toh*

You must pay duty on this.

**Abra esta maleta.**
*ah-brah ehs-tah mah-leh-tah*

Open this bag.

### YOU MAY SEE…

| | |
|---|---|
| **ADUANAS** | customs |
| **ARTÍCULOS LIBRES DE IMPUESTOS** | duty-free goods |
| **ARTÍCULOS QUE DECLARAR** | goods to declare |
| **NADA QUE DECLARAR** | nothing to declare |
| **CONTROL DE PASAPORTES** | passport control |
| **POLICÍA** | police |

## ESSENTIAL

| | |
|---|---|
| Where's...? | **¿Dónde está...?** <u>dohn</u>•deh ehs•<u>tah</u>... |
| the ATM | **el cajero automático** |
| | ehl kah•<u>kheh</u>•roh awtoh•<u>mah</u>•tee•koh |
| the bank | **el banco** ehl <u>bahn</u>•koh |
| the currency | **la casa de cambio** lah <u>kah</u>•sah deh |
| exchange office | <u>kahm</u>•beeyoh |
| When does the bank open/close? | **¿A qué hora abre/cierra el banco?** |
| | ah keh <u>oh</u>•rah <u>ah</u>•breh/<u>seeyeh</u>•rrah ehl bahn•koh |
| I'd like to change dollars/pounds into... | **Quiero cambiar dólares/libras a...** |
| | <u>keeyeh</u>•roh kahm•<u>beeyahr</u> <u>doh</u>•lah•rehs/<u>lee</u>•brahs ah... |
| I'd like to cash traveler's checks [cheques]. | **Quiero cobrar cheques de viajero.** |
| | <u>keeyeh</u>•roh koh•<u>brahr cheh</u>•kehs deh beeyah•<u>kheh</u>•ro |

For Currency, see page 17.

## At the Bank

| | |
|---|---|
| I'd like to change money/get a cash advance. | **Quiero cambiar dinero/un adelanto de efectivo.** |
| | <u>keeyeh</u>•roh kahm•<u>beeyahr</u> dee•<u>neh</u>•roh/oon |
| | ah•deh•<u>lahn</u>•toh deh eh•fehk•<u>tee</u>•boh |
| What's the exchange rate? | **¿Cuál es el tipo de cambio?** |
| | kwahl ehs ehl <u>tee</u>•poh deh <u>kahm</u>•beeyoh |
| How much is the fee? | **¿Cuánto es la tasa?** <u>kwahn</u>•toh ehs lah <u>tah</u>•sah |
| I think there's a mistake. | **Creo que hay un error.** <u>kreh</u>•oh keh aye |
| | oon eh•<u>rrohr</u> |

| | |
|---|---|
| I lost my traveler's checks [cheques]. | **He perdido los cheques de viajero.** |
| | *eh pehr·dee·doh lohs cheh·kehs deh beeyah·kheh·ro* |
| My card was lost. | **Se me ha perdido la tarjeta.** |
| | *seh meh ah pehr·dee·doh lah tahr·kheh·tah* |
| My card was stolen. | **Me han robado la tarjeta.** |
| | *meh ahn roh·bah·doh lah tahr·kheh·tah* |
| My card doesn't work. | **Mi tarjeta no funciona.** |
| | *mee tahr·kheh·tah noh foon·seeyoh·nah* |

## YOU MAY SEE...

| | |
|---|---|
| **INTRODUCIR TARJETA AQUÍ** | insert card here |
| **CANCELAR** | cancel |
| **BORRAR** | clear |
| **INTRODUCIR** | enter |
| **CLAVE** | PIN |
| **RETIRAR FONDOS** | withdraw funds |
| **DE CUENTA CORRIENTE** | from checking [current] account |
| **DE CUENTA DE AHORROS** | from savings account |
| **RECIBO** | receipt |

ATMs are located throughout Latin America. Cash can be obtained from ATMs with Visa™, American Express® and many other international cards. Instructions are often given in English. Debit cards are also becoming a more accepted method of payment. Whether using a credit card or debit card, make sure you have a PIN (personal identification number) and that it is four digits. If you have an alphabetic PIN, be aware that Latin American ATMs may not have letters on the keypad.

Banks offer the best exchange rates but you can also change money at travel agencies and hotels. Remember to bring your passport when you want to change money. Each country also has its own currency, see the currency table on pages 17 and 18.

| Country | Currency |
| --- | --- |
| **Argentina** | peso argentino _peh•soh ahr•khehn•tee•noh_ |
| **Bolivia** | boliviano _boh•lee•beeyah•noh_ |
| **Chile** | peso chileno _peh•soh chee•leh•noh_ |
| **Colombia** | peso colombiano _peh•soh coh•lohm•beeyah•noh_ |
| **Costa Rica** | colón costarricense _koh•lon kohs•tah•rree•sehn•seh_ |
| **Cuba** | peso cubano _peh•soh koo•bah•noh_ |
| **Ecuador** | dólar estadounidense (American dollar) _doh•lahr ehs•tah•doh•oo•nee•dehn•seh_ |
| **El Salvador** | colón salvadoreño _koh•lon sahl•bah•doh•reh•nyo_ |
| **Guatemala** | quetzal _keht•sahl_ |
| **Honduras** | lempira _lem•pee•ra_ |
| **Mexico** | peso mexicano _peh•soh meh•khee•kah•noh_ |
| **Nicaragua** | córdoba _kohr•doh•bah_ |

| Panama | balboa *bal·boh·ah* |
| Paraguay | guaraní *gua·ra·nee* |
| Peru | nuevo sol *nweh·boh sohl* |
| Puerto Rico | dólar estadounidense (American dollar) *doh·lahr ehs·tah·doh·oo·nee·dehn·seh* |
| Dominican Republic | peso dominicano *peh·soh doh·mee·nee·kah·noh* |
| Uruguay | peso uruguayo *peh·soh oo·roo·gway·eeyo* |
| Venezuela | bolívar *boh·lee·bahr* |

## Getting Around

### ESSENTIAL

| How do I get to town? | **¿Cómo se llega a la ciudad?** *koh·moh seh yeh·gah ah lah seew·dahd* |
| Where's…? | **¿Dónde está…?** *dohn·deh ehs·tah…* |
| the airport | **el aeropuerto** *ehl ah·eh·roh·pwehr·toh* |
| the train [railway] station | **la estación de tren** *lah ehs·tah·seeyohn deh trehn* |

| the bus station | **la estación de autobuses** |
| | *lah ehs·tah·<u>seeyohn</u> deh awtoh·<u>boo</u>·ses* |
| the metro [underground] station | **la estación de metro** |
| | *lah ehs·tah·<u>seeyohn</u> dch <u>meh</u>·troh* |

| How far is it? | **¿A qué distancia está?** |
| | *ah keh dees·<u>tahn</u>·seeyah ehs·<u>tah</u>* |
| Where do I buy a ticket? | **¿Dónde se compra el boleto?** |
| | *<u>dohn</u>·deh seh <u>kohm</u>·prah ehl boh·<u>leh</u>·toh* |
| A one-way/round-trip [return] ticket to... | **Un boleto de ida/ida y vuelta a...** |
| | *oon boh·<u>leh</u>·toh deh <u>ee</u>·dah/<u>ee</u>·dah ee <u>bwehl</u>·tah ah...* |
| How much? | **¿Cuánto es?** *<u>kwahn</u>·toh ehs* |
| Is there a discount? | **¿Hacen descuento?** |
| | *<u>ah</u>·sen dehs·<u>kwehn</u>·toh* |
| Which...? | **¿De qué...?** *deh keh...* |
| gate | **puerta de embarque** |
| | *<u>pwehr</u>·tah deh ehm·<u>bahr</u>·keh* |
| line | **línea** *<u>lee</u>·neh·ah* |
| platform | **andén** *ahn·<u>dehn</u>* |
| Where can I get a taxi? | **¿Dónde puedo tomar un taxi?** |
| | *<u>dohn</u>·deh <u>pweh</u>·doh toh·<u>mahr</u> oon <u>tah</u>·xee* |
| Take me to this address. | **Lléveme a esta dirección.** |
| | *<u>yeh</u>·beh·meh ah <u>ehs</u>·tah dee·rehk·<u>seeyohn</u>* |
| Where's the car rental [hire]? | **¿Dónde está el alquiler de autos?** |
| | *<u>dohn</u>·deh ehs·<u>tah</u> ehl ahl·kee·<u>lehr</u> deh <u>ahoo</u>·tohs* |
| Can I have a map? | **¿Podría darme un mapa?** |
| | *poh·<u>dree</u>·ah <u>dahr</u>·meh oon <u>mah</u>·pah* |

## Tickets

| | |
|---|---|
| When's...to Quito? | **¿Cuándo sale...a Quito?** |
| | *kwahn·doh <u>sah</u>·leh...ah <u>kee</u>·toh* |
| the (first) bus | **el (primer) autobús** *ehl (pree·<u>mehr</u>) awtoh·<u>boos</u>* |
| the (next) flight | **el (próximo) vuelo** *ehl (<u>proh</u>·xee·moh) bweh·loh* |
| the (last) train | **el (último) tren** *ehl (<u>ool</u>·tee·moh) trehn* |
| Where do I buy a ticket? | **¿Dónde se compra el boleto?** |
| | *dohn·deh seh <u>kohm</u>·prah ehl boh·<u>leh</u>·toh* |
| One/Two ticket(s), please. | **Un/Dos boleto(s), por favor.** |
| | *oon/dohs boh·<u>leh</u>·toh(s) pohr fah·<u>bohr</u>* |
| For today/tomorrow. | **Para hoy/mañana.** *<u>pah</u>·rah oy/mah·<u>nyah</u>·nah* |
| A...ticket. | **Un boleto...** *oon boh·<u>leh</u>·toh...* |
| one-way | **de ida** *deh <u>ee</u>·dah* |
| round-trip [return] | **de ida y vuelta** *deh <u>ee</u>·dah ee <u>bwehl</u>·tah* |
| first class | **de primera clase** *deh pree·<u>meh</u>·rah <u>klah</u>·she* |
| business class | **clase ejecutiva** *<u>kla</u>·seh ehkhe·koo·<u>ti</u>·vah* |
| economy class | **de clase económica** *deh <u>klah</u>·seh eh·koh·**<u>noh</u>**·mee·kah* |
| How much? | **¿Cuánto es?** |
| | *<u>kwahn</u>·toh ehs* |
| Is there a discount for...? | **¿Hacen descuento a...?** |
| | *ah·sehn dehs·<u>kwehn</u>·toh ah...* |
| children | **los niños** *lohs <u>nee</u>·nyohs* |
| students | **los estudiantes** *lohs ehs·too·<u>deeyahn</u>·tehs* |
| senior citizens | **los jubilados** *lohs khoo·bee·<u>lah</u>·dohs* |
| tourists | **turistas** *too·<u>rees</u>·tahs* |
| The express bus/express train, please. | **El autobús/tren exprés, por favor.** *ehl ahoohtoh·<u>boos</u>/trehn ehx·<u>prehs</u>, pohr fah·<u>bor</u>* |
| The local bus/train, please. | **El autobús/tren local, por favor.** *ehl ahoohtoh·<u>boos</u>/trehn loh·<u>kahl</u>, pohr fah·<u>bor</u>* |

| I have an e-ticket. | **Tengo un boleto electrónico.** |
| | *tehn•goh oon boh•leh•toh eh•lehk•troh•nee•koh* |
| Can I buy a ticket on the bus/train ? | **¿Puedo comprar el boleto a bordo del autobús/tren?** *pweh•doh kohm•prahr ehlbo•leh•toh ah bohr•doh dehl awtoh•boos/trehn* |
| Do I have to stamp the ticket before boarding? | **¿Tengo que sellar el boleto antes de abordar?** *tehn•goh keh sehyar ehl boh•leh•toh ahn•tes deh ah•bohr•dahr* |
| How long is this ticket valid? | **¿Cuál es la vigencia de este boleto?** *kwahl ehs lah vikhen•seeya deh ehs teh boh•leh•toh* |
| Can I return on the same ticket? | **¿Puedo volver con el mismo boleto?** *pweh•doh vohl•behr kohn ehl meez•moh boh•leh•toh* |
| I'd like to…my reservation. | **Quiero…mi reserva.** *keeyeh•roh…mee reh•sehr•bah* |
| cancel | **cancelar** *kahn•seh•lahr* |
| change | **cambiar** *kahm•beeyahr* |
| confirm | **confirmar** *kohn•feer•mahr* |

For Time, see page 173.

For Days, see page 174.

## Plane

### Airport Transfer

| How much is a taxi to the airport? | **¿Cuánto cuesta el trayecto en taxi al aeropuerto?** *kwahn•toh kwehs•tah ehl trah•yehk•toh ehn tah•xee ahl ah•eh•roh•pwehr•toh* |
| To…Airport, please. | **Al aeropuerto de…, por favor.** *ahl ah•eh•roh•pwehr•toh deh…pohr fah•bohr* |
| My airline is… | **Mi línea aérea es…** *mee lee•neh•ah ah•eh•reh•ah ehs…* |
| My flight leaves at… | **Mi vuelo sale a la/las…** *mee bweh•loh sah•leh ah lah/lahs* |

| | |
|---|---|
| I'm in a rush. | **Tengo prisa.** tehn•goh pree•sah |
| Can you take an alternate route? | **¿Puede tomar otro camino?** pweh•deh toh•mahr oh•troh kah•mee•noh |
| Can you drive faster/slower? | **¿Puede ir más deprisa/despacio?** pweh•deh eer mahs deh•pree•sah/dehs•pah•seeyoh |

For Grammar, see page 166.

For Time, see page 173.

## YOU MAY HEAR...

| | |
|---|---|
| **¿Con qué línea aérea viaja?** kohn keh lee•neh•ah ah•eh•reh•ah beeyah•khah | What airline are you flying? |
| **¿Nacional o internacional?** nah•seeyoh•nahl oh een•tehr•nah•seeyoh•nahl | Domestic or international? |
| **¿Qué terminal?** keh tehr•mee•nahl | What terminal? |

## YOU MAY SEE...

| | |
|---|---|
| **LLEGADAS** | arrivals |
| **SALIDAS** | departures |
| **RECLAMO DE EQUIPAJE** | baggage claim |
| **VUELOS NACIONALES** | domestic flights |
| **VUELOS INTERNACIONALES** | international flights |
| **MOSTRADOR DE PREEMBARQUE** | check-in |
| **PREEMBARQUE ELECTRÓNICO** | e-ticket check-in |
| **PUERTAS DE EMBARQUE** | departure gates |

## Checking In

| | |
|---|---|
| Where's check-in? | **¿Dónde está el mostrador de preembarque?** *dohn•deh ehs•tah ehl mohs•trah•dohr deh preh•ehm•bahr•keh* |
| My name is... | **Me llamo...** *meh yah•moh...* |
| I'm going to... | **Voy a...** *boy ah...* |
| I have... | **Tengo...** *tehn•goh* |
| one suitcase | **una maleta** *oo•nah mah•leh•tah* |
| two suitcases | **dos maletas** *dohs mah•leh•tahs* |
| one piece of hand luggage | **una pieza de equipaje de mano** *oo•nah peeeh•sah deh eh•kee•pa•kheh deh mah•noh* |
| How much luggage is allowed? | **¿Cuánto equipaje está permitido?** *kwahn•toh eh•kee•pah•kheh ehs•tah pehr•mee•tee•doh* |
| Is that pounds or kilos? | **¿Son libras o kilos?** *sohn lee•brahs oh kee•lohs* |
| Which terminal/gate ? | **¿De qué terminal/puerta de embarque?** *deh keh tehr•mee•nahl/pwehr•tah deh ehm•bahr•keh* |
| I'd like a window/an aisle seat. | **Quiero un asiento de ventana/pasillo.** *keeyeh•roh oon ah•seeyehn•toh deh behn•tah•nah/ pah•see•yoh* |
| When do we leave/arrive ? | **¿A qué hora salimos/llegamos?** *ah keh oh•rah sah•lee•mohs/yeh•gah•mohs* |

| | |
|---|---|
| Is the flight delayed? | **¿Tiene retraso el vuelo?** |
| | *teeyeh·nehreh·trah·soh ehl bweh·loh* |
| How late? | **¿Cuánto retraso tiene?** |
| | *kwahn·tohreh·trah·soh teeyeh·neh* |

## YOU MAY HEAR...

**¡Siguiente!** *see·geeyehn·teh*
Next!

**Su pasaporte/boleto, por favor.** *soo pah·sah·pohr·teh/boh·leh·toh pohr fah·bohr*
Your passport/ ticket, please.

**¿Va a registrar el equipaje?** *bah ah reh·khees·trahr ehl eh·kee·pah·kheh*
Are you checking any luggage?

**Lleva exceso de equipaje.** *yeh·bah ehx·seh·soh deh eh·kee·pah·kheh*
You have excess luggage.

**Eso es demasiado grande para equipaje de mano.** *eh·soh ehs deh·mah·seeyah·doh grahn·deh pah·rah eh·kee·pah·kheh deh mah·noh*
That's too large for a carry-on [to carry on board].

**¿Hizo las maletas usted?** *ee·soh lahs mah·leh·tahs oos·ted*
Did you pack these bags yourself?

**¿Le entregó alguien algún paquete?** *leh ehn·treh·goh ahl·geeyehn ahl·goon pah·keh·teh*
Did anyone give you anything to carry?

**Vacíese los bolsillos.** *bah·see·eh·seh lohs bohl·see·yohs*
Empty your pockets.

**Quítese los zapatos.** *kee·teh·seh lohs sah·pah·tohs*
Take off your shoes.

**Se está efectuando el embarque del vuelo...** *seh ehs·tah eh·fehk·too·ahn·doh ehl ehm·bahr·keh dehl bweh·loh...*
Now boarding flight...

## Luggage

| Where is/are...? | ¿Dónde está/están...? |
| --- | --- |
| | *dohn-deh ehs-tah/ehs-tahn...* |
| the luggage carts [trolleys] | **los carritos para el equipaje** *lohs kah-rree-tohs pah-rah ehl eh-kee-pah-kheh* |
| the luggage lockers | **los casilleros para equipaje** *lohs kah-see-yeh-rohs pa-rah eh-kee-pah-kheh* |
| the baggage claim | **el reclamo de equipaje** *ehl reh-klah-moh deh eh-kee-pah-kheh* |
| My luggage has been lost. | **Han perdido mi equipaje.** *ahn pehr-dee-doh mee eh-kee-pah-kheh* |
| My luggage has been stolen. | **Me han robado el equipaje.** *meh ahn roh-bah-doh ehl eh-kee-pah-kheh* |
| My suitcase is damaged. | **Mi maleta ha sufrido daños.** *mee mah-leh-tah ah soo-free-doh dah-nyohs* |

## Finding your Way

| Where is/are...? | ¿Dónde está/están...? |
| --- | --- |
| | *dohn-deh ehs-tah/ehs-tahn...* |
| the currency exchange | **la casa de cambio** *lah kah-sah deh kahm-beeyoh* |
| the car hire | **el alquiler de autos** *ehl ahl-kee-lehr deh ahoo-tohs* |
| the exit | **la salida** *lah sah-lee-dah* |
| the taxis | **los taxis** *lohs tah-xees* |
| Is there...into town? | **¿Hay...que vaya a la ciudad?** *aye... keh bah-yah ah lah seew-dahd* |
| a bus | **un autobus** *oon awtoh-boos* |
| a train | **un tren** *oon trehn* |
| a metro [underground] | **un metro** *oon meh-troh* |

For Asking Directions, see page 35.

## Train

| | |
|---|---|
| Where's the train [railway] station? | **¿Dónde está la estación de tren?** _dohn_•deh ehs•_tah_ lah ehs•tah•_seeyohn_ deh trehn |
| How far is it? | **¿A qué distancia está?** ah keh dees•_tahn_•seeyah ehs•_tah_ |
| Where is/are…? | **¿Dónde está/están…?** _dohn_•deh ehs•_tah_/ehs•_tahn_… |
| the ticket office | **la boletería** lah boh•leh•teh•_ree_•a |
| the information desk | **el mostrador de información** ehl mohs•trah•_dohr_ deh een•fohr•mah•_seeyohn_ |
| the luggage lockers | **los casilleros para equipaje** lohs kah•see•yeh•rohs _pa_•rah eh•kee•_pah_•kheh |
| the platforms | **los andenes** lohs ahn•_deh_•nehs |
| Can I have a schedule [timetable]? | **¿Podría darme un horario?** poh•_dree_•ah dahr•meh oon oh•rah•_reeyoh_ |

---

**YOU MAY SEE…**

| | |
|---|---|
| **ANDENES** | platforms |
| **INFORMACIÓN** | information |
| **RESERVAS** | reservations |
| **SALA DE ESPERA** | waiting room |
| **LLEGADAS** | arrivals |
| **SALIDAS** | departures |

| How long is the trip? | **¿Cuánto dura el viaje?** |
| | _kwahn_•toh _doo_•rah ehl _beeyah_•kheh |
| Is it a direct train? | **¿Es un tren directo?** ehs oon trehn dee•_rehk_•toh |
| Do I have to change | **¿Tengo que cambiar de trenes?** |
| trains? | _tehn_•goh keh kahm•_beeyahr_ deh _treh_•nehs |
| Is the train on time? | **¿Es puntual el tren?** ehs poon•_twahl_ ehl trehn |

For Tickets, see page 20.

The railway system is not fully developed in Latin America but most Latin American countries have a local and national rail service. Mexico and Argentina have almost no passenger rail service and are serviced by multiple private intercity bus lines. For more on bus transport, see page 28.

## Departures

| Which track [platform] | **¿De qué andén sale el tren a…?** |
| for the train to…? | deh keh ahn•_dehn_ _sah_•leh ehl trehn ah… |
| Is this the track | **¿Es éste el andén/tren a…?** |
| [platform]/train to…? | ehs _ehs_•teh ehl ahn•_dehn_/trehn ah… |
| Where is track | **¿Dónde está el andén…?** |
| [platform]…? | _dohn_•deh ehs•_tah_ ehl ahn•_dehn_… |
| Where do I change | **¿Dónde tengo que cambiar para…?** |
| for…? | _dohn_•deh _tehn_•goh keh kahm•_beeyahr_ _pah_•rah… |

## On Board

| Can I sit here/open | **¿Le importa si me siento aquí/abro la ventana?** |
| the window? | leh eem•_pohr_•tah see meh _seeyehn_•toh ah•_kee_/_ah_•broh |
| | lah ben•_tah_•nah |
| That's my seat. | **Ése es mi asiento.** _eh_•seh ehs mee ah•_seeyehn_•toh |
| Here's my reservation. | **Aquí está mi reserva.** ah•_kee_ ehs•tah mee reh•_sehr_•ba |

## YOU MAY HEAR...

| | |
|---|---|
| **¡Todos a bordo!** _toh·dohs ah bohr·doh_ | All aboard! |
| **Boletos, por favor.** _bo·leh·tohs pohr fah·bohr_ | Tickets, please. |
| **Tiene que cambiar de tren en...** | You have to change |
| _teeyeh·neh keh kahm·beeyahr deh trehn ehn..._ | trains at... |
| **Próxima parada: Constitución.** | Next stop, Constitución. |
| _proh·xee·mah pah·rah·dah khons·tee·tu·seeyohn_ | |

## Bus

| | |
|---|---|
| Where's the bus station? | **¿Dónde está la estación de autobuses?** _dohn·deh ehs·tah lah ehs·tah·seeyohn deh awtoh·boo·sehs_ |
| How far is it? | **¿A qué distancia está?** _ah keh dees·tahn·seeyah ehs·tah_ |
| How do I get to...? | **¿Cómo se llega a...?** _koh·moh seh yeh·gah ah..._ |
| Is this the bus to...? | **¿Es éste el autobús a...?** _ehs ehs·teh ehl awtoh·boos ah..._ |
| What's the fare to...? | **¿Cuál es la tarifa a...?** _kwahl ehs lah tah·ree·fah ah..._ |
| Can you tell me when to get off? | **¿Podría decirme cuándo me tengo que bajar?** _poh·dree·ah deh·seer·meh kwahn·doh meh tehn·goh keh bah·khahr_ |
| Do I have to change buses? | **¿Tengo que hacer transbordo?** _tehn·goh keh ah·sehr trahnz·bohr·doh_ |
| How many stops to...? | **¿Cuántas paradas hay hasta...?** _kwahn·tahs pah·rah·dahs aye ahs·tah..._ |
| Stop here, please! | **¡Pare aquí, por favor!** _pah·reh ah·kee pohr fah·bohr_ |

For Tickets, see page 20.

The bus service in Latin America is extensive. For local service within a town, you usually pay as you board the bus. The fare will vary according to the length of the trip.

Note that buses can be called by various different names within a country and these names can also vary from country to country:

| | |
|---|---|
| Mexico | **camión, micro, pecera** |
| Peru | **micro, combi, bus** |
| Chile | **micro, liebre** |
| Central America | **camión, guagua** |

## YOU MAY SEE...

| | |
|---|---|
| **PARADA DE AUTOBUSES** | bus stop |
| **PARADA** | request stop |
| **SUBIR/BAJAR** | enter/exit |
| **MARCAR BOLETO** | stamp your ticket |

## Metro

| | |
|---|---|
| Where's the metro [underground] station? | **¿Dónde está la estación de metro?** _dohn_•deh ehs•_tah_ lah ehs•tah•_seeyohn_ deh _meh_•troh |
| A map, please. | **Un plano, por favor.** oon _plah_•noh pohr fah•_bohr_ |
| Which line for. . .? | **¿Qué línea tengo que tomar para...?** keh _lee_•neh•ah _tehn_•goh keh toh•_mahr_ _pah_•rah. . . |
| Which direction? | **¿Qué dirección?** keh dee•rehk•_seeohn_ |
| Do I have to transfer [change]? | **¿Tengo que hacer transbordo?** _tehn_•goh keh ah•_sehr_ trahnz•_bohr_•doh |
| Is this the metro [train] to. . .? | **¿Es éste el tren a...?** ehs _ehs_•teh ehl trehn ah. . . |
| Where are we? | **¿Dónde estamos?** _dohn_•deh ehs•_tah_•mohs |

For Tickets, see page 20.

---

**Metro** (subway) systems are not widespread in Latin America, and many cities do not have them. Buenos Aires (Argentina), Mexico City, Guadalajara and Monterrey (all in Mexico) are some cities that do have **metro** systems.

**Metros** in Latin America are easy to use and are reasonably priced. All **metro** systems operate on a one-way, per-ride basis.

---

## Boat & Ferry

| | |
|---|---|
| When is the ferry to. . .? | **¿Cuándo sale el ferry a...?** _kwahn_•doh _sah_•leh ehl feh•_rree_ ah. . . |
| Can I take my car? | **¿Puedo llevar el coche?** _pweh_•doh yeh•_bahr_ ehl _koh_•cheh |
| What time is the next sailing? | **¿A qué hora sale el siguiente barco?** ah keh _oh_•rah _sah_•leh ehl see•_geeyehn_•teh _buhr_•koh |
| Can I book a seat/cabin? | **¿Puedo reservar un asiento/una cabina?** _pweh_•doh reh•sehr•_bahr_ oon ah•_seeyehn_•toh/_oo_•nah kah•_bee_•nah |

| How long is the crossing? | **¿Cuánto dura el traslado?** _kwahn•toh_ _doo•rah ehl trahs•lah•doh_ |

For Tickets, see page 20.

---

**YOU MAY SEE...**

| **BALSA SALVAVIDAS** | life boat |
| **CHALECO SALVAVIDAS** | life jacket |

---

In Latin America there are some destinations with ferry service.
In Mexico, for example, there are ferries traveling from Cozumel
Island to Playa del Carmen, and from Isla Mujeres to Cancun. In
Argentina, there are ferries from Buenos Aires to Montevideo, Colonia
and Piriapolis (Uruguay).

## Taxi

| Where can I get a taxi? | **¿Dónde puedo tomar un taxi?** _dohn•deh pweh•doh toh•mahr oon tah•xee_ |
| Can you send a taxi? | **¿Puede enviar un taxi?** _pweh•deh ehn•beeyar oon tahk•see_ |
| Do you have the number for a taxi? | **¿Tiene el número de alguna empresa de taxi?** _teeyeh•neh ehl noo•meh•roh deh ahl•goo•nah ehm•preh•sah deh tah•xee_ |
| I'd like a taxi now/ for tomorrow at... | **Quiero un taxi ahora/para mañana a la(s)...** _keeyeh•roh oon tah•xee ah•oh•rah/ pah•rah mah•nyah•nah ah lah(s)..._ |
| Pick me up at (place/time)... | **Recójame en/a la(s)...** _reh•koh•khah•meh ehn/ah lah(s)..._ |

| | |
|---|---|
| I'm going to... | **Voy...** *boy...* |
| this address | **a esta dirección** *ah ehs·tah dee·rehk·seeyohn* |
| the airport | **al aeropuerto** *ahl ah·eh·roh·pwehr·toh* |
| the train [railway] station | **a la estación de tren** *ah lah ehs·tah·seeyohn deh trehn* |
| I'm late. | **Llego tarde.** *yeh·goh tahr·deh* |
| Can you drive faster/slower? | **¿Puede ir más deprisa/despacio?** *pweh·deh eer mahs deh·pree·sah/dehs·pah·seeyoh* |
| Stop/Wait here. | **Pare/Espere aquí.** *pah·reh/ehs·peh·reh ah·kee* |
| How much? | **¿Cuánto es?** *kwahn·toh ehs* |
| You said it would cost... | **Dijo que costaría...** *dee·khoh keh kohs·tah·ree·ah...* |
| Keep the change. | **Quédese con el cambio.** *keh·deh·seh kohn ehl kahm·beeyoh* |

For Grammar, see page 166.

---

**YOU MAY HEAR...**

**¿Adónde se dirige?**
*ah·dohn·deh seh dee·ree·kheh*

Where to?

**¿Cuál es la dirección?**
*kwahl ehs lah dee·rehk·seeyohn*

What's the address?

In major Latin American cities, taxis are reasonably priced. Extra fees are usually charged for trips to the airport, bus station, and train station and also for extra luggage.

In most parts of Latin America taxis do not have meters, and travelers should discuss the fare beforehand.

## Bicycle & Motorbike

| | |
|---|---|
| I'd like to rent [hire]... | **Quiero alquilar...** _keeyeh_·roh ahl·kee·_lahr_... |
| a bicycle | **una bicicleta** _oo_·nah bee·see·_kleh_·tah |
| a moped | **un ciclomotor** oon see·kloh·moh·_tohr_ |
| a motorcycle | **una motocicleta** _oo_·nah moh·toh·see·_kleh_·tah |
| How much per day/week? | **¿Cuánto cuesta por día/semana?** _kwahn_·toh _kwehs_·tah pohr _dee_·ah/seh·_mah_·nah |
| Can I have a helmet/lock? | **¿Puede darme un casco/candado?** _pweh_·deh _dahr_·meh oon _kahs_·koh/kahn·_dah_·doh |

## Car Hire

| | |
|---|---|
| Where's the car rental [hire]? | **¿Dónde está el alquiler de autos?** _dohn_·deh ehs·_tah_ ehl ahl·kee·_lehr_ deh _ahoo_·tohs |
| I'd like... | **Quiero...** _keeyeh_·roh... |
| a cheap/small car | **un auto económico/pequeño** oon _ahoo_·toh eh·koh·_noh_·mee·koh/peh·_keh_·nyoh |
| an automatic/ a manual | **un auto automático/con transmisión manual** oon _ahoo_·toh awtoh·_mah_·tee·koh/kohn trahnz·mee·_seeyohn_ mah·noo·_ahl_ |
| air conditioning | **un auto con aire acondicionado** oon _ahoo_·toh kohn _ayee_·reh ah·kohn·dee·seeyoh·_nah_·doh |
| a car seat | **un asiento de niño** oon ah·_seeyehn_·toh deh _nee_·nyoh |

| How much...? | **¿Cuánto cobran...?** _kwahn·toh koh·brahn..._ |
| per day/week | **por día/semana** _pohr dee·ah/seh·mah·nah_ |
| for...days | **por...días** _pohr... dee·ahs_ |
| per kilometer | **por kilómetro** _pohr kee·loh·meh·troh_ |
| for unlimited mileage | **por kilometraje ilimitado** _pohr kee·loh·meh·trah·kheh ee·lee·mee·tah·doh_ |
| with insurance | **con el seguro** _kohn ehl seh·goo·roh_ |
| Are there any discounts? | **¿Ofrecen algún descuento?** _oh·freh·sehn ahl·goon dehs·kwehn·toh_ |

In Spain and some Latin American countries, **coger** means to catch or get, e.g. **¿Dónde puedo coger un taxi?** (Where can I catch a cab?). However, in many countries in Latin America, **coger** is a vulgarity for 'to have sex'. Travelers to Latin America should always use **tomar**, e.g. **¿Dónde puedo tomar un taxi?**

## YOU MAY HEAR...

| **¿Tiene permiso de conducir internacional?** _teeyeh·neh pehr·mee·soh deh kohn·doo·seer een·tehr·nah·seeyoh·nahl_ | Do you have an international driver's license? |
| **Su pasaporte, por favor.** _soo pah·sah·pohr·teh pohr fah·bohr_ | Your passport, please. |
| **¿Quiere seguro?** _keeyeh·reh seh·goo·roh_ | Do you want insurance? |
| **Tiene que dejar un depósito.** _teeyeh·neh keh deh·khahr oon deh·poh·see·toh_ | I'll need a deposit. |
| **Firme aquí.** _feer·meh ah·kee_ | Sign here. |

## Fuel Station

| | |
|---|---|
| Where's the fuel station? | **¿Dónde está la gasolinera?** _dohn_·deh ehs·_tah_ lah gah·soh·lee·_neh_·rah |
| Fill it up. | **Lleno.** _yeh_·noh |
| ...liters/galons, please. | **...litros/galones, por favor. ...** _lee_·trohs/gah·_loh_·nehs pohr fah·bohr |
| I'll pay in cash/by credit card. | **Voy a pagar en efectivo/con tarjeta de crédito.** boy ah pah·_gahr_ ehn eh·fehk·_tee_·boh/kohn tahr·_kheh_·tah deh _kreh_·dee·toh |

**YOU MAY SEE...**

| | |
|---|---|
| **NORMAL** | regular |
| **SÚPER** | super |
| **DIÉSEL** | diesel |

## Asking Directions

| | |
|---|---|
| Is this the way to...? | **¿Es ésta la ruta a...?** _ehs_ ehs·tah lah _rooh_·tah ah... |
| How far is it to...? | **¿A qué distancia está...?** ah keh dees·_tahn_·seeyah ehs·_tah_... |
| Where's...? | **¿Dónde está...?** _dohn_·deh ehs·_tah_... |
| ...Street | **la calle...** lah _kah_·yeh... |
| this address | **esta dirección** _ehs_·tah dee·rek·_seeyohn_ |
| the highway [motorway] | **la autopista** lah aw·toh·_pees_·tah |
| Can you show me on the map? | **¿Me lo puede indicar en el mapa?** meh loh _pweh_·deh een·dee·_kahr_ ehn ehl _mah_·pah |
| I'm lost. | **Me he perdido.** meh eh pehr·_dee_·doh |

## YOU MAY HEAR...

| | |
|---|---|
| **todo recto** _toh-doh rehk-toh_ | straight ahead |
| **a la izquierda** _ah lah ees-keeyehr-dah_ | left |
| **a la derecha** _ah lah deh-reh-chah_ | right |
| **en/doblando la esquina** | on/around the corner |
| _ehn/doh-blahn-doh lah ehs-kee-nah_ | |
| **frente a** _frehn-teh ah_ | opposite |
| **detrás de** _deh-trahs deh_ | behind |
| **al lado de** _ahl lah-doh deh_ | next to |
| **después de** _dehs-pwehs deh_ | after |
| **al norte/sur** _ahl nohr-teh/soor_ | north/south |
| **al este/oeste** _ahl ehs-teh/oh-ehs-teh_ | east/west |
| **en el semáforo** _en ehl seh-mah-foh-roh_ | at the traffic light |
| **en el cruce** _en ehl kroo-seh_ | at the intersection |

## Parking

| | |
|---|---|
| Can I park here? | **¿Puedo estacionar aquí?** |
| | _pweh-doh es-tah-seeo-nahr ah-kee_ |
| Where's the parking garage/parking lot [car park]? | **¿Dónde está el garaje/estacionamiento?** |
| | _dohn-deh ehs-tah ehl gah-rah-kheh/_ |
| | _es-tah-seeo-nah-meeyehn-toh_ |
| Where's the parking meter? | **¿Dónde está el parquímetro?** _dohn-deh ehs-tah_ |
| | _ehl pahr-kee-meh-troh_ |
| How much...? | **¿Cuánto cobran...?** _kwahn-toh koh-brahn..._ |
| per hour | **por hora** _pohr oh-rah_ |
| per day | **por día** _pohr dee-ah_ |
| for overnight | **por la noche** _pohr lah noh-cheh_ |

## YOU MAY SEE...

 **PROHIBIDO ADELANTAR**     no passing zone

 **PARE**     stop

 **CALLE DE SENTIDO ÚNICO**     one-way street

 **CEDA EL PASO**     yield [give way]

 **ENTRADA PROHIBIDA**     no entry

 **ESTACIONAMIENTO PROHIBIDO**     no parking

 **FINAL DEL CARRIL LATERAL DERECHO**     right lane ends (merge left)

 **VELOCIDAD MÁXIMA**     maximum speed limit

## Breakdown & Repair

My car broke down/ won't start.     **El auto se me ha descompuesto/no arranca.** *ehl ahoo·toh seh meh ah des·kom·pwes·toh/noh ah·rrahn·kah*

Can you fix it (today)?     **¿Puede arreglarlo (hoy mismo)?** *pweh·deh ah·rreh·glahr·loh (oy meez·moh)*

When will it be ready?     **¿Cuándo estará listo?** *kwahn·doh ehs·tah·rah lees·toh*

How much?     **¿Cuánto es?** *kwahn·toh ehs*

I have a puncture/flat tyre (tire).     **Tengo una ponchadura/llanta ponchada** *tehn·goh oo·na pohn·chah·doo·rah/yahn·tah pohn·chah·dah*

### Accidents

| | |
|---|---|
| There was an accident. | **Ha habido un accidente.** *ah ah·bee·doh oon ahk·see·dehn·teh* |
| Call an ambulance/ the police. | **Llame a una ambulancia/la policía.** *yah·meh ah oo·nah ahm·boo·lahn·seeyah/lah poh·lee·see·ah* |

Many towns have zones where parking is allowed.
Public parking is noted by a street sign with an **E**
(for **estacionamiento**). Traffic authorities may enforce payment of
fines on the spot for illegal parking.

## Places to Stay

### ESSENTIAL

| | |
|---|---|
| Can you recommend a hotel? | **¿Puede recomendarme un hotel?** *pweh·deh reh·koh·mehn·dahr·meh oon oh·tehl* |
| I have a reservation. | **Tengo una reserva.** *tehn·goh oo·nah reh·sehr·bah* |
| My name is… | **Me llamo…** *meh yah·moh…* |
| Do you have a room…? | **¿Tienen habitaciones…?** *teeyeh·nehn ah·bee·tah·seeyoh·nehs…* |
| for one/two | **individuales/dobles** *een·dee·bee·doo·ah·lehs/doh·blehs* |
| with a bathroom | **con baño** *kohn bah·nyoh* |
| with air-conditioning | **con aire acondicionado** *kohn ayee· reh ah·kohn·dee·seeyoh·nah·doh* |
| For… | **Para…** *pah·rah…* |
| tonight | **esta noche** *ehs·tah noh·cheh* |

| | |
|---|---|
| two nights | **dos noches** *dohs <u>noh</u>·chehs* |
| one week | **una semana** *<u>oo</u>·nah seh·<u>mah</u>·nah* |
| How much? | **¿Cuánto es?** *<u>kwahn</u>·toh ehs* |
| Is there anything cheaper? | **¿Hay alguna tarifa más barata?** *aye ahl·<u>goo</u>·nah tah·<u>ree</u>·fah mahs bah·<u>rah</u>·tah* |
| When's check-out? | **¿A qué hora hay que desocupar la habitación?** *ah keh <u>oh</u>·rah aye keh deh·soh·koo·<u>pahr</u> lah ah·bee·tah·<u>seeyohn</u>* |
| Can I leave this in the safe? | **¿Puedo dejar esto en la caja fuerte?** *<u>pweh</u>·doh deh·<u>khahr</u> ehs·toh ehn lah <u>kah</u>·khah <u>fwehr</u>·teh* |
| Can I leave my bags? | **¿Podría dejar mi equipaje?** *poh·<u>dree</u>·ah deh·<u>khahr</u> mee eh·kee·<u>pah</u>·kheh* |
| Can I have the bill/ a receipt? | **¿Me da la factura/un recibo?** *meh dah lah fahk·<u>too</u>·rah/oon reh·<u>see</u>·boh* |
| I'll pay in cash/by credit card. | **Voy a pagar en efectivo/con tarjeta de crédito.** *boy ah pah·<u>gahr</u> ehn eh·fehk·<u>tee</u>·boh/ kohn tahr·<u>kheh</u>·tah deh <u>kreh</u>·dee·toh* |

## Somewhere to Stay

| | |
|---|---|
| Can you recommend...? | **¿Puede recomendarme...?** *<u>pweh</u>·deh reh·koh·mehn·<u>dahr</u>·meh* |
| a hotel | **un hotel** *oon oh·<u>tehl</u>* |
| a hostel | **un hostal** *oon oh·<u>stahl</u>* |
| a campsite | **un campamento** *oon kahm·pah·<u>mehn</u>·toh* |
| a bed and breakfast | **un alojamiento y desayuno** *oon al·oh·kha·meeyehn·to ee deh·sah·yoo·noh* |
| What is it near? | **¿Qué hay cerca?** *keh aye <u>sehr</u>·kah* |
| How do I get there? | **¿Cómo se llega allí?** *<u>koh</u>·moh seh <u>yeh</u>·gah ah·<u>yee</u>* |

A variety of places to stay are available in Latin America. Hotels are rated from one to five stars, with five stars being the most expensive and having the most amenities. Other options include spas, resorts, apartment rentals and lodges. Visit the local **Oficina de turismo** (Tourist Information Office) or a local travel agency for recommendations.

## At the Hotel

| | |
|---|---|
| I have a reservation. | **Tengo una reserva.** _tehn_•goh _oo_•nah reh•_sehr_•bah |
| My name is... | **Me llamo...** meh _yah_•moh... |
| Do you have a room...? | **¿Tiene una habitación...?** _teeyeh_•neh _oo_•nah ah•bee•tah•_seeyohn_... |
| for one/two | **individual/doble** een•dee•bee•_dwahl_/_doh_•bleh |
| with a bathroom [toilet]/shower | **con un baño/una ducha** kohn oon _bah_•nyoh/_oo_•nah _doo_•chah |
| with air conditioning | **con aire acondicionado** kohn _ayee_•reh ah•kohn•dee•seeyoh•_nah_•doh |
| with a single/double bed | **con una cama/cama matrimonial** kohn una _kah_•mah/_kah_•mah mah•tree•moh•_neeyahl_ |
| that's smoking/non-smoking | **para fumadores/no fumadores** _pah_•rah foo•mah•_doh_•rehs/noh foo•mah•_doh_•rehs |
| For... | **Para...** _pah_•rah... |
| tonight | **esta noche** _ehs_•tah _noh_•cheh |
| two nights | **dos noches** dohs _noh_•chehs |
| a week | **una semana** _oo_•nah seh•_mah_•nah |
| Does the hotel have...? | **¿Tiene el hotel...?** _teeyeh_•neh ehl oh•_tehl_... |
| a computer | **una computadora** oona kohm•poo•tah•_doh_•rah |
| an elevator [a lift] | **un ascensor** oon ah•sehn•_sohr_ |
| (wireless) internet | **acceso (inalámbrico) a Internet** |

| | | |
|---|---|---|
| service | | *ahk·seh·soh (een·ah·lahm·bree·koh) ah een·tehr·neht* |
| room service | **servicio de habitación** | |
| | | *sehr·bee·seeyoh deh ah·bee·tah·seeyohn* |
| a pool | **una piscina** *oo·nah pees·see·nah* | |
| a gym | **un gimnasio** *oon kheem·nah·seeyoh* | |
| I need... | **Necesito...** *neh·seh·see·toh...* | |
| an extra bed | **otra cama** *oh·trah kah·mah* | |
| a cot | **un catre** *oon kah·treh* | |
| a crib | **una cuna** *oo·nah koo·nah* | |

For Numbers, see page 171.

---

## YOU MAY HEAR...

**Su pasaporte/tarjeta de crédito,
por favor.** *soo pah·sah·pohr·teh/
tahr·kheh·tah deh kreh·dee·toh pohr fah·bohr*

Your passport/
credit card, please.

**Rellene este formulario.**
*reh·yeh·neh ehs·teh fohr·moo·lah·reeyoh*

Fill out this form.

**Firme aquí.** *feer·meh ah·kee*

Sign here.

## Price

| How much per night/week? | **¿Cuánto cuesta por noche/semana?** |
| | _kwahn·toh kwehs·tah pohr noh·cheh/seh·mah·nah_ |
| Does that include breakfast/sales tax [VAT]? | **¿Incluye el precio el desayuno/IVA?** |
| | _een·kloo·yeh ehl preh·seeyoh_ |
| | _ehl deh·sah·yoo·noh/ee·bah_ |
| Are there any discounts? | **¿Ofrecen algún descuento?** |
| | _oh·freh·sehn ahl·goon dehs·kwehn·toh_ |

## Preferences

| Can I see the room? | **¿Puedo ver la habitación?** |
| | _pweh·doh behr lah ah·bee·tah·seeyohn_ |
| I'd like a…room. | **Me gustaría una habitación…** |
| | _meh goos·tah·ree·ah oo·na ah·bee·tah·seeyohn_ |
| better | **mejor** _meh·khor_ |
| bigger | **más grande** _mahs grahn·de_ |
| cheaper | **más económica** _mahs eh·koh·noh·mee·kah_ |
| quieter | **más tranquila** _mahs trahn·kee·lah_ |
| I'll take it. | **La tomo.** _lah toh·moh_ |
| No, I won't take it. | **No, no la tomaré.** _noh, noh lah toh·mah·reh_ |

## Questions

| Where's…? | **¿Dónde está…?** _dohn·deh ehs·tah…_ |
| the bar | **el bar** _ehl bahr_ |
| the bathroom [toilet] | **el baño** _ehl bah·nyoh_ |
| the elevator [lift] | **el ascensor** _ehl ahs·sehn·sohr_ |
| Can I have…? | **¿Puede darme…?** _pweh·deh dahr·meh…_ |
| a blanket | **una manta** _oo·nah mahn·tah_ |
| an iron | **una plancha** _oo·nah plahn·chah_ |
| the room key/key card | **la llave/tarjeta de la habitación** _lah yah·beh/_ |
| | _tahr·kheh·tah deh lah ah·bee·tah·seeyohn_ |
| a pillow | **una almohada** _oo·nah ahl·moh·ah·dah_ |

| soap | **jabón** *khah·bohn* |
| toilet paper | **papel higiénico** *pah·pehl ee·kheeyeh·nee·koh* |
| a towel | **una toalla** *oo·nah toh·ah·yah* |
| Do you have an adapter for this? | **¿Tiene un adaptador para esto?** *teeyeh·neh oon ah·dahp·tah·dohr pah·rah ehs·toh* |
| How do I turn on the lights? | **¿Cómo enciendo las luces?** *koh·moh ehn·seeyehn·doh lahs loo·sehs* |
| Can you wake me at…? | **¿Podría despertarme a la/las…?** *poh·dree·ah dehs·pehr·tahr·meh ah lah/lahs…* |
| Can I leave this in the safe? | **¿Puedo dejar esto en la caja fuerte?** *pweh·doh deh·khahr ehs·toh ehn lah kah·khah fwehr·teh* |
| Can I have my things from the safe? | **¿Podría darme mis cosas de la caja fuerte?** *poh·dree·ah dahr·meh mees koh·sahs deh lah kah·khah fwehr·teh* |
| Is there mail [post]/ a message for me? | **¿Hay correo/algún mensaje para mí?** *aye koh·rreh·oh/ahl·goon mehn·sah·kheh pah·rah mee* |
| Do you have a laundry service? | **¿Tienen servicio de lavandería?** *teeyeh·nehn sehr·bee·seeoh deh lah·bahn·deh·reeyah* |

When asking for a public restroom, it's more common and polite to use the term **servicio**. The term **baño** tends to be used when asking for a private bathroom such as in a home or a hotel room. Native speakers sometimes use both words interchangeably, but you will almost always see **servicio** on a sign.

## Problems

| There's a problem. | **Hay un problema.** *aye oon proh·bleh·mah* |
| I lost my key/ key card. | **He perdido la llave/llave electrónica.** *eh pehr·dee·doh lah yah·beh/yah·beh eh·lehk·troh·nee·kah* |

## YOU MAY SEE...

| | |
|---|---|
| **EMPUJAR/TIRAR** | push/pull |
| **BAÑO/SERVICIO** | bathroom/restroom [toilet] |
| **DUCHA** | shower |
| **ASCENSOR** | elevator [lift] |
| **ESCALERAS** | stairs |
| **LAVANDERÍA** | laundry |
| **NO MOLESTAR** | do not disturb |
| **PUERTA DE INCENDIOS** | fire door |
| **SALIDA (DE EMERGENCIA)** | exit (emergency) |

I'm locked out of the room. **He dejado la llave dentro de la habitación.** *eh deh·khah·doh lah yah·beh dehn·troh deh lah ah·bee·tah·seeyohn*

There's no hot water/toilet paper. **No hay agua caliente/papel higiénico.** *no aye ah·gwah kah·leeyehn·teh/pah·pehl ee·kheeyeh·nee·koh*

The room is dirty. **La habitación está sucia.** *lah ah·bee·tah· seeyohn ehs·tah soo·seeyah*

There are bugs in the room. **Hay insectos en la habitación.** *aye een·sehk·tohs ehn lah ah·bee·tah·seeyohn*

...doesn't work. **...no funciona.** *...no foon·seeyoh·nah*

Can you fix...? **¿Pueden arreglar...?** *pweh·dehn ah·rreh·glahr...*

the air conditioning **el aire acondicionado** *ehl ayee·reh ah·kohn·dee·seeyoh·nah·doh*

the fan **el ventilador** *ehl behn·tee·lah·dohr*

the heat [heating] **la calefacción** *lah kah·leh·fahk·seeyohn*

the light **la luz** *lah loos*

the TV **la televisión** *lah teh·leh·bee·seeyohn*

the toilet **el retrete** *ehl reh·treh·teh*

I'd like another room. **Quiero otra habitación.** *keeyeh·roh oh·trah ah·bee·tah·seeyohn*

## Checking Out

| | |
|---|---|
| When's check-out? | **¿A qué hora hay que desocupar la habitación?**<br>*ah keh oh•rah aye keh deh•soh•koo•pahr lah*<br>*ah•bee•tah•seeyohn* |
| Can I leave my<br>bags here until…? | **¿Puedo dejar mi equipaje aquí hasta…?** *pweh•doh*<br>*deh•khahr mee eh•kee•pah•kheh ah•kee ahs•tah…* |
| Can I have an<br>itemized bill/a<br>receipt? | **¿Puede darme una factura detallada/un recibo?**<br>*pweh•deh dahr•meh oo•nah*<br>*fahk•too•rah deh•tah•yah•dah/oon reh•see•boh* |
| I think there's a mistake. | **Creo que hay un error.** *kreh•oh keh aye oon eh•rrohr* |
| I made… phone calls. | **He hecho…llamadas.** *eh eh•choh… yah•mah•dahs* |
| I took…from<br>the mini-bar. | **He tomado…del minibar.**<br>*eh toh•mah•doh…dehl mee•nee•bar* |
| I'll pay in cash/by<br>credit card. | **Voy a pagar en efectivo/con tarjeta de crédito.**<br>*boy ah pah•gahr ehn eh•fehk•tee•boh/kohn*<br>*tahr•kheh•tah deh kreh•dee•toh* |

## Renting

| | |
|---|---|
| I reserved an<br>apartment/a room. | **He reservado un apartamento/una habitación.**<br>*eh reh•sehr•bah•doh oon ah•pahr•tah•mehn•toh/oo•nah*<br>*ah•bee•tah•seeyohn* |

| My name is... | **Me llamo...** *meh yah·moh...* |
| Can I have the key/key card? | **¿Puede darme la llave/llave electrónica?** *pweh·deh dahr·meh lah yah·beh/yah·beh eh·lehk·troh·nee·kah* |

| Are there...? | **¿Hay...?** *aye...* |
| dishes | **platos** *plah·tohs* |
| pillows | **almohadas** *ahl·moh·ah·dahs* |
| sheets | **sábanas** *sah·bah·nahs* |
| towels | **toallas** *toh·ah·yahs* |
| utensils | **cubiertos** *koo·beeyehr·tohs* |
| When do I put out the bins/recycling? | **¿Cuándo saco la basura/el reciclado?** *kwahn·doh sah·koh lah bah·soo·rah/ ehl reh·see·klah·doh* |
| ...is broken. | **...está roto** *m***/rota** *f ... ehs·tah roh·toh/roh·tah* |
| How does... work? | **¿Cómo funciona...?** *koh·moh foon·seeyoh·nah...* |
| the air conditioner | **el aire acondicionado** *ehl ayee·rehah·kohn·dee·seeyoh·nah·doh* |
| the dishwasher | **el lavavajillas** *ehl lah·bah·bah·khee·yahs* |
| the freezer | **el congelador** *ehl kohn·kheh·lah·dohr* |
| the heater | **la calefacción** *lah kah·leh·fahk·seeyohn* |
| the microwave | **el microondas** *ehl mee·kroh·ohn·dahs* |
| the refrigerator | **el refrigerador** *ehl reh·free·kheh·rah·dohr* |
| the stove | **el horno** *ehl ohr·noh* |
| the washing machine | **la lavadora** *lah lah·bah·doh·rah* |

## Domestic Items

| I need... | **Necesito...** *neh·seh·see·toh...* |
| an adapter | **un adaptador** *oon ah·dahp·tah·dohr* |
| aluminum [kitchen] foil | **papel de aluminio** *pah·pehl deh ah·loo·mee·neeyoh* |
| a bottle opener | **un abrebotellas** *oon ah·breh·boh·teh·yahs* |

| a broom | **una escoba** _oo_•nah ehs•_koh_•bah |
|---|---|
| a can opener | **un abrelatas** oon ah•breh•_lah_•tahs |
| cleaning supplies | **productos de limpieza** proh•_dook_•tohs deh leem•_peeyeh_•sah |
| a corkscrew | **un sacacorchos** oon sah•kah•_kohr_•chohs |
| detergent | **detergente** deh•tehr•_khehn_•teh |
| dishwashing liquid | **líquido lavavajillas** _lee_•kee•doh lah•bah•bah•_khee_•yahs |
| bin bags | **bolsas de basura** _bohl_•sahs deh bah•_soo_•rah |
| a lightbulb | **una bombilla** _oo_•nah bohm•_bee_•yah |
| matches | **fósforos** _fohs_•foh•rohs |
| a mop | **un trapeador** oon trah•peh•ah•_dohr_ |
| napkins | **servilletas** sehr•bee•_yeh_•tahs |
| paper towels | **papel de cocina** pah•_pehl_ deh koh•_see_•nah |
| plastic wrap [cling film] | **film transparente** feelm trahns•pah•_rehn_•teh |
| a plunger | **un desatascador** oon deh•sah•tahs•kah•_dohr_ |
| scissors | **tijeras** tee•_kheh_•rahs |
| a vacuum cleaner | **una aspiradora** _oo_•nah ahs•pee•rah•_doh_•rah |

For In the Kitchen, see page 80.

For Oven Temperature, see page 177.

## At the Hostel

| Is there a bed available? | **¿Hay camas disponibles?** ahy _kah_•mahs dees•poh•_nee_•blehs |
|---|---|
| Can I have...? | **¿Me puede dar...?** meh _pweh_•deh dahr... |
| a single/double room | **una habitación individual/doble** _oo_•nah ah•bee•tah•_seeyohn_ een•dee•bee•doo•_ahl_/_doh_•bleh |
| a blanket | **una manta** _oo_•nah _mahn_•tah |
| a pillow | **una almohada** _oo_•nah ahl•moh•_ah_•dah |
| sheets | **sábanas** _sah_•bah•nahs |
| a towel | **una toalla** _oo_•nah toh•_ah_•yah |

**Electrical outlets** have different voltages in different countries throughout Latin America. For example, Paraguay's electric current is 220 volts, Venezuela's is 120 volts and Mexico has both. You should check the voltage for the country you wish to visit, and bring a converter and/or an adapter for your appliances.

**Tipping** in hotels and bars is customary in Latin America, however, there is no standard or expected rate. The amount of the tip is voluntary.

There are many hostels around Latin America, so finding an inexpensive place to stay should be easy. Hostels are an inexpensive option that have dormitory-style rooms and, sometimes, private or semi-private rooms. Some offer private bathrooms, though most have shared facilities.

There is usually a self-service kitchen on site. Reservations are recommended in advance in larger cities and popular destinations during the high season.

| | | |
|---|---|---|
| Do you have lockers? | **¿Tiene casilleros?** | _teeyeh_•ne kah•see•_yeh_•rohs |
| When do you lock up? | **¿A qué hora cierran las puertas?** | |
| | _ah_ keh oh•rah _seeyeh_•rrahn lahs _pwehr_•tahs | |
| Do I need a | **¿Necesito una tarjeta de socio?** | |
| membership card? | neh•seh•_see_•toh _oo_•nah tahr•_kheh_•tah de _soh_•seeyoh | |
| Here's my | **Aquí tiene mi carné internacional de estudiante.** | |
| International | _ah_•_kee_ _teeyeh_•neh mee kahr•_neh_ | |
| Student Card. | een•tehr•nah•seeyoh•_nahl_ deh ehs•too•_deeyahn_•teh | |

## Going Camping

| | | |
|---|---|---|
| Can I camp here? | **¿Puedo acampar aquí?** | _pweh_•doh ah•kahm•_pahr_ ah•_kee_ |
| Where's the campsite? | **¿Dónde está el cámping?** | _dohn_•deh ehs•_tah_ |
| | ehl _kahm_•peeng | |

| | |
|---|---|
| What is the charge per day/week? | **¿Cuánto cobran por día/semana?** _kwahn_•toh _koh_•brahn pohr _dee_•ah/seh•_mah_•nah |
| Are there…? | **¿Hay…?** _aye_… |
| cooking facilities | **instalaciones para cocinar** eens•tah•lah•_seeyoh_•nehs pah•rah koh•see•_nahr_ |
| electric outlets | **enchufes eléctricos** ehn•_choo_•fehs eh•_lehk_•tree•kohs |
| laundry facilities | **servicio de lavandería** sehr•_bee_•seeyoh deh lah•bahn•deh•_ree_•ah |
| showers | **duchas** _doo_•chahs |
| tents for rent [hire] | **tiendas de alquiler** _teeyehn_•dahs deh ahl•kee•_lehr_ |
| Where can I empty the chemical toilet? | **¿Dónde puedo vaciar el inodoro químico?** _dohn_•deh _pweh_•doh bah•see•_yahr_ ehl ee•noh•_doh_•roh _kee_•mee•koh |

For Domestic Items, see page 46.

---

### YOU MAY SEE…

| | |
|---|---|
| **AGUA POTABLE** | drinking water |
| **PROHIBIDO ACAMPAR** | no camping |
| **PROHIBIDO HACER HOGUERAS/BARBACOAS** | no fires/ barbecues |

# Communications

## ESSENTIAL

| | |
|---|---|
| Where's an internet cafe? | **¿Dónde hay un cibercafé?** _dohn·deh aye oon see·behr·kah·feh_ |
| Can I access the internet here/ check e-mail ? | **¿Puedo acceder a Internet/revisar el correo electrónico?** _pweh·doh ahk·seh·dehr ah een·tehr·neht/reh·bee·sahr ehl koh·rreh·oh eh·lehk·troh·nee·koh_ |
| How much per (half) hour? | **¿Cuánto cuesta por (media) hora?** _kwahn·toh kwehs·tah pohr (meh·deeyah) oh·rah_ |
| How do I connect/ log on? | **¿Cómo entro al sistema/inicio la sesión?** _koh·moh ehn·troh ahl sees·teh·mah/ee·nee·seeyoh lah seh·seeyohn_ |
| A phone card, please. | **Una tarjeta telefónica, por favor.** _oo·nah tahr·kheh·tah teh·leh·foh·nee·kah pohr fah·bohr_ |
| Can I have your phone number? | **¿Me puede dar su número de teléfono?** _meh pweh·deh dahr soo noo·meh·roh deh teh·leh·foh·noh_ |
| Here's my number/ e-mail address. | **Aquí tiene mi número/dirección de correo electrónico.** _ah·kee teeyeh·neh mee noo·meh·roh/ dee·rehk·seeyohn deh koh·rreh·oh eh·lehk·troh·nee·koh_ |
| Call me. | **Llámeme.** _yah·meh·meh_ |
| E-mail me. | **Envíeme un correo.** _ehn·bee·eh·meh oon koh·rreh·oh_ |
| Hello. This is… | **Hola. Soy…** _oh·lah soy…_ |
| Can I speak to…? | **¿Puedo hablar con…?** _pweh·doh ah·blahr kohn…_ |
| Can you repeat that? | **¿Puede repetir eso?** _pweh·deh reh·peh·teer eh·soh_ |
| I'll call back later. | **Llamaré más tarde.** _yah·mah·reh mahs tahr·deh_ |
| Bye. | **Adiós.** _ah·deeyohs_ |

| Where's the post office? | **¿Dónde está la oficina de correos?** |
| | *dohn-deh ehs-tah lah oh-fee-see-nah deh koh-rreh-ohs* |
| I'd like to send this to… | **Quiero mandar esto a…** *keeyeh-roh* |
| | *mahn-dahr ehs-toh ah…* |

## Online

| Where's an internet cafe? | **¿Dónde hay un cibercafé?** |
| | *dohn-deh aye oon see-behr-kah-feh* |
| Does it have wireless internet? | **¿Tiene Internet inalámbrico?** |
| | *teeyeh-neh een-tehr-neht een-ah-lahm-bree-koh* |
| What is the WiFi password? | **¿Cuál es la contraseña de WiFi?** *kwahl ehs* |
| | *lah kohn-trah-seh-nya deh WiFi* |
| Is the WiFi free? | **¿Es gratis el WiFi?** *ehs grah-tees ehl WiFi* |
| Do you have bluetooth? | **¿Tiene bluetooth?** *teeyeh-ne bloo-tooth* |
| How do I turn the computer on/off? | **¿Cómo enciendo/apago la computadora?** *koh-moh* |
| | *ehn-seeyen-doh/ah-pah-goh lah kohm-poo-tah-doh-rah* |
| Can I…? | **¿Puedo…?** *pweh-doh…* |
| access the internet | **acceder a Internet** *ahk-seh-dehr ah een-tehr-neht* |
| check e-mail | **revisar el correo electrónico** *reh-bee-sahr ehl* |
| | *koh-rreh-oh eh-lehk-troh-nee-koh* |
| print | **imprimir** *eem-pree-meer* |
| plug in/charge my laptop/iPhone/iPad/BlackBerry? | **conectar/cargar mi laptop/iPhone/iPad/BlackBerry?** *koh-nehk-tahr/kahr-gahr mee lahp tohp/* |
| | *aye fohn/aye pahd/blahk beh-rree* |
| access Skype? | **acceder a Skype?** *ahk-seh-dehr ah ehs-kype* |
| How much per (half) hour? | **¿Cuánto cuesta por (media) hora?** |
| | *kwahn-toh kwehs-tah pohr (meh-deeyah) oh-rah* |
| How do I…? | **¿Cómo…?** *koh-moh…* |
| connect/disconnect | **me conecto/me desconecto** |
| | *meh koh-nehk-toh/meh dehs-koh-nehk-toh* |

| log on/off | **inicio/cierro la sesión** *ee·<u>nee</u>·seeyoh/<u>seeyeh</u>·rroh lah seh·<u>seeyohn</u>* |
| type this symbol | **escribo este símbolo** *ehs·<u>kree</u>·boh ehs·teh <u>seem</u>·boh·loh* |
| What's your e-mail? | **¿Cuál es su dirección de correo electrónico?** *kwahl ehs soo dee·rehk·<u>seeyohn</u> deh koh·<u>rreh</u>·oh eh·lehk·<u>troh</u>·nee·koh* |
| My e-mail is… | **Mi dirección de correo electrónico es…** *mee dee·rehk·<u>seeyohn</u> deh koh·<u>rreh</u>·oh eh·lehk·<u>troh</u>·nee·koh ehs…* |
| Do you have a scanner? | **¿Tiene escáner?** *<u>teeyeh</u>·neh ehs·<u>kah</u>·nehr* |

## Social Media

| Are you on Facebook/Twitter? | **¿Estás en Facebook/Twitter?** *ehs·<u>tahs</u> ehn <u>fays</u>·book/<u>twee</u>·tehr* |
| What's your user name? | **¿Cuál es tu nombre de usuario?** *kwahl ehs too <u>nohm</u>·breh deh oo·<u>swah</u>·reeoh* |
| I'll add you as a friend. | **Te agregaré como amigo(a).** *teh ah·greh·gah·<u>reh</u> koh·moh ah·<u>mee</u>·goh(ah)* |
| I'll follow you on Twitter. | **Te seguiré en Twitter.** *teh seh·gee·<u>reh</u> ehn twee·tehr* |
| Are you following…? | **¿Estás siguiendo…?** *ehs·<u>tahs</u> see·<u>geeyehn</u>·doh* |
| I'll put the pictures on Facebook/Twitter. | **Pondré fotos en Facebook/Twitter.** *pohn·<u>dreh</u> foh·tohs ehn <u>fays</u>·book/<u>twee</u>·tehr* |
| I'll tag you in the pictures. | **Te etiquetaré en las fotos.** *teh eh·tee·keh·tah·<u>reh</u> ehn lahs <u>foh</u>·tohs* |

## Phone

| A phone card/prepaid phone, please. | **Una tarjeta telefónica/Un teléfono prepago, por favor.** *<u>oo</u>·nah tahr·<u>kheh</u>·tah teh·leh·<u>foh</u>·nee·kah/oon teh·<u>leh</u>·foh·noh preh·<u>pah</u>·goh pohr fah·<u>bohr</u>* |
| How much? | **¿Cuánto es?** *<u>kwahn</u>·toh ehs* |
| Where's the pay phone? | **¿Dónde está el teléfono público?** *<u>dohn</u>·deh ehs·<u>tah</u> ehl teh·<u>leh</u>·foh·noh <u>poo</u>·blee·koh* |

## YOU MAY SEE...

| | |
|---|---|
| **CERRAR** | close |
| **BORRAR** | delete |
| **CORREO ELECTRÓNICO** | e-mail |
| **SALIR** | exit |
| **AYUDA** | help |
| **MENSAJERO INSTANTÁNEO** | instant messenger |
| **INTERNET** | internet |
| **INICIO DE SESIÓN** | login |
| **NUEVO (MENSAJE)** | new (message) |
| **ENCENDER/APAGAR** | on/off |
| **ABRIR** | open |
| **IMPRIMIR** | print |
| **GUARDAR** | save |
| **ENVIAR** | send |
| **NOMBRE DE USUARIO/CONTRASEÑA** | username/password |
| **INTERNET INALÁMBRICO** | wireless internet |

| | |
|---|---|
| What's the area code/country code for...? | **¿Cuál es el prefijo/código de país para...?** <br> *kwahl ehs ehl preh·fee·khoh/ koh·dee·goh deh pah·ees pah·rah...* |
| What's the number for Information? | **¿Cuál es el número de información?** <br> *kwahl ehs ehl noo·meh·roh deh een·fohr·mah·seeyohn* |
| I'd like the number for... | **Quiero que me dé el número de teléfono de...** <br> *keeyeh·roh keh meh deh ehl noo·meh·roh deh teh·leh·foh·noh deh...* |
| I'd like to call collect [reverse the charges]. | **Quiero hacer una llamada por cobrar [hacer el cargo]** *keeyeh·roh ah·sehr oo·nah yah·mah·dah pohr koh·brahr [ah·sehr ehl kahr·goh]* |
| My phone doesn't work here. | **Mi teléfono no funciona aquí.** <br> *mee teh·leh·foh·noh no foon·seeyoh·nah ah·kee* |

| What network are you on? | **¿En qué red estás?** *ehn keh rehd ehs-tahs* |
| Is it 3G? | **¿Es 3G?** *ehs trehs kheh* |
| I have run out of credit/minutes. | **Se me acabó el crédito/Se me acabaron los minutos.** *seh meh ah-kah-boh ehl kreh-dee-toh/ seh meh ah-kah-bah-rohn lohs mee-noo-tohs* |
| Can I buy some credit? | **¿Puedo comprar más crédito?** *pweh-doh kohm-prahr mahs kreh-dee-toh* |
| Do you have a phone charger? | **¿Tiene cargador de teléfono?** *teeyeh-neh kahr-gah-dohr deh teh-leh-foh-noh* |
| Can I have your number? | **¿Me puede dar su número de teléfono?** *meh pweh-deh dahr soo noo-meh-roh deh teh-leh-foh-noh* |
| Here's my number. | **Aquí tiene mi número.** *ah-kee teeyeh-neh mee noo-meh-roh* |
| Please call me. | **Llámame, por favor.** *yah-mah-meh pohr fah-bohr* |
| Please text me. | **Envíame un mensaje de texto, por favor.** *ehn-beeyah-meh oon mehn-sah-kheh deh tehx-toh poh fah-bohr* |
| I'll call you. | **Lo m/La f llamaré.** *loh/lah yah-mah-reh* |
| I'll text you. | **Te enviaré un mensaje de texto.** *teh ehn-beeyah-re oon mehn-sah-kheh deh tehx-toh* |

## Telephone Etiquette

| Hello. This is… | **Hola. Soy…** *oh-lah soy…* |
| Can I speak to…? | **¿Puedo hablar con…?** *pweh-doh ah-blahr kohn…* |
| Extension… | **Extensión…** *ehks-tehn-seeyohn…* |
| Speak louder/more slowly, please. | **Hable más alto/despacio, por favor.** *ah-bleh mahs ahl-toh/dehs-pah-seeyoh pohr fah-bohr* |
| Can you repeat that? | **¿Puede repetir eso?** *pweh-deh reh-peh-teer eh-soh* |
| I'll call back later. | **Llamaré más tarde.** *yah-mah-reh mahs tuhr-deh* |
| Bye. | **Adiós.** *ah-deeyohs* |

Public phones are generally either coin or card operated, though
coin operated phones are becoming less common. Phone cards
can be purchased in post offices, newsstands and supermarkets.
For international calls, calling cards are the most economical.
You can also make long distance calls at **locutorios** (call centers);
these also offer internet, fax and wireless phone charging services at
reasonable prices. International hotel call rates can be very expensive.
To call the U.S. or Canada from Latin America, dial 00 + 1 + area code
+ phone number. To call the U.K. from Latin America, dial 00 + 44 +
area code (minus the first 0) + phone number.

## Fax

| | |
|---|---|
| Can I send/receive a fax here? | **¿Puedo enviar/recibir un fax aquí?** _pweh•doh ehn•bee•ahr/reh•see•beer oon fahx ah•kee_ |
| What's the fax number? | **¿Cuál es el número de fax?** _kwahl ehs ehl noo•meh•roh deh fahx_ |
| Please fax this to… | **Por favor envíe este fax a…** _pohr fah•bohr ehn•bee•eh ehs•teh fahx ah…_ |

## YOU MAY HEAR...

| | |
|---|---|
| **¿Quién llama?** keeyehn <u>yah</u>•mah | Who's calling? |
| **Espere.** ehs•<u>peh</u>•reh | Hold on. |
| **Le paso.** leh <u>pah</u>•soh | I'll put you through. |
| **No está.** noh ehs•<u>tah</u> | He/She is not here. |
| **No puede atenderlo** m/ **atenderla** f **en este momento.** noh <u>pweh</u>•deh ah•tehn•<u>dehr</u>•loh/ ah•tchn•dehr•lah ehn ehs•teh moh•<u>mehn</u>•toh | He/She can't come to the phone. |
| **¿Quiere dejarle un mensaje?** <u>keeyeh</u>•reh deh•<u>khahr</u>•leh oon mehn•<u>sah</u>•kheh | Would you like to leave a message? |
| **Vuelva a llamar más tarde/en diez minutos.** <u>bwehl</u>•bah ah yah•<u>mahr</u> mahs <u>tahr</u>•deh/ehn deeyehs mee•<u>noo</u>•tohs | Call back later/in 10 minutes. |
| **¿Lo** m/**La** f **puede llamar él/ella a usted?** loh/lah <u>pweh</u>•deh yah•<u>mahr</u> ehl/ <u>eh</u>•yah ah oos•<u>tehd</u>? | Can he/she call you back? |
| **¿Me da su número?** meh dah soo <u>noo</u>•meh•roh | What's your number? |

## Post

| | |
|---|---|
| Where's the post office/mailbox [postbox]? | **¿Dónde está la oficina/el buzón de correos?** <u>dohn</u>•deh ehs•<u>tah</u> lah oh•fee•<u>see</u>•nah/ehl boo•<u>sohn</u> deh koh•<u>rreh</u>•ohs |
| A stamp for this postcard/letter to... | **Una estampilla para esta postal/carta a...** oona ehs•tam•<u>pee</u>•yah <u>pah</u>•rah <u>ehs</u>•tah pohs•<u>tahl</u>/ <u>kahr</u>•tah ah... |
| How much? | **¿Cuánto es?** <u>kwahn</u>•toh ehs |

| | |
|---|---|
| I want to send this package by airmail/express. | **Quiero mandar este paquete por correo aéreo/urgente.** _keeyeh_•roh mahn•_dahr_ ehs•teh pah•_keh_•teh pohr koh•rreh•oh ah•_eh_•reh•oh/oor•_khen_•teh |
| A receipt, please. | **Un recibo, por favor.** oon reh•_see_•boh pohr fah•_bohr_ |

### YOU MAY HEAR...

**Rellene la declaración para la aduana.**
reh•_yeh_•neh lah deh•klah•rah•_seeyohn_
_pah_•rah lah ah•doo•_ah_•nah

Fill out the customs
declaration form.

**¿Qué valor tiene?** keh bah•_lohr_ teeyeh•neh

What's the value?

**¿Qué hay dentro?** keh aye _dehn_•troh

What's inside?

**Oficinas de Correos** (post offices) in Latin America offer more than just standard postal services. You may be able to fax, scan and e-mail documents and send money orders from the local post office. The services available vary by location.

# Food & Drink

## ESSENTIAL

| | |
|---|---|
| Can you recommend a good restaurant/bar? | **¿Puede recomendarme un buen restaurante/bar?** _pweh_•deh reh•koh•mehn•_dahr_ •meh oon bwehn rehs•taw•_rahn_•teh/bahr |
| Is there a traditional/inexpensive restaurant nearby? | **¿Hay un restaurante típico/barato cerca de aquí?** _aye oon rehs•taw•_rahn_•teh _tee_•pee•koh/bah•_rah_•toh _sehr_•kah deh ah•_kee_ |
| A table for one/two, please. | **Una mesa para uno/dos..., por favor.** _oo_•nah _meh_•sah _pah_•rah oo•noh/dohs pohr fah•_bohr_ |
| Can we sit...? | **¿Podemos sentarnos...?** poh•_deh_•mohs sehn•_tahr_•nohs... |
| here/there | **aquí/allá** ah•_kee_/ah•_ya_ |
| outside | **afuera** ah•_fweh_•rah |
| in a non-smoking area | **en una zona de no fumadores** ehn _oo_•nah _soh_•nah deh noh foo•mah•_doh_•rehs |
| I'm waiting for someone. | **Estoy esperando a alguien.** ehs•_toy_ ehs•peh•_rahn_•doh ah _ahl_•geeyehn |
| Where's the restroom [toilet]? | **¿Dónde están los servicios?** _dohn_•deh ehs•_tahn_ lohs sehr•_bee_•seeohs |
| A menu, please. | **Una carta, por favor.** _oo_•nah _kahr_•tah pohr fah•_bohr_ |
| What do you recommend? | **¿Qué me recomienda?** keh meh reh•koh•_meeyehn_•dah |
| I'd like... | **Quiero...** _keeyeh_•roh... |
| Some more..., please. | **Quiero más..., por favor.** _keeyeh_•roh mahs...pohr fah•_bohr_ |
| Enjoy your meal! | **¡Buen provecho!** bwen proh•_beh_•choh |
| The check [bill], please. | **La cuenta, por favor.** lah _kwen_•tah pohr fah•_bohr_ |

| Is service included? | **¿Está incluido el servicio?** |
| | *ehs·tah een·kloo·ee·doh ehl sehr·bee·seeyoh* |
| Can I pay by credit card? | **¿Puedo pagar con tarjeta de crédito?** |
| | *pweh·doh pah·gahr kohn tahr·kheh·tah deh kreh·dee·toh* |
| Can I have a receipt? | **¿Podría darme un recibo?** |
| | *poh·dree·ah dahr·meh oon reh·see·boh* |
| Thank you! | **¡Gracias!** *grah·seeyahs* |

## Where to Eat

| Can you recommend...? | **¿Puede recomendarme...?** |
| | *pweh·deh reh·koh·mehn·dahr·meh...* |
| a restaurant | **un restaurante** *oon rehs·taw·rahn·teh* |
| a bar | **un bar** *oon bahr* |
| a cafe | **un café** *oon kah·feh* |
| a fast-food place | **un restaurante de comida rápida** *oon rehs·taw·rahn·teh deh koh·mee·dah rah·pee·dah* |
| a cheap restaurant | **un restaurante económico** *oon rehs·taw·rahn·teh eh·koh·noh·mee·koh* |
| an expensive restaurant | **un restaurante caro** *oon rehs·taw·rahn·teh kah·ro* |
| a restaurant with a good view | **un restaurante con buena vista** *oon rehs·taw·rahn·teh kohn bweh·nah bees·tah* |
| an authentic/a non-touristy restaurant | **un restaurante auténtico/no turístico** *oon rehs·taw·rahn·teh ahw·tehn·tee·koh/noh too·rees·tee·koh* |

## Reservations & Preferences

| I'd like to reserve a table... | **Quiero reservar una mesa...** |
| | *keeyeh·roh reh·sehr·bahr oo·nah meh·sah...* |
| for two | **para dos** *pah·rah dohs* |
| for this evening | **para esta noche** *pah·rah ehs·tah noh·cheh* |

| | |
|---|---|
| for tomorrow at... | **para mañana a la/las...** |
| | *pah·rah mah·nyah·nah ah lah/lahs...* |
| A table for two, please. | **Una mesa para dos, por favor.** |
| | *oo·nah meh·sah pah·rah dohs pohr fah·bohr* |
| We have a reservation. | **Tenemos una reserva.** |
| | *teh·neh·mohs oo·nah reh·sehr·bah* |
| My name is... | **Me llamo...** *meh yah·moh...* |
| Can we sit...? | **¿Podríamos sentarnos...?** |
| | *poh·dree·ah·mohs sehn·tahr·nohs...* |
| here/there | **aquí/allá** *ah·kee/ah·ya* |
| outside | **afuera** *ah·fweh·rah* |
| in a non-smoking area | **en una zona de no fumadores** |
| | *ehn oo·nah soh·nah deh noh foo·mah·doh·rehs* |
| by the window | **al lado de la ventana** |
| | *ahl lah·doh de lah behn·tah·nah* |
| in the sun | **en el sol** *ehn ehl sohl* |
| in the shade | **en la sombra** *ehn lah sohm·brah* |

## YOU MAY HEAR...

| | |
|---|---|
| **¿Tiene reserva?** | Do you have |
| *teeyeh·neh reh·sehr·bah* | a reservation? |
| **¿Cuántos son?** *kwahn·tohs sohn* | How many? |
| **¿Fumador o no fumador?** | Smoking or |
| *foo·mah·dohr oh noh foo·mah·dohr* | non-smoking? |
| **¿Está listo _m_/lista _f_ para pedir?** | Are you ready to order? |
| *ehs·tah lees·toh/lees·tah pah·rah peh·deer?* | |
| **¿Qué va a tomar?** *keh bah ah toh·mahr* | What would you like? |
| **Le recomiendo...** *leh reh·koh·meeyehn·doh...* | I recommend... |
| **Buen provecho.** *bwen proh·beh·choh* | Enjoy your meal. |

| Where's the restroom [toilet]? | **¿Dónde están los servicios?** |
| | _dohn_·deh ehs·_tahn_ lohs sehr·_bee_·seeohs |

## How to Order

| Waiter/Waitress! | **¡Camarero _m_/Camarera _f_!** |
| | kah·mah·_reh_·roh/kah·mah·_reh_·rah |
| We're ready to order. | **Estamos listos para pedir.** |
| | ehs·_tah_·mohs _lees_·tohs _pah_·rah peh·_deer_ |
| The wine list, please. | **La carta de vinos, por favor.** |
| | lah _kahr_·tah deh _bee_·nohs pohr fah·_bohr_ |
| I'd like... | **Quiero...** _keeyeh_·roh... |
| a bottle of... | **una botella de...** _oo_·nah boh·_teh_·yah deh... |
| a carafe of... | **una jarra de...** _oo_·nah _jah_·rrah deh... |
| a glass of... | **un vaso de...** oon _bah_·soh deh... |
| The menu, please. | **La carta, por favor.** lah _kahr_·tah pohr fah·_bohr_ |
| Do you have...? | **¿Tiene...?** _teeyeh_·neh... |
| a menu in English | **una carta en inglés** _oo_·nah _kahr_·tah ehn een·_glehs_ |
| a fixed-price menu | **el menú del día** ehl meh·_noo_ dehl _dee_·ah |
| a children's menu | **una carta para niños** |
| | _oo_·nah _kahr_·tah _pah_·rah _nee_·nyohs |
| What do you recommend? | **¿Qué me recomienda?** |
| | keh meh reh·koh·_meeyehn_·dah |

| | | |
|---|---|---|
| What's this? | **¿Qué es esto?** *keh ehs ehs•toh* | |
| What's in it? | **¿Qué lleva?** *keh yeh•bah* | |
| Is it spicy? | **¿Es picante?** *ehs pee•kahn•the* | |
| I'd like... | **Quiero...** *keeyeh•roh...* | |
| More..., please. | **Más..., por favor.** *mahs...pohr fah•bohr* | |
| With/Without... | **Con/Sin...** *kohn/seen...* | |
| I can't have... | **No puedo tomar...** *noh pweh•doh toh•mahr...* | |
| rare | **muy poco cocido m/cocida f** | |
| | *mooy poh•koh koh•sih•doh/koh•sih•dah* | |
| medium | **término medio** *tehr•meeh•noh meh•deeyoh* | |
| well-done | **bien cocido m/cocida f** | |
| | *beeyehn koh•sih•doh/koh•sih•dah* | |
| It's to go [take away]. | **Es para llevar.** *ehs pah•rah yeh•bahr* | |

For Drinks, see page 82.

---

**YOU MAY SEE...**

| | |
|---|---|
| **PROPINA** | cover charge |
| **MENÚ DEL DÍA** | menu of the day |
| **SERVICIO (NO) INCLUIDO** | service (not) included |
| **ESPECIALIDADES DE LA CASA** | specials |

---

## Cooking Methods

| | |
|---|---|
| baked | **al horno** *ahl ohr•noh* |
| boiled | **hervido m/hervida f** *ehr•bee•doh/ehr•bee•dah* |
| braised | **a fuego lento** *ah fweh•goh lehn•toh* |
| breaded | **empanado m/empanada f** |
| | *ehm•pah•nah•doh/ehm•pah•nah•dah* |
| creamed | **con crema** *kohn kreh•mah* |
| diced | **cortado en daditos** *kohr•tah•doh ehn dah•dee•tohs* |

| | |
|---|---|
| fileted | **cortado en filetes** kohr·_tah_·doh ehn fee·_leh_·tehs |
| fried | **frito** m/**frita** f _free_·toh/_free_·tah |
| grilled | **a la plancha** ah lah _plahn_·chah |
| poached | **escalfado** m/**escalfada** f _ehs·kahl·_fah_·doh/ehs·kahl·_fah_·dah |
| roasted | **asado** m/**asada** f ah·_sah_·doh/ah·_sah_·dah |
| sautéed | **salteado** m/**salteada** f _sahl·teh·ah·doh/sahl·teh·ah·dah |
| smoked | **ahumado** m/**ahumada** f _ah_·oo·mah·doh/_ah_·oo·mah·dah |
| steamed | **al vapor** ahl bah·_pohr_ |
| stewed | **guisado** m/**guisada** f gee·_sah_·doh/gee·_sah_·dah |
| stuffed | **relleno** m/**rellena** f reh·_yeh_·noh/reh·_yeh_·nah |

## Dietary Requirements

| | |
|---|---|
| I'm... | **Soy...** soy... |
| diabetic | **diabético** m/**diabética** f dee·ah·_beh_·tee·koh/dee·ah·_beh_·tee·kah |
| lactose intolerant | **intolerante a la lactosa** een·toh·leh·_rahn_·teh ah lah lahk·_toh_·sah |
| vegetarian | **vegetariano** m/**vegetariana** f beh·kheh·tah·_reeyah_·noh/beh·kheh·tah·_reeyah_·nah |
| vegan | **vegetariano estricto** beh·kheh·tah·_reeyah_·noh ehs·_treek_·toh |
| I'm allergic to... | **Soy alérgico** m/**alérgica** f **a...** soy ah·_lehr_·khee·koh/ah·_lehr_·khee·kah ah... |
| I can't eat... | **No puedo comer...** noh _pweh_·doh koh·_mehr_... |
| dairy products | **productos lácteos** proh·_dook_·tohs lahk·teh·ohs |
| gluten | **gluten** _gloo_·tehn |
| nuts | **frutos secos** _froo_·tohs _seh_·kohs |
| pork | **carne de cerdo** _kahr_·neh deh _sehr_·doh |

64

| shellfish | **mariscos** *mah·rees·kohs* |
| spicy foods | **comidas picantes** *koh·mee·dahs pee·kahn·tehs* |
| wheat | **trigo** *tree·goh* |
| Is it halal/kosher ? | **¿Es halal/kosher ?** *ehs ah·lahl/koh·sehr* |
| Do you have...? | **¿Tiene...?** *teeyeh·neh* |
| skimmed milk | **leche descremada** *leh·cheh dehs·kreh·mah·dah* |
| whole milk | **leche entera** *leh·cheh ehn·teh·rah* |
| soya milk | **leche de soya** *leh·cheh deh soh·yah* |

## Dining with Children

| Do you have children's portions? | **¿Sirven raciones para niños?** *seer·behn rah·seeyoh·nehs pah·rah nee·nyohs* |
| A highchair/child's seat, please. | **Una silla alta/para niños, por favor.** *oo·nah see·yah ahl·tah/pah·rah nee·nyohs pohr fah·bohr* |
| Where can I feed/change the baby? | **¿Dónde puedo darle de comer/cambiar al niño?** *dohn·deh pweh·doh dahr·leh deh koh·mehr/kahm·beeyahr ahl nee·nyoh* |
| Can you warm this? | **¿Puede calentar esto?** *pweh·deh kah·lehn·tahr ehs·toh* |

For Traveling with Children, see page 146.

## How to Complain

| How much longer will our food be? | **¿Cuánto más tardará la comida?** *kwahn·toh mahs tahr·dah·rah lah koh·mee·dah* |
| We can't wait any longer. | **No podemos esperar más.** *noh poh·deh·mohs ehs·peh·rahr mahs* |
| We're leaving. | **Nos vamos.** *nohs bah·mohs* |
| I didn't order this. | **Esto no es lo que pedí.** *ehs·toh noh ehs loh keh peh·dee* |
| I ordered... | **Pedí...** *peh·dee...* |
| I can't eat this. | **No puedo comerme esto.** *noh pweh·doh koh·mehr·meh ehs·toh* |

| This is too... | **Esto está demasiado...** |
| | *ehs·toh ehs·tah deh·mah·seeyah·doh...* |
| cold/hot | **frío/caliente** *free·oh/kah·leeyehn·teh* |
| salty/spicy | **salado/picante** *sah·lah·doh/pee·kahn·teh* |
| tough/bland | **duro/soso** *doo·roh/soh·soh* |
| This isn't clean/fresh. | **Esto no está limpio/fresco.** |
| | *ehs·toh noh ehs·tah leem·peeyoh/frehs·koh* |

## Paying

| The check [bill], please. | **La cuenta, por favor.** *lah kwehn·tah pohr fah·bohr* |
| Separate checks [bills], please. | **Cuentas separadas, por favor.** |
| | *kwehn·tahs seh·pah·rah·dahs pohr fah·bohr* |
| It's all together. | **Póngalo todo junto.** |
| | *pohn·gah·loh toh·doh khoon·toh* |
| Is service included? | **¿Está incluido el servicio?** |
| | *ehs·tah een·kloo·ee·doh ehl sehr·bee·seeyoh* |
| What's this amount for? | **¿De qué es esta cantidad?** |
| | *deh keh ehs ehs·tah kahn·tee·dahd* |
| I didn't have that. I had... | **Yo no tomé eso. Tomé...** |
| | *yoh noh toh·meh eh·soh toh·meh...* |
| Can I pay by credit card? | **¿Puedo pagar con tarjeta de crédito?** *pweh·doh* |
| | *pah·gahr kohn tahr·kheh·tah deh kreh·dee·toh* |
| Can I have a receipt/ an itemized bill? | **¿Podría darme un recibo/una cuenta detallada?** |
| | *poh·dree·ah dahr·meh oon reh·see·boh/oo·nah* |
| | *kwehn·tah deh·tah·yah·dah* |

Although restaurants are generally required to include service charges as part of the bill, a tip is also expected. A tip of 10% of the bill is customary for the waiter.

| That was delicious! | **¡Estuvo delicioso!** ehs·_too_·boh deh·lee·_seeyoh_·soh |
| I've already paid. | **Ya pagué** yah pah·_gweh_ |

## Meals & Cooking

**El desayuno** (breakfast) is usually served from 7:00 – 10:00 a.m. **El almuerzo** (lunch), generally the largest meal of the day, is served from 1:00– 4:00 p.m. **La cena** (dinner) is typically a light meal, and is usually served after 8:00 p.m.

## Breakfast

| | |
| --- | --- |
| **el agua** ehl _ah_·gwah | water |
| **el bollo** ehl _boh_·yoh | muffin |
| **el café/el té...** ehl kah·_feh_/ehl teh... | coffee/tea... |
| **con azúcar** kohn ah·_soo_·kahr | with sugar |
| **con edulcorante artificial** kohn eh·dool·koh·_rahn_·teh ahr·tee·fee·_seeyahl_ | with artificial sweetener |
| **con leche** kohn _leh_·cheh | with milk |
| **descafeinado** dehs·kah·feyee·_nah_·doh | decaf |
| **solo** _soh_·loh | black |
| **los cereales (calientes/fríos)** lohs seh·reh·_ah_·lehs (kah·_leeyehn_·tehs/_free_·ohs) | (cold/hot) cereal |
| **los fiambres** lohs fee·_ahm_·brehs | cold cuts [charcuterie] |
| **las frutas** lahs _froo_·tahs | fruits |
| **la granola** lah grah·_noh_·lah | granola [muesli] |
| **la harina de avena** lah ah·_ree_·nah deh ah·_beh_·nah | oatmeal |

| | |
|---|---|
| **el huevo...** *ehl weh·boh...* | egg... |
| **duro/pasado por agua** | hard-/soft-boiled |
| *doo·roh/pah·sah·doh pohr ah·gwah* | |
| **frito** *free·toh* | fried |
| **revuelto** *reh·bwehl·toh* | scrambled |
| **el jugo de...** *ehl khoo·goh deh...* | ...juice |
| **manzana** *mahn·sah·nah* | apple |
| **pomelo** *poh·meh·loh* | grapefruit |
| **naranja** *nah·rahn·khah* | orange |
| **la leche** *lah leh·cheh* | milk |
| **la mantequilla** *lah mahn·teh·kee·yah* | butter |
| **la mermelada/la jalea** | jam/jelly |
| *lah mehr·meh·lah·dah/khah·leh·ah* | |
| **el pan** *ehl pahn* | bread |
| **el panecillo** *ehl pah·neh·see·yoh* | roll |
| **el panqueque** *ehl pahn·keh·keh* | pancakes |
| **el queso** *ehl keh·soh* | cheese |
| **la salchicha** *lah sahl·chee·chah* | sausage |
| **el sándwich** *ehl sahn·weech* | sandwich |
| **mixto** *meex·toh* | with ham and cheese |
| **de pollo** *deh poh·yoh* | with chicken |
| **de huevo** *deh weh·boh* | with egg |

| | |
|---|---|
| **el tocino** *ehl toh-see-noh* | bacon |
| **la tortilla...** *lah tohr-tee-yah...* | omelet... |
| **de papas** *deh pah-pahs* | with potato (and sometimes onion) |
| **de jamón** *deh khah-mohn* | with ham |
| **de queso** *deh keh-soh* | with cheese |
| **de hongos** *deh ohn-gohs* | with mushrooms |
| **la tostada** *lah tohs-tah-dah* | toast |
| **el yogur** *ehl yoh-goor* | yogurt |

## Appetizers

| | |
|---|---|
| **las aceitunas (rellenas)** *lahs ah-seyee-too-nahs (reh-yeh-nahs)* | (stuffed) olives |
| **las albóndigas** *lahs ahl-bohn-dee-gahs* | meatballs |
| **las anchoas en vinagre** *lahs an-choh-ahs ehn bee-nah-greh* | anchovies marinated in garlic and olive oil |
| **el bacalao** *ehl bah-kah-laoh* | dried salt cod |
| **las brochetas** *lahs broh-cheh-tahs* | grilled, skewered meat |
| **los caracoles** *lohs kah-rah-koh-lehs* | snails |
| **el ceviche** *ehl seh-bee-cheh* | raw fish marinated in lime |
| **los champiñones al ajillo** *lohs chahm-pee-nyoh-nehs ahl ah-khee-yoh* | mushrooms fried in olive oil with garlic |
| **las croquetas** *lahs kroh-keh-tahs* | croquettes with various fillings |
| **las empanadas...** *lahs ehm-pah-nah-dahs...* | flour dough stuffed... |
| **de carne** *deh kahr-neh* | with meat |
| **de pollo** *deh poh-yoh* | with chicken |
| **de queso** *deh keh-soh* | with cheese |
| **las langostinos al ajillo** *lohs lahn-gohs-tee-nohs ahl ah-khee-yoh* | broiled shrimp in garlic |
| **el mondongo** *ehl mon-dohn-goh* | tripe in hot paprika sauce |

**los pescados fritos**      fried fish
*lohs pehs•kah•dohs free•tohs*

**los pimientos** *lohs pee•meeyehn•tohs*      peppers

**los quesos** *lohs keh•sohs*      cheese platter

**el tamal** *ehl tah•mahl*      corn and cornmeal dough
stuffed with a meat mixture

**la tortilla española**      potato omelet
*lah tohr•tee•yah ehs•pah•nyoh•lah*

> **Piqueos** are snacks, similar to appetizers, served in cafes, bars
> and restaurants. Many bars have their own specialties and each
> country has its own typical **piqueo**.

## Soup

| | |
|---|---|
| **el gazpacho** *ehl gahs•pah•choh* | cold tomato soup |
| **el sancochado** *ehl sahn•koh•chah•doh* | boiled meat with cabbage, corn, potatoes, turnip |
| **la sopa...** *lah soh•pah...* | ...soup |
|    **de espárragos** *deh ehs•pah•rrah•gohs* | asparagus |
|    **de frijoles** *deh frih•khoh•les* | bean |
|    **de mariscos** *deh mah•rees•kohs* | seafood |
|    **de pollo** *deh poh•yoh* | chicken |
|    **de tomate** *deh toh•mah•teh* | tomato |
|    **de verduras** *deh behr•doo•rahs* | vegetables |
|    **de zapallo** *deh sah•pah•yoh* | squash |

## Fish & Seafood

| | |
|---|---|
| **la almeja** *lah ahl•meh•khah* | clam |
| **la anchoa** *lah an•cho•ah* | fresh baby anchovy |

**el arenque** *ehl ah·rehn·keh* — herring
**el atún** *ehl ah·toon* — tuna
**el bacalao** *ehl bah·kah·laoh* — cod
**el besugo** *ehl beh·soo·goh* — sea bream
**la caballa** *lah kah·bah·yah* — mackerel
**el cangrejo** *ehl kahn·greh·khoh* — crab
**ceviche** *seh·bee·cheh* — ceviche (cold fish marinated with citrus fruits)

   **de pescado** *deh pehs·kah·do* — fish
   **de langostinos** *deh lahn·gohs·tee·nohs* — shrimp
   **de pulpo** *deh pool·poh* — octopus
   **de conchas** *deh kohn·chahs* — scallops
   **mixto** *meex·toh* — mixed seafood
**el chicharrón de calamar** — deep-fried squid
*ehl chee·chah·rrohn deh kah·lah·mahr*
**las cigalas** *lahs see·gah·lahs* — crayfish
**las cigalas cocidas** — boiled crayfish
*lahs see·gah·lahs koh·see·dahs*
**la cojinova** *lah koh·khee·noh·bah* — yellowtail
**las conchas** *lahs kohn·chahs* — scallops
**la corvina** *lah kohr·bee·nah* — meagre
**los langostinos** *lohs lahn·gohs·tee·nohs* — shrimp
**la langosta** *lah lahn·gohs·tah* — lobster
**el lenguado** *ehl lehn·gwah·doh* — sole
**la lubina** *lah loo·bee·nah* — sea bass
**los mejillones** *lohs meh·khee·yoh·nehs* — mussels
**los mejillones en escabeche** *lohs* — mussels in a
*meh·khee·yohn·ehs ehn ehs·kah·beh·cheh* — marinade
**la merluza** *lah mehr·loo·sah* — hake
**el mero** *ehl meh·roh* — grouper
**la ostra** *lah ohs·trah* — oyster

| | |
|---|---|
| **el pez espada** *ehl pehs ehs•pah•dah* | swordfish |
| **el pulpo** *ehl pool•poh* | octopus |
| **el pulpo al olivo** *ehl pool•poh ahl oh•lee•boh* | octopus with olive |
| **el salmón** *ehl sahl•mohn* | salmon |
| **el tiburón** *ehl tee•boo•rohn* | shark |
| **la tilapia** *lah tee•lah•peeya* | tilapia |
| **la trucha** *lah troo•chah* | trout |

**Ceviche** is a specialty dish of many Latin American countries. It is made by marinating raw fish with lemons and limes. The citrus adds flavor and cooks the fish without heat. The preparation includes onions and hot peppers, and it can be served with corn and sweet potato. **Ceviche** is always served cold.

There are many different kinds of **ceviche** depending on the country or city. The most well-known is the one made with fish. However you can also find **ceviche** made with shellfish, squid and shrimp.

## Meat & Poultry

| | |
|---|---|
| **el bife ancho** *ehl bee•feh ahn•choh* | rib eye steak |
| **el bife angosto** *ehl bee•feh ahn•gohs•toh* | strip steak |
| **el bisté** *ehl bees•teh* | beef steak |
| **la carne** *lah kahr•neh* | meat |
| **la carne de cerdo** *lah kahr•neh deh sehr•doh* | pork |
| **la carne molida** *lah kahr•neh moh•lee•dah* | ground beef |
| **la carne de res** *lah kahr•neh deh rehs* | beef |
| **el chorizo** *ehl choh•ree•soh* | highly-seasoned pork sausage |
| **la chuleta** *lah choo•leh•tah* | chop |
| **la codorniz** *lah koh•dohr•nees* | quail |
| **el conejo** *ehl koh•neh•khoh* | rabbit |

**el cordero** *ehl kohr-deh-roh* — lamb

**las costillas de cerdo** — pork ribs
*lahs kohs-tee-yahs deh sehr-doh*

**la falda de buey** *lah fahl-dah deh bwehy* — beef flank steak

**el filete** *ehl fee-leh-teh* — steak

**el guiso de riñones** — kidney stew
*ehl gee-soh deh ree-nyoh-nehs*

**el hígado** *ehl ee-gah-doh* — liver

   **de cordero** *deh kohr-deh-roh* — lamb

   **de pollo** *deh poh-yoh* — chicken

   **de res** *deh rehs* — beef

**el jamón** *ehl khah-mohn* — ham

**el jamón ibérico** *ehl khah-mohn ee-beh-ree-koh* — aged Iberian ham

**el jamón serrano** *ehl khah-mohn seh-rrah-noh* — dry-cured serrano ham

**el lomo** *ehl loh-moh* — steak

**las mollejas de ternera** — veal sweetbread
*lahs moh-yeh-khahs deh tehr-neh-rah*

**la morcilla** *lah mohr-see-yah* — blood sausage

**las patas de cerdo** *lahs pah-tahs deh sehr-doh* — pig's feet [trotters]

**el pato** *ehl pah-toh* — duck

**el pavo** *ehl pah-boh* — turkey

**el pollo** *ehl poh-yoh* — chicken

**el pollo frito** *ehl poh-yoh free-toh* — fried chicken

**el riñón** *ehl ree-nyohn* — kidney

**la salchicha** *lah sahl-chee-chah* — sausage

**el salchichón** *ehl sahl-chee-chohn* — salami-type sausage

**el solomillo** *ehl soh-loh-mee-yoh* — sirloin

**la ternera** *lah tehr-neh-rah* — veal

**el tocino** *ehl toh-see-noh* — bacon

**la trucha ahumada** — smoked trout
*lah troo-chah ah-ooh-mah-dah*

**el venado** *ehl beh-nah-doh* — venison

Argentina is famous for its **asado**, or barbecued meat.
The **asado** is a typical food all over the country. It includes
several different cuts of beef and sometimes includes chicken, and
occasionally pork.
**Asado** is typically spiced with **chimichurri**, a sauce made with garlic,
red pepper, parsley, hot pepper, onion, thyme, and bay leaves. It is
usually served with red wine.

## Vegetables & Staples

| | |
|---|---|
| **la albahaca** *lah ahl·bah·ah·kah* | basil |
| **la aceituna** *lah ah·seyee·too·nah* | olive |
| **la acelga** *lah ah·sehl·gah* | chard |
| **el aguacate** *ehl ah·gwah·khah·teh* | avocado |
| **el ajo** *ehl ah·khoh* | garlic |
| **la alcachofa** *lah ahl·kah·choh·fah* | artichoke |
| **la alcaparra** *lah ahl·kah·pah·rrah* | caper |
| **la almendra** *lah ahl·mehn·drah* | almond |
| **el anís** *ehl ah·nees* | aniseed |
| **el apio** *ehl ah·peeyoh* | celery |
| **el arroz...** *ehl ah·rrohs...* | rice... |
| **árabe** *ah·rah·beh* | with noodles and raisins |
| **con frijoles** *kohn free·khoh·les* | with beans |
| **a la jardinera** *ah lah khar·dee·neh·rah* | with corn and peas |
| **con mariscos** *kohn mah·rees·kohs* | with mariscos |
| **con pollo** *kohn poh·yoh* | with chicken |
| **la arveja** *lah ar·beh·kha* | pea |
| **el azafrán** *ehl ah·sah·frahn* | saffron |
| **el azúcar** *ehl ah·soo·kahr* | sugar |
| **la berenjena** *lah beh·rehn·kheh·nah* | eggplant [aubergine] |

| | |
|---|---|
| **el brócoli** *ehl broh•koh•lee* | broccoli |
| **los brotes de soja** | bean sprouts |
| *lohs broh•tehs deh soh•khah* | |
| **el calabacín** *ehl kah•lah•bah•seen* | zucchini [courgette] |
| **el camote** *ehl kah•moh•teh* | yam |
| **la cebolla** *lah seh•boh•yah* | onion |
| **el champiñón (a la plancha/salteado)** | (grilled/sautéed ) mushroom |
| *ehl chahm•pee•nyohn (ah lah* | |
| *plahn•chah/sahl•teh•ah•doh)* | |
| **la coliflor** *lah koh•lee•flohr* | cauliflower |
| **el espárrago** *ehl ehs•pah•rrah•goh* | asparagus |
| **la espinaca** *lah ehs•pee•nah•kah* | spinach |
| **los frijoles** *lah free•kho•lehs* | beans |
| **las habas** *lahs ah•bahs* | broad beans |
| **la harina** *lah ah•ree•nah* | flour |
| **el hongo** *ehl ohn•goh* | mushroom |
| **la lechuga** *lah leh•choo•gah* | lettuce |
| **la lenteja** *lah lehn•teh•khah* | lentil |
| **el maíz** *ehl mah•ees* | corn |
| **la mantequilla (con/sin sal)** | butter (with/without salt) |
| *lah mahn•teh•kee•yah (kohn/seen sahl)* | |
| **la margarina** *lah mahr•gah•ree•nah* | margarine |
| **la menestra** *lah meh•nehs•trah* | vegetable stew |
| **el pan** *ehl pahn* | bread |
| **la papa** *lah pah•pah* | potato |
| **la pasta** *lah pahs•tah* | pasta |
| **el pepino** *ehl peh•pee•noh* | cucumber |
| **el perejil** *ehl peh•reh•kheel* | parsley |
| **la pimienta negra** | black pepper |
| *lah pee•meeyehn•tahneh•grah* | |
| **el pimiento relleno** | stuffed pepper |
| *ehl pee•meeyehn•toh reh•yeh•noh* | |

**el pimiento rojo/verde** *ehl pee‑meeyehn‑toh roh‑khoh/behr‑deh*    red/green pepper

**el repollo** *ehl reh‑poh‑yoh*    cabbage

**el tomate** *ehl toh‑mah‑teh*    tomato

**la vainita** *lah bahy‑nee‑tah*    green bean

**la verdura** *lah behr‑doo‑rah*    vegetable

**la zanahoria** *lah sah‑nah‑oh‑reeyah*    carrot

## Fruit

**el damasco** *ehl dah‑mahs‑koh*    apricot

**el arándano** *ehl ah‑rahn‑dah‑noh*    blueberry

**el arándano rojo** *ehl ah‑rahn‑dah‑noh roh‑khoh*    cranberry

**la banana** *lah bah‑nah‑nah*    banana

**la cereza** *lah seh‑reh‑sah*    cherry

**la ciruela** *lah see‑rweh‑lah*    plum

**la chirimoya** *lah chee‑ree‑moh‑yah*    chirimoya

**el coco** *ehl koh‑koh*    coconut

**el durazno** *ehl duh‑rahs‑noh*    peach

**la frambuesa** *lah frahm‑bweh‑sah*    raspberry

**la fresa** *lah freh‑sah*    strawberry

**la fruta** *lah froo‑tah*    fruit

**la granadilla** *lah grah‑nah‑dee‑yah*    sweet passion fruit

| **la guayaba** *lah gwah·yah·bah* | guava |
| **el kiwi** *ehl kee·wee* | kiwi |
| **la lima** *lah lee·mah* | lime |
| **el limón** *ehl lee·mohn* | lemon |
| **el mamey** *ehl mah·mehy* | mamey |
| **el mango** *ehl mahn·goh* | mango |
| **la mandarina** *luh mahn·dah·ree·nah* | tangerine |
| **la manzana** *lah mahn·sah·nah* | apple |
| **el maracuyá** *ehl mah·rah·coo·yah* | passion fruit |
| **el melón** *ehl meh·lohn* | melon |
| **la naranja** *lah nah·rahn·khah* | orange |
| **la nectarina** *lah nehk·tah·ree·nah* | nectarine |
| **la papaya** *lah pah·pah·yah* | papaya |
| **la pera** *lah peh·rah* | pear |
| **la piña** *lah pee·nyah* | pineapple |
| **el pomelo** *ehl poh·meh·loh* | grapefruit |
| **la sandía** *lah sahn·dee·ah* | watermelon |
| **el tamarindo** *ehl tah·mah·reen·doh* | tamarind |
| **el tangelo** *ehl tahn·geh·loh* | sour orange |
| **la uva** *lah oo·bah* | grape |

## Cheese

| **el queso...** *ehl keh·soh...* | ...cheese |
| **blanco/fresco** *blahn·koh/frehs·koh* | white cheese |
| **blando** *blahn·doh* | soft, mild-flavored |
| **cremoso** *kreh·moh·soh* | cream |
| **curado** *koo·rah·doh* | ripe |
| **de leche de cabra** *deh leh·cheh deh kah·brah* | from goat's milk |
| **duro** *doo·roh* | hard |
| **fuerte** *fwehr·teh* | strong |
| **manchego** *mahn·cheh·goh* | hard cheese from Manchego sheep's milk |

| | | |
|---|---|---|
| **parmesano** *par·meh·sah·noh* | | parmesan |
| **rallado** *rah·yah·doh* | | grated |
| **requesón** *reh·keh·sohn* | | cottage |
| **suave** *swah·beh* | | mild |
| **tipo roquefort** *tee·poh roh·qeh·fohrt* | | blue |

## Dessert

| | |
|---|---|
| **el alfajor** *ehl ahl·fah·khor* | sweet dough filled with caramel and sprinkled with powder sugar |
| **el arroz con leche** *ehl ah·rros kohn leh·cheh* | rice pudding |
| **el brazo de gitano** *ehl brah·soh deh khee· tah·noh* | sponge cake roll with cream filling |
| **el buñuelo** *ehl boo·nyweh·loh* | thin, deep-fried fritter, covered in sugar |
| **el churro** *ehl choo·rroh* | deep-fried fritter sprinkled with sugar |
| **el dulce de leche** *ehl dool·seh deh leh·cheh* | cooked sugared milk |
| **el flan** *ehl flahn* | caramel custard |
| **la galleta** *lah gah·yeh·tah* | cookie [biscuit] |
| **la gelatina** *lah geh·lah·tee·nah* | jello® [jelly] |
| **el helado** *ehl eh·lah·doh* | ice cream |
| **la leche frita** *lah leh·cheh free·tah* | fried milk custard |
| **la mantecada** *lah mahn·teh·kah·dah* | small sponge cake |
| **la manzana asada** *lah mahn·sah·nah ah·sah·dah* | baked apple |
| **el panqueque** *ehl pahn·keh·keh* | crepe (used in sweet or savory dishes) |
| **el pastel de manzana** *ehl pahs·tehl deh mahn·sah·nah* | apple pie |
| **el pastel de queso** *ehl pahs·tehl deh keh·soh* | cheesecake |

| **el pie de limón** *ehl pah·ee deh lee·mohn* | keylime pie |
| **el sorbete** *ehl sohr·beh·teh* | sorbet |

## Sauces & Condiments

| **la sal** *lah sahl* | salt |
| **pimienta** *pee·meeyehn·tah* | pepper |
| **mostaza** *mohs·tah·sah* | mustard |
| **cátsup** *kaht·soop* | ketchup |

## At the Market

| Where are the carts [trolleys]/baskets? | **¿Dónde están los carritos/las cestas?** *dohn·deh ehs·tahn lohs kah·rree·tohs/lahs sehs·tahs* |
| Where is ...? | **¿Donde está...?** *dohn·deh ehs·tah...* |
| I'd like some of that/this. | **Quiero un poco de eso/esto.** *keeyeh·roh oon poh·koh deh eh·soh/ehs·toh* |
| Can I taste it? | **¿Puedo probarlo?** *pweh·doh proh·bahr·loh* |
| I'd like... | **Quiero...** *keeyeh·roh...* |
|   a kilo/half-kilo of... | **un kilo/medio kilo de...** *oon kee·loh/meh·deeyoh kee·loh deh...* |
|   a liter of... | **un litro de...** *oon lee·troh deh...* |
|   a piece of... | **un trozo de...** *oon troh·soh deh...* |
|   a slice of... | **una rodaja de...** *oo·nah roh·dah·khah deh...* |
| More./Less. | **Más./Menos.** *mahs/meh·nohs* |
| How much? | **¿Cuánto es?** *kwahn·toh ehs* |
| Where do I pay? | **¿Dónde se paga?** *dohn·deh seh pah·gah* |
| A bag, please. | **Una bolsa, por favor.** *oo·nah bohl·sah pohr fah·bohr* |
| I'm being helped. | **Ya me están atendiendo.** *yah meh ehs·tahn ah·tehn·dyehn·doh* |

For Conversion Tables, see page 176.

For Currency, see page 17.

## In the Kitchen

| | | |
|---|---|---|
| bottle opener | **el destapador** | ehl dehs•tah•pah•_dohr_ |
| bowl | **el bol** | ehl bohl |
| can opener | **el abrelatas** | ehl ah•breh•_lah_•tahs |
| corkscrew | **el sacacorchos** | ehl sah•kah•_kohr_•chohs |
| cup | **la taza** | lah _tah_•sah |
| fork | **el tenedor** | ehl teh•neh•_dohr_ |

In Latin America, food is often purchased at local family-run markets. These are excellent places for regional and specialty foods, fresh fruit and vegetables, meat and baked goods. **Supermercados** (large grocery store chains) are also common, but these are usually found in big cities. These stores have a larger selection than regular supermarkets, and are often less expensive. Measurements in Latin America are metric— and that applies to the weight of food too. If you tend to think in pounds and ounces, it's worth brushing up on what the metric equivalent is before you go shopping for fruit and veg in markets and supermarkets. Five hundred grams, or half a kilo, is a common quantity to order, and that converts to just over a pound (17.65 ounces, to be precise).

## YOU MAY HEAR...

**¿Necesita ayuda?** *eh·seh·see·tah ah·yoo·dah*     Can I help you?
**¿Qué desea?** *keh deh·seh·ah*     What would you like?
**¿Algo más?** *ahl·goh mahs*     Anything else?
**Son... pesos** *sohn... peh·sohs*     That's... pesos.

## YOU MAY SEE...

| | |
|---|---|
| **CONSUMIR PREFERENTEMENTE ANTES DE...** | best if used by... |
| **CALORÍAS** | calories |
| **SIN GRASA** | fat free |
| **CONSERVAR EN REFRIGERACIÓN** | keep refrigerated |
| **PUEDE CONTENER RASTROS DE...** | may contain traces of... |
| **SE PUEDE COCER O CALENTAR EN HORNO DE MICROONDAS** | microwavable |
| **FECHA LÍMITE DE VENTA...** | sell by... |
| **APTO PARA VEGETARIANOS** | suitable for vegetarians |

| | |
|---|---|
| frying pan | **la sartén** *lah sahr·tehn* |
| glass | **el vaso** *ehl bah·soh* |
| (steak) knife | **el cuchillo (de carne)** *ehl koo·chee·yoh (deh kahr·neh)* |
| measuring cup/spoon | **la taza/la cuchara medidora** *lah tah·sah/ lah koo·chah·rah meh·dee·doh·rah* |
| napkin | **la servilleta** *lah sehr·bee·yeh·tah* |
| plate | **el plato** *ehl plah·toh* |
| pot | **la olla** *lah oh·yah* |
| saucepan | **la cacerola** *lah kah·seh·roh·lah* |
| spatula | **la espátula** *lah ehs·pah·too·lah* |
| spoon | **la cuchara** *lah koo·chah·rah* |

## Drinks

### ESSENTIAL

| | |
|---|---|
| The wine list/drink menu, please. | **La carta de vinos/bebidas, por favor.** _kahr·tah deh bee·nohs/beh·bee·dahs pohr fah·bohr_ |
| What do you recommend? | **¿Qué me recomienda?** _keh meh reh·koh·meeyehn·dah_ |
| I'd like a bottle/glass of red/white wine. | **Quiero una botella/una copa de vino tinto/blanco.** _keeyeh·roh oo·nah boh·teh·yah/oo·nah koh·pah deh bee·noh teen·toh/blahn·koh_ |
| The house wine, please. | **El vino de la casa, por favor.** _ehl bee·noh deh lah kah·sah pohr fah·bohr_ |
| Another bottle/glass, please. | **Otra botella/Otra copa, por favor.** _oh·trah boh·teh·yah/oh·trah koh·pah pohr fah·bohr_ |
| I'd like a local beer. | **Quiero una cerveza local.** _keeyeh·roh oo·nah sehr·beh·sah loh·khal_ |
| Let me buy you a drink. | **¿Puedo invitarle a una copa?** _pweh·doh een·bee·tahr·leh ah oo·nah koh·pah_ |
| Cheers! | **¡Salud!** _sah·lood_ |
| A coffee/tea, please. | **Un café/té, por favor.** _oon kah·feh/teh pohr fah·bohr_ |
| Black coffee. | **Café solo.** _kah·feh soh·loh_ |

### Non-alcoholic Drinks

| | |
|---|---|
| **el agua (con/sin gas)** _ehl ah·gwah (kohn/seen gahs)_ | (sparkling/still ) water |
| **el café** _ehl kah·feh_ | coffee |
| **la chicha** _lah chee·chah_ | a cold drink made from corn |
| **el chocolate caliente** _ehl choh·koh·lah·teh kah·leeyehn·teh_ | hot chocolate |

82

| With... | **Con...** kohn... | |
| milk | **leche** _leh_•cheh | |
| sugar | **azúcar** ah•_soo_•kahr | |
| artificial sweetener | **edulcorante artificial** | |
| | eh•dool•khoh•_rahn_•teh ahr•tee•fce•_seeyahl_ | |
| A..., please. | **Un...,  por favor.** oon...pohr fah•_bohr_ | |
| juice | **jugo** _khoo_•goh | |
| soda | **refresco** reh•_frehs_•koh | |
| (sparkling/still) | **agua (con/sin gas)** _ah_•gwah (kohn/seen gahs) | |
| water | | |

| | | |
|---|---|---|
| **el granizado** ehl grah•nee•_sah_•doh | iced drink |
| **el jugo** ehl _khoo_•goh | juice |
| **la leche** lah _leh_•cheh | milk |
| **la limonada** lah lee•moh•_nah_•dah | lemonade |
| **el refresco** ehl reh•_frehs_•koh | soda |
| **el té (con hielo)** ehl teh (kohn _eeyeh_•loh) | (iced) tea |

Many Latin Americans love coffee and drink it throughout the day. Tap water is not always safe to drink, though many locals drink it at home. Travelers are recommended always to drink bottled water. Restaurants will almost always serve bottled water with meals, unless you specifically request **agua del grifo**, tap water.
Juice is usually served with breakfast, but it's not common to drink it at lunch or dinner.

## YOU MAY HEAR...

**¿Qué desea beber?**
*keh deh-seh-ah beh-behr*

**¿Con leche o azúcar?**
*kohn leh-cheh oh ah-soo-kahr*

**¿Agua con gas o sin gas?**
*ah-gwah kohn gahs oh seen gahs*

What would you
like to drink?

With milk or
sugar?

Sparkling or still
water?

## Aperitifs, Cocktails & Liqueurs

| | |
|---|---|
| **el coñac** *ehl koh-nyahk* | brandy |
| **la ginebra** *lah khee-neh-brah* | gin |
| **el jerez fino** *ehl kheh-rehs fee-noh* | pale, dry sherry |
| **el jerez oloroso** *ehl kheh-rehs oh-loh-roh-soh* | dark, heavy sherry |
| **el licor** *ehl lee-kohr* | liqueur |
| **el oporto** *ehl oh-pohr-toh* | port |
| **el ron** *ehl rohn* | rum |
| **la sangría** *lah sahn-gree-ah* | wine punch |
| **el tequila** *ehl teh-kee-lah* | tequila |

There are many popular brands of beer in Latin America, such
as **Águila**® in Colombia, **Polar**® in Venezuela and **Quilmes**® in
Argentina. Each brand usually has several classes and types of beer
available, though most will be a lager-type beer.
The classes of beer include **clásica**, a light, pale, pilsner-type lager;
**especial**, a heavier pilsner-type lager; **negra**, a dark, malty lager; and
**extra**, a heavy, high-alcohol lager.

**el vodka** *ehl bohd·kah*          vodka
**el whisky** *ehl wees·kee*          whisky

## Beer

**la cerveza...** *lah sehr·beh·sah...*          ...beer
  **en botella/de barril**          bottled/draft
  *ehn boh·teh·yah/deh bah·rreel*
  **local/extranjera** *loh·khal/ehx·trahn·kheh·rah* local/imported
  **negra/ligera** *neh·grah/lee·kheh·rah*          dark/light
  **rubia/pilsner** *roo·beeyah/peelz·nehr*          lager/pilsner
  **sin alcohol** *seen ahl·koh·ohl*          non-alcoholic

## Wine

**el cava** *ehl kah·bah*          sparkling wine
**el champán** *ehl chahm·pahn*          champagne
**el vino...** *ehl bee·noh...*          ...wine
  **de la casa/de mesa**          house/table
  *deh lah kah·sah/dehmeh·sah*
  **espumoso** *ehs·poo·moh·soh*          sparkling
  **tinto/blanco** *teen·toh/blahn·koh*          red/white
  **seco/dulce** *seh·koh/dool·seh*          dry/sweet

Latin America has many land areas under vine. Chile is probably
the most famous wine-producing country in Latin America. Their
wine culture has existed for centuries and there is a wide selection of
global wine varieties.

In Latin America, vineyards are called **viñedos** and the chambers
where the wine is kept are called **bodegas**.

## On the Menu

| | | |
|---|---|---|
| **el aceite** *ehl ah‧seyee‧teh* | | oil |
| **el aceite de oliva** *ehl ah‧seyee‧teh deh oh‧lee‧bah* | | olive oil |
| **la aceituna** *lah ah‧seyee‧too‧nah* | | olive |
| **la acelga** *lah ah‧sehl‧gah* | | chard |
| **la achicoria** *lah ah‧chee‧koh‧reeyah* | | chicory |
| **el agua** *ehl ah‧gwah* | | water |
| **el aguacate** *ehl ah‧gwah‧kah‧teh* | | avocado |
| **el ajo** *ehl ah‧khoh* | | garlic |
| **el ajo chalote** *ehl ah‧khoh chah‧loh‧teh* | | shallot |
| **la albahaca** *lah ahl‧bah‧ah‧kah* | | basil |
| **la albóndiga** *lah ahl‧bohn‧dee‧gah* | | meatball |
| **la alcachofa** *lah ahl‧kah‧choh‧fah* | | artichoke |
| **la alcaparra** *lah ahl‧kah‧pah‧rrah* | | caper |
| **la almeja** *lah ahl‧meh‧khah* | | clam |
| **la almendra** *lah ahl‧mehn‧drah* | | almond |
| **el almíbar** *ehl ahl‧mee‧bahr* | | syrup |
| **las ancas de rana** *lahs ahn‧kahs deh rah‧nah* | | frog's legs |
| **la anchoa** *lah ahn‧choh‧ah* | | anchovy |
| **la anguila** *lah ahn‧gee‧lah* | | eel |
| **la angula** *lah ahn‧goo‧lah* | | baby eel |
| **el anís** *ehl ah‧nees* | | aniseed |
| **el aperitivo** *ehl ah‧peh‧ree‧tee‧boh* | | appetizer [starter] |
| **el apio** *ehl ah‧peeyoh* | | celery |
| **el arándano** *ehl ah‧rahn‧dah‧noh* | | blueberry |
| **el arándano rojo** *ehl ah‧rahn‧dah‧noh roh‧khoh* | | cranberry |
| **el arenque** *ehl ah‧rehn‧keh* | | herring |
| **el arroz** *ehl ah‧rrohs* | | rice |
| **el arroz integral** *ehl ah‧rrohs een‧teh‧grahl* | | whole grain rice |

| | |
|---|---|
| **el arroz salvaje** *ehl ah•rrohs sahl•bah•kheh* | wild rice |
| **la arveja** *lah ar•beh•kha* | pea |
| **el asado** *ehl ah•sah•doh* | roast |
| **las asaduras** *lahs ah•sah•doo•rahs* | organ meat [offal] |
| **el atún** *ehl ah•toon* | tuna |
| **la avellana** *lah ah•beh•yah•nah* | hazelnut |
| **la avena** *lah ah•beh•nah* | oat |
| **las aves** *lahs ah•behs* | poultry |
| **el azafrán** *ehl ah•sah•frahn* | saffron |
| **el azúcar** *ehl ah•soo•kahr* | sugar |
| **el bacalao** *bah•kah•lao* | cod |
| **la banana** *lah bah•nah•nah* | banana |
| **los barquillos** *lohs bahr•kee•yohs* | wafers/ice cream cones |
| **la batata** *lah bah•tah•tah* | sweet potato |
| **el batido** *ehl bah•tee•doh* | milk shake |
| **la bebida** *lah beh•bee•dah* | drink |
| **la berenjena** *lah beh•rehn•kheh•nah* | eggplant [aubergine] |
| **la berraza** *lah beh•rrah•sah* | parsnip |
| **el berro** *ehl beh•rroh* | watercress |
| **la berza** *lah behr•sah* | kale |
| **el besugo** *ehl beh•soo•goh* | sea bream |
| **el bollo** *ehl boh•yoh* | pastry |
| **el bollo** *ehl boh•yoh* | muffin |
| **el brandy** *ehl brahn•dee* | brandy |
| **el brócoli** *ehl broh•koh•lee* | broccoli |
| **los brotes de soja** *lohs broh•tehs deh soh•khah* | bean sprouts |
| **el buey** *ehl bwehy* | ox |
| **el buñuelo** *ehl boo•nyweh•loh* | fritter |
| **la caballa** *lah kah•bah•yah* | mackerel |
| **la cabra** *lah kah•brah* | goat |
| **el cabrito** *ehl kah•bree•toh* | young goat |

| | |
|---|---|
| **el café** *ehl kah·feh* | coffee |
| **el café solo** *ehl kah·feh soh·loh* | espresso |
| **el calabacín** *ehl kah·lah·bah·seen* | zucchini [courgette] |
| **la calabaza** *lah kah·lah·bah·sah* | pumpkin |
| **el calamar** *ehl kah·lah·mahr* | squid |
| **el caldo** *ehl kahl·doh* | broth |
| **la canela** *lah kah·neh·lah* | cinnamon |
| **el cangrejo** *ehl kahn·greh·khoh* | crab |
| **el capuchino** *ehl kah·poo·chee·noh* | cappuccino |
| **el caracol** *ehl kah·rah·kohl* | snail |
| **el caramelo** *ehl kah·rah·meh·loh* | candy [sweet] |
| **la carne** *lah kahr·neh* | meat |
| **la carne de cangrejo** *lah kahr·neh deh kahn·greh·khoh* | crabmeat |
| **la carne de cerdo** *lah kahr·neh deh sehr·doh* | pork |
| **la carne molida** *lah kahr·neh moh·lee·dah* | ground beef |
| **la carne de res** *lah kahr·neh deh rehs* | beef |
| **el carnero** *ehl kahr·neh·roh* | mutton |
| **las carrilladas** *lahs kah·rree·yah·dahs* | cow's cheeks |
| **casero** *kah·seh·roh* | homemade |
| **la castaña** *lah kahs·tah·nyah* | chestnut |
| **el cava** *ehl kah·bah* | sparkling wine |
| **la cebolla** *lah seh·boh·yah* | onion |
| **la cebolleta** *lah seh·boh·yeh·tah* | scallion [spring onion] |
| **los cebollinos** *lohs seh·boh·yee·nohs* | chives |
| **la cecina de bovino** *lah seh·see·nah deh boh·bee·noh* | corned beef |
| **el centeno** *ehl sehn·teh·noh* | rye |
| **el centollo** *ehl sehn·toh·yoh* | spider crab |
| **el cereal** *ehl seh·reh·ahl* | cereal |
| **la cereza** *lah seh·reh·sah* | cherry |

| | |
|---|---|
| **la cerveza** *lah sehr·beh·sah* | beer |
| **ceviche** *seh·bee·cheh* | ceviche (cold fish dish marinated with citrus fruits) |
| **de pescado** *deh pehs·kah·do* | fish |
| **de langostinos** *deh lahn·gohs·tee·nohs* | shrimp |
| **de pulpo** *deh pool·poh* | octopus |
| **de conchas** *deh kohn·chahs* | scallops |
| **mixto** *meex·toh* | mixed seafood |
| **el champiñón** *ehl chahm·pee·nyohn* | mushroom |
| **el champán** *ehl chahm·pahn* | champagne |
| **la chirivía** *lah chee·ree·bee·ah* | parsnip |
| **el chocolate** *ehl choh·koh·lah·teh* | chocolate |
| **el chocolate caliente** *ehl choh·koh·lah·teh kah·leeyehn·teh* | hot chocolate |
| **el chorizo** *ehl choh·ree·soh* | highly-seasoned pork sausage |
| **la chuleta** *lah choo·leh·tah* | chop |
| **el chuletón** *ehl choo·leh·tohn* | T-bone steak |
| **el ciervo** *ehl seeyehr·boh* | deer |
| **la cigala** *lah see·gah·lah* | crayfish |
| **el cilantro** *ehl see·lahn·troh* | cilantro [coriander] |
| **la ciruela** *lah see·rweh·lah* | plum |
| **la ciruela pasa** *lah see·rweh·lah pah·sah* | prune |
| **el clavo de olor** *ehl klah·boh deh oh·lohr* | clove |
| **el cochinillo** *ehl koh·chee·nee·yoh* | suckling pig |
| **el coco** *ehl koh·koh* | coconut |
| **la codorniz** *lah koh·dohr·nees* | quail |
| **la col** *lah kohl* | cabbage |
| **las coles de Bruselas** *lahs koh·lehs deh broo·seh·lahs* | Brussels sprouts |
| **la coliflor** *lah koh·lee·flohr* | cauliflower |
| **el comino** *ehl koh·mee·noh* | cumin |

| | |
|---|---|
| **la compota** *lah kohm-poh-tah* | stewed fruit |
| **con alcohol** *kohn ahl-koh-ohl* | with alcohol |
| **con crema** *kohn kreh-mah* | with cream |
| **las conchas** *lahs kohn-chahs* | scallop |
| **el condimento** *ehl kohn-dee-mehn-toh* | relish |
| **el conejo** *ehl koh-neh-khoh* | rabbit |
| **el congrio** *ehl kohn-greeyoh* | conger eel |
| **el consomé** *ehl kohn-soh-meh* | consommé |
| **el coñac** *ehl koh-nyahk* | brandy |
| **el corazón** *ehl koh-rah-sohn* | heart |
| **el cordero** *ehl kohr-deh-roh* | lamb |
| **la codorniz** *lah koh-dohr-nees* | quail |
| **el coriandro** *ehl koh-reeyahn-droh* | coriander |
| **la crema** *lah kreh-mah* | cream |
| **la crema agria** *lah kreh-mah ah-greeyah* | sour cream |
| **la crema montada** *lah kreh-mah mohn-tah-dah* | whipped cream |
| **la croqueta** *lah kroh-keh-tah* | croquette |
| **el cruasán** *ehl krwah-sahn* | croissant |
| **crudo** *kroo-doh* | raw |
| **los dátiles** *lohs dah-tee-lehs* | dates |
| **descafeinado** *dehs-kah-feyey-nah-doh* | decaffeinated |
| **el durazno** *ehl duh-rahs-noh* | peach |
| **el edulcorante artificial** *ehl eh-dool-koh-rahn-teh ahr-tee-fee-seeyahl* | artificial sweetener |
| **la empanada** *lah ehm-pah-nah-dah* | pastry filled with meat, chicken, tuna or vegetables |
| **el encurtido** *ehl ehn-koor-tee-doh* | pickled |
| **la endibia** *lah ehn-dee-beeyah* | endive |
| **el eneldo** *ehl eh-nehl-doh* | dill |
| **la ensalada** *lah ehn-sah-lah-dah* | salad |

**la escarola** *lah ehs·kah·<u>roh</u>·lah* — escarole [chicory]

**el espagueti** *ehl ehs·pah·<u>geh</u>·tee* — spaghetti

**la espaldilla** *lah ehs·pahl·<u>dee</u>·yah* — shoulder

**el espárrago** *ehl ehs·<u>pah</u>·rrah·qoh* — asparagus

**las especias** *lahs ehs·<u>peh</u>·seeyahs* — spices

**la espinaca** *lah ehs·pee·<u>nah</u>·kah* — spinach

**el estragón** *ehl ehs·trah·<u>gohn</u>* — tarragon

**el faisán** *ehl fayee·<u>sahn</u>* — pheasant

**la falda de ternera** *lah <u>fahl</u>·dah deh tehr·<u>neh</u>·rah* — beef brisket

**los fiambres** *lohs <u>feeyahm</u>·brehs* — cold cuts [charcuterie]

**el fideo** *ehl fee·<u>deh</u>·oh* — noodle

**el filete** *ehl fee·<u>leh</u>·teh* — steak

**el flan** *ehl flahn* — caramel custard

**el fletán** *ehl fleh·<u>tahn</u>* — halibut

**la frambuesa** *lah frahm·<u>bweh</u>·sah* — raspberry

**la fresa** *lah <u>freh</u>·sah* — strawberry

**la fruta** *lah <u>froo</u>·tah* — fruit

**los frutos secos** *lohs <u>froo</u>·tohs <u>seh</u>·kohs* — nuts

**la galleta** *lah gah·<u>yeh</u>·tah* — cookie [biscuit]

**la galleta salada** *lah gah·yeh·tah sah·<u>lah</u>·dah* — cracker

**el ganso** *ehl <u>gahn</u>·soh* — wild goose

**el garbanzo** *ehl gahr·<u>bahn</u>·soh* — chickpea

**el gazpacho** *ehl gahs·<u>pah</u>·choh* — cold tomato-based soup

**la ginebra** *lah khee·<u>neh</u>·brah* — gin

**el gofre** *ehl <u>goh</u>·freh* — waffle

**la granada** *lah grah·<u>nah</u>·dah* — pomegranate

**el granizado** *ehl grah·nee·<u>sah</u>·doh* — iced drink

**la granola** *lah grah·<u>noh</u>·lah* — granola [muesli]

**la grosella espinosa** *lah groh·<u>seh</u>·yah ehs·pee·<u>noh</u>·sah* — gooseberry

| | |
|---|---|
| **la grosella negra** *lah groh·seh·yah neh·grah* | black currant |
| **la grosella roja** *lah groh·seh·yah roh·khah* | red currant |
| **la guayaba** *lah gwah·yah·bah* | guava |
| **la guinda** *lah geen·dah* | sour cherry |
| **la guindilla en polvo** | chili pepper |
| *lah geen·dee·yah ehn pohl·boh* | |
| **el guirlache** *ehl geer·lah·cheh* | nougat |
| **la hamburguesa** *lah ahm·boor·geh·sah* | hamburger |
| **la harina** *lah ah·ree·nah* | flour |
| **la harina de avena** | oatmeal |
| *lah ah·ree·nah deh ah·beh·nah* | |
| **la harina de maíz** | cornmeal |
| *lah ah·ree·nah deh mah·ees* | |
| **el helado** *ehl eh·lah·doh* | ice cream |
| **el (cubito de) hielo** | ice (cube) |
| *ehl (kooh·bee·toh deh) eeyeh·loh* | |
| **el hígado** *ehl ee·gah·doh* | liver |
| **el higo** *ehl ee·goh* | fig |
| **el hinojo** *ehl ee·noh·khoh* | fennel |
| **la hoja de laurel** *lah oh·khah deh lawoo·rehl* | bay leaf |
| **el hueso** *ehl weh·soh* | bone |
| **el huevo** *ehl weh·boh* | egg |
| **el hongo** *ehl ohn·goh* | mushroom |
| **el jabalí** *ehl khah·bah·lee* | wild boar |
| **la jalea** *lah khah·leh·ah* | jelly |
| **el jamón** *ehl khah·mohn* | ham |
| **el jengibre** *ehl khehn·khee·breh* | ginger |
| **el jerez** *ehl kheh·rehs* | sherry |
| **la judía** *lah khoo·dee·ah* | bean |
| **el jugo** *ehl khoo·goh* | juice |
| **el ketchup** *ehl keht·choop* | ketchup |

**el kiwi** *ehl kee·wee*                                   kiwi
**la langosta** *lah lahn·gohs·tah*                         lobster
**el langostino** *ehl lahn·gohs·tee·noh*                   shrimp
**la leche** *lah leh·cheh*                                 milk
**la leche de soja** *lah leh·cheh deh soh·khah*            soymilk [soya milk]
**la lechuga** *lah leh·choo·gah*                           lettuce
**la lengua** *lah lehn·gwah*                               tongue
**el lenguado** *ehl lehn·gwah·doh*                         sole
**la lenteja** *lah lehn·teh·khah*                          lentil
**el licor** *ehl lee·kohr*                                 liqueur
**el licor de naranja** *ehl lee·kohr*                      orange liqueur
*deh nah·rahn·khah*
**los licores** *lohs lee·kohr·ehs*                         spirits
**la liebre** *lah leyee·breh*                              hare
**la lima** *lah lee·mah*                                   lime
**el limón** *ehl lee·mohn*                                 lemon
**la limonada** *lah leeh·moh·nah·dah*                      lemonade
**la lombarda** *lah lohm·bahr·dah*                         red cabbage
**el lomo** *ehl loh·moh*                                   loin
**la lubina** *lah loo·bee·nah*                             (sea) bass
**los macarrones** *lohs mah·kah·rrohn·ehs*                 macaroni

| | |
|---|---|
| **la maicena** *lah mayee·seh·nah* | cornmeal |
| **el maíz** *ehl mah·ees* | sweet corn |
| **la mandarina** *lah mahn·dah·ree·nah* | tangerine |
| **el mango** *ehl mahn·goh* | mango |
| **el maní** *ehl mah·nee* | peanut |
| **la mantequilla** *lah mahn·teh·kee·yah* | butter |
| **la manzana** *lah mahn·sah·nah* | apple |
| **la margarina** *lah mahr·gah·ree·nah* | margarine |
| **el marisco** *ehl mah·rees·koh* | shellfish |
| **la mayonesa** *lah mah·yoh·neh·sah* | mayonnaise |
| **el mazapán** *ehl mah·sah·pahn* | marzipan |
| **el mejillón** *ehl meh·khee·yohn* | mussel |
| **la mejorana** *lah meh·khoh·rah·nah* | marjoram |
| **la melaza** *lah meh·lah·sah* | molasses |
| **el melón** *ehl meh·lohn* | melon |
| **la menta** *lah mehn·tah* | mint |
| **el menudillo** *ehl meh·noo·dee·yoh* | giblet |
| **el merengue** *ehl meh·rehn·geh* | meringue |
| **la merluza** *lah mehr·loo·sah* | hake |
| **la mermelada** *lah mehr·meh·lah·dah* | marmalade/jam |
| **el mero** *ehl meh·roh* | grouper |
| **la miel** *lah meeyehl* | honey |
| **el mondongo** *ehl mon·dohn·goh* | tripe |
| **la molleja** *lah moh·yeh·khah* | sweetbread |
| **la morcilla** *lah mohr·see·yah* | black pudding |
| **la mostaza** *lah mohs·tah·sah* | mustard |
| **el nabo** *ehl nah·boh* | turnip |
| **la naranja** *lah nah·rahn·khah* | orange |
| **las natillas** *lahs nah·tee·yahs* | custard |
| **la nuez** *lah nwehs* | walnut |
| **la nuez moscada** *lah nwehs mohs·kah·dah* | nutmeg |

| | |
|---|---|
| **el oporto** *ehl oh-pohr-toh* | port |
| **el orégano** *ehl oh-reh-gah-noh* | oregano |
| **la ostra** *lah ohs-trah* | oyster |
| **la pecana** *lah peh-kah-nah* | pecan |
| **la paella** *lah pah-eh-yah* | rice dish |
| **la paletilla** *lah pah-leh-tee-yah* | shank |
| **el palmito** *ehl pahl-mee-toh* | palm heart |
| **el pan** *ehl pahn* | bread |
| **el panecillo** *ehl pah-neh-see-yoh* | roll |
| **la papa** *lah pah-pah* | potato |
| **las papas fritas** *lahs pah-pahs free-tahs* | French fries, potato [chips] |
| **la papaya** *lah pah-pah-yah* | papaya |
| **la paprika** *lah pah-pree-kah* | paprika |
| **la pasa** *lah pah-sah* | raisin |
| **la pasta** *lah pahs-tah* | pasta |
| **el pastel** *ehl pahs-tehl* | pie |
| **el pastel de queso** *ehl pahs-tehl deh keh-soh* | cheesecake |
| **la pata** *lah pah-tah* | leg |
| **las patas de cerdo** *lahs pah-tahs deh sehr-doh* | pig's feet [trotters] |
| **el paté** *ehl pah-teh* | pâté |
| **el pato** *ehl pah-toh* | duck |
| **el pato salvaje** *ehl pah-toh sahl-bah-kheh* | wild duck |
| **el pavo** *ehl pah-boh* | turkey |
| **la pechuga (de pollo)** *lah peh-choo-gah (deh poh-yoh)* | breast (of chicken) |
| **el pepinillo** *ehl peh-pee-nee-yoh* | pickle |
| **el pepino** *ehl peh-pee-noh* | cucumber |
| **la pera** *lah peh-rah* | pear |
| **la perca** *lah pehr-kah* | sea perch |
| **la perdiz** *lah pehr-dees* | partridge |

**el perejil** *ehl peh·reh·kheel* — parsley

**el perro caliente** — hot dog
*ehl peh·rroh kah·leeyehn·teh*

**el pescadito** *ehl pehs·kah·dee·toh* — small fish

**el pescado** *ehl pehs·kah·doh* — fish

**el pescado frito** *ehl pehs·kah·doh free·toh* — fried fish

**pescado y marisco** — seafood
*pehs·kah·doh ee mah·rees·koh*

**el pez espada** *ehl pes ehs·pah·dah* — swordfish

**el pichón** *ehl pee·chohn* — young pigeon

**pilsner** *peelz·nehr* — pilsner (beer)

**el pimentón** *ehl pee·mehn·tohn* — paprika

**la pimienta** *lah pee·meeyehn·tah* — pepper (seasoning)

**la pimienta negra** — black pepper
*lah pee·meeyehn·tah neh·grah*

**la pimienta inglesa** *lah* — allspice
*pee·meeyehn·tah een·gleh·sah*

**el pimiento** *ehl pee·meeyehn·toh* — pepper (vegetable)

**la piña** *lah pee·nyah* — pineapple

**los piñones** *lohs pee·nyohn·ehs* — pine nuts

**la pintada** *lah peen·tah·dah* — guinea fowl

**la pizza** *lah peet·sah* — pizza
**el pollo** *ehl poh·yoh* — chicken
**el pollo frito** *ehl poh·yoh free·toh* — fried chicken
**el pomelo** *ehl poh·meh·loh* — grapefruit
**el puerro** *ehl pweh·rroh* — leek
**el pulpo** *ehl pool·poh* — octopus
**el queso** *ehl keh·soh* — cheese
**el queso de cabra** *ehl keh·soh deh kah·brah* — goat cheese
**el queso crema** *ehl keh·soh kreh·mah* — cream cheese
**el queso roquefort** *ehl keh·soh roh·keh·fohrt* — blue cheese
**el rábano** *ehl rah·bah·noh* — radish
**el rabo de buey** *ehl rah·boh deh bwehy* — oxtail
**el rape** *ehl rah·peh* — monkfish
**los ravioles** *lohs rah·beeyoh·lehs* — ravioli
**la raya** *lah rah·yah* — skate
**el refresco** *ehl reh·frehs·koh* — soda
**relleno** *reh·yeh·noh* — stuffed/stuffing
**la remolacha** *lah reh·moh·lah·chah* — beet
**el repollo** *ehl reh·poh·yoh* — cabbage
**el requesón** *ehl reh·keh·sohn* — cottage cheese
**los retoños de bambú**
*lohs reh·toh·nyohs deh bahm·boo* — bamboo shoots

**el riñón** *ehl ree·nyohn* — kidney
**el róbalo** *ehl roh·bah·loh* — haddock
**el romero** *ehl roh·meh·roh* — rosemary
**el ron** *ehl rohn* — rum
**la rosquilla** *lah rohs·kee·yah* — doughnut
**rubia** *roo·beeyah* — lager (beer)
**el ruibarbo** *ehl rwee·bahr·boh* — rhubarb
**la sal** *lah sahl* — salt
**el salame** *ehl sah·lah·meh* — salami

| | |
|---|---|
| **la salchicha** *lah sahl•chee•chah* | sausage |
| **el salmón** *ehl sahl•mohn* | salmon |
| **el salmonete** *ehl sahl•moh•neh•teh* | red mullet |
| **la salsa** *lah sahl•sah* | sauce |
| **la salsa agridulce** *lah sahl•sah ah•gree•dool•seh* | sweet and sour sauce |
| **la salsa al ajo** *lah sahl•sah ahl ah•kho* | garlic sauce |
| **la salsa picante** *lah sahl•sah pee•kahn•teh* | hot pepper sauce |
| **la salsa de soja** *lah sahl•sah deh soh•khah* | soy sauce |
| **la salvia** *lah sahl•beeyah* | sage |
| **la sandía** *lah sahn•dee•ah* | watermelon |
| **el sándwich** *ehl sahnd•weech* | sandwich |
| **la sangría** *lah sahn•gree•ah* | wine punch |
| **la sardina** *lah sahr•dee•nah* | sardine |
| **la semilla** *lah seh•mee•yah* | seed |
| **la semilla de soja** *lah seh•mee•yah deh soh•khah* | soybean [soya bean] |
| **el sésamo** *ehl seh•sah•moh* | sesame |
| **los sesos** *lohs seh•sohs* | brains |
| **la sidra** *lah see•drah* | cider |
| **la soja** *lah soh•khah* | soy [soya] |
| **el solomillo** *ehl soh•loh•mee•yoh* | sirloin |
| **la sopa** *lah soh•pah* | soup |
| **el sorbete** *ehl sohr•beh•teh* | sorbet |
| **el suero de leche** *ehl sweh•roh deh leh•cheh* | buttermilk |
| **el té** *ehl teh* | tea |
| **la ternera** *lah tehr•neh•rah* | veal |
| **el tequila** *ehl teh•kee•lah* | tequila |
| **el tiburón** *ehl tee•boo•rohn* | shark |
| **tinto** *teen•toh* | red (wine) |
| **el tocino** *ehl toh•see•noh* | bacon |

| | |
|---|---|
| **el tofu** *ehl <u>toh</u>·foo* | tofu |
| **el tomate** *ehl toh·<u>mah</u>·teh* | tomato |
| **el tomillo** *ehl toh·<u>mee</u>·yoh* | thyme |
| **la tónica** *lah <u>toh</u>·nee·kah* | tonic water |
| **la torta** *lah <u>tohr</u>·tah* | cake |
| **la tortilla** *lah tohr·<u>tee</u>·yah* | omelet |
| **la tostada** *lah tohs·<u>tah</u>·dah* | toast |
| **el trigo** *ehl <u>tree</u>·goh* | wheat |
| **la trucha** *lah <u>troo</u>·chah* | trout |
| **las trufas** *lahs <u>troo</u>·fahs* | truffles |
| **la uva** *lah <u>oo</u>·bah* | grape |
| **la vainilla** *lah bayee·<u>nee</u>·yah* | vanilla |
| **la vainita** *lah bay·<u>nee</u>·tah* | green bean |
| **el venado** *ehl beh·<u>nah</u>·doh* | venison |
| **la verdura** *lah behr·<u>doo</u>·rah* | vegetable |
| **el vermut** *ehl behr·<u>moot</u>* | vermouth |
| **el vinagre** *chl bee·<u>nah</u>·greh* | vinegar |
| **el vino** *ehl <u>bee</u>·noh* | wine |
| **el vino dulce** *ehl bee·noh <u>dool</u>·seh* | dessert wine |
| **el vodka** *ehl <u>bohd</u>·kah* | vodka |
| **el whisky** *chl <u>wees</u>·kee* | whisky |
| **el whisky escocés** *ehl <u>wees</u>·kee ehs·koh·<u>sehs</u>* | scotch |
| **la yema/clara de huevo** *lah <u>yeh</u>·mah/<u>klah</u>·rah deh <u>weh</u>·boh* | egg yolk/white |
| **el yogur** *ehl yoh·goor* | yogurt |
| **la zanahoria** *lah sah·nah·<u>oh</u>·reeyah* | carrot |
| **la zarzamora** *lah sahr·sah·<u>moh</u>·rah* | blackberry |

# People

## ESSENTIAL

| | |
|---|---|
| Hello! | **¡Hola!** _oh-lah_ |
| How are you? | **¿Cómo está?** _koh-moh ehs-tah_ |
| Fine, thanks. | **Bien, gracias.** _beeyehn grah-seeyahs_ |
| Excuse me! (to get attention) | **¡Disculpe!** _dihs-koohl-peh_ |
| Do you speak English? | **¿Habla inglés?** _ah-blah een-glehs_ |
| What's your name? | **¿Cómo se llama?** _koh-moh seh yah-mah_ |
| My name is... | **Me llamo...** _meh yah-moh..._ |
| Nice to meet you. | **Encantado _m_/Encantada _f_.** _ehn-kahn-tah-doh/ehn-kahn-tah-dah_ |
| Where are you from? | **¿De dónde es usted?** _deh dohn-deh ehs oos-tehd_ |
| I'm from the U.S./U.K. | **Soy de Estados Unidos/del Reino Unido.** _soy deh ehs-tah-dohs oo-nee-dohs/dehl reyee-noh oo-nee-doh_ |
| What do you do? | **¿A qué se dedica?** _ah keh seh deh-dee-kah_ |
| I work for... | **Trabajo para...** _trah-bah-khoh pah-rah..._ |
| I'm a student. | **Soy estudiante.** _soy ehs-too-deeyahn-teh_ |
| I'm retired. | **Estoy jubilado _m_/jubilada _f_.** _ehs-toy khoo-bee-lah-doh/khoo-bee-lah-dah_ |
| Do you like...? | **¿Le gusta...?** _leh goos-tah..._ |
| Goodbye. | **Adiós.** _ah-deeyohs_ |
| See you later. | **Hasta luego.** _ah-stah lweh-goh_ |

In Spanish, there are a number of ways of expressing 'you' that take different verb forms: **tú** (singular, informal), **usted** (singular, formal) and **ustedes** (plural). When addressing strangers, always use the more formal **usted** (singular) as opposed to the more familiar **tú** (singular), until told otherwise.

If you know someone's title, it is considered polite to use it, e.g., **doctor** (male doctor), **doctora** (female doctor). You can also simply say **Señor** (Mr.), **Señora** (Mrs.) or **Señorita** (Miss).

## Language Difficulties

| | |
|---|---|
| Do you speak English? | **¿Habla inglés?** _ah_-blah een-_glehs_ |
| Does anyone here speak English? | **¿Hay alguien que hable inglés?** aye _ahl_-geeyen keh _ah_-bleh een-_glehs_ |
| I don't speak (much) Spanish. | **No hablo (mucho) español.** noh _ah_-bloh (_moo_-choh) ehs-pah-_nyol_ |
| Can you speak more slowly? | **¿Puede hablar más despacio?** _pweh_-deh ah-_blahr_ mahs dehs-_pah_-seeyoh |
| Can you repeat that? | **¿Podría repetir eso?** poh-_dree_-ah reh-peh-_teer eh_-soh |
| Excuse me? | **¿Cómo?** _koh_-moh |
| What was that? | **¿Qué ha dicho?** keh ah _dee_-choh |
| Can you spell it? | **¿Podría deletrearlo?** poh-_dree_-ah deh-leh-treh-_ahr_-loh |
| Please write it down. | **Escríbamelo, por favor.** ehs-_kree_-bah-meh-loh pohr fah-_bohr_ |
| Can you translate this into English for me? | **¿Podría traducirme esto al inglés?** poh-_dree_-ah trah-doo-_seer_-meh _ehs_-toh ahl een-_glehs_ |
| What does this/that mean? | **¿Qué significa esto/eso?** keh seeg-nee-_fee_-kah _ehs_-toh/_eh_-soh |
| I understand. | **Entiendo.** ehn-_teeyehn_-doh |

| | | |
|---|---|---|
| I don't understand. | **No entiendo.** | noh ehn·_teeyehn_·doh |
| Do you understand? | **¿Entiende?** | ehn·_teeyehn_·deh |

---

### YOU MAY HEAR...

**Hablo muy poco inglés.**
_ah_·bloh mooy _poh_·koh een·_glehs_

I only speak a little English.

**No hablo inglés.** noh _ah_·bloh een·_glehs_

I don't speak English.

---

## Making Friends

| | | |
|---|---|---|
| Hello! | **¡Hola!** | _oh_·lah |
| Good morning. | **Buenos días.** | _bweh_·nohs _dee_·ahs |
| Good afternoon. | **Buenas tardes.** | _bweh_·nahs _tahr_·dehs |
| Good evening. | **Buenas noches.** | _bweh_·nahs _noh_·chehs |
| My name is... | **Me llamo...** | meh _yah_·moh... |
| What's your name? | **¿Cómo se llama?** | _koh_·moh seh _yah_·mah |
| I'd like to introduce you to... | **Quiero presentarle a...** | _keeyeh_·roh preh·sehn·_tahr_·leh ah... |
| Pleased to meet you. | **Encantado m/Encantada f.** | ehn·kahn·_tah_·doh/ehn·kahn·_tah_·dah |

| How are you? | **¿Cómo está?** _koh·moh ehs·tah_ |
| Fine, thanks. | **Bien gracias. ¿Y usted?** |
| And you? | _beeyehn grah·seeyahs ee oos·tehd_ |

> When first meeting someone in Latin America always greet him
> or her with **hola** (hello), **buenos días** (good morning) or **buenas
> tardes** (good afternoon). Latin Americans even extend this general
> greeting to strangers when in elevators, waiting rooms and other small
> public spaces. A general acknowledgment or reply is expected from all.
> When leaving, say **adiós** (goodbye).

## Travel Talk

| I'm here... | **Estoy aquí...** _ehs·toy ah·kee..._ |
| on business | **en viaje de negocios** |
| | _ehn beeyah·kheh deh neh·goh·seeyohs_ |
| on vacation | **de vacaciones** _deh bah·kah·seeyoh·nehs_ |
| [holiday] | |
| studying | **estudiando** _ehs·too·deeyahn·doh_ |
| I'm staying for... | **Voy a quedarme...** _boy ah keh·dahr·meh..._ |
| I've been here... | **Llevo aquí...** _yeh·boh ah·kee..._ |
| a day | **un día** _oon dee·ah_ |
| a week | **una semana** _oo·nah seh·mah·nah_ |
| a month | **un mes** _oon mehs_ |
| Where are you from? | **¿De dónde es usted?** _deh dohn·deh ehs oos·tehd_ |
| I'm from... | **Soy de...** _soy deh..._ |

For Numbers, see page 171.

## Personal

| Who are you with? | **¿Con quién vino?** _kohn keeyehn beeh·noh_ |
| I'm here alone. | **Vine solo** _m_/**sola** _f._ _beeh·neh soh·loh/soh·lah_ |

| | |
|---|---|
| I'm with my… | **Vine con mi…** _beeh_·neh kohn mee… |
| husband/wife | **marido/mujer** mah·_ree_·doh/moo·_khehr_ |
| boyfriend/girlfriend | **novio** _m_/**novia** _f_ _noh_·beeyoh/_noh_·beeyah |
| friend(s)/ | **amigo(s)/colega(s)** |
| colleague(s) | ah·_mee_·goh(s)/koh·_leh_·gah(s) |
| When's your | **¿Cuándo es su cumpleaños?** |
| birthday? | _kwahn_·doh ehs soo koom·pleh·_ah_·nyohs |
| How old are you? | **¿Qué edad tiene usted?** |
| | keh eh·_dahd_ _teeyeh_·neh oos·_tehd_ |
| I'm… | **Tengo…años.** _tehn_·goh…_ah_·nyohs |
| Are you married? | **¿Está casado** _m_/**casada** _f_**?** |
| | ehs·_tah_ kah·_sah_·doh/kah·_sah_·dah |
| I'm… | **Estoy…** ehs·_toy_… |
| single | **soltero** _m_/**soltera** _f_ sohl·_teh_·roh/sohl·_teh_·rah |
| in a relationship | **en una relación** ehn _oo_·nah reh·lah·_seeyohn_ |
| married | **casado** _m_/**casada** _f_ kah·_sah_·doh/kah·_sah_·dah |
| divorced | **divorciado** _m_/**divorciada** _f_ |
| | dee·bohr·_seeyah_·doh/dee·bohr·_seeyah_·dah |
| separated | **separado** _m_/**separada** _f_ |
| | seh·pah·_rah_·doh/seh·pah·_rah_·dah |
| I'm widowed. | **Soy viudo** _m_/**viuda** _f_ |
| | soy _beeyoo_·doh/_beeyoo_·dah |
| Do you have children/ | **¿Tiene hijos/nietos?** |
| grandchildren? | _teeyeh_·neh _ee_·khohs/_neeyeh_·tohs |

For Numbers, see page 171.

## Work & School

| | |
|---|---|
| What do you do? | **¿A qué se dedica?** ah keh seh deh·_dee_·kah |
| What are you studying? | **¿Qué estudia?** keh ehs·_too_·deeyah |
| I'm studying Spanish. | **Estudio español.** ehs·_too_·deeyoh ehs·pah·_nyohl_ |

| I... | **Yo...** _yoh_... |
|---|---|
| work full-time/ part-time | **trabajo a tiempo completo/parcial** _trah·bah·khoh ah teeyehm·poh kohm·pleh·toh/pahr·seeyahl_ |
| am unemployed | **estoy sin empleo** _ehs·toy seehn ehm·pleh·oh_ |
| work at home | **trabajo desde casa** _trah·bah·khoh dehz·deh kah·sah_ |
| Who do you work for? | **¿Para quién trabaja?** _pah·rah keeyehn trah·bah·khah_ |
| I work for... | **Trabajo para...** _trah·bah·khoh pah·rah..._ |
| Here's my business card. | **Aquí tiene mi tarjeta.** _ah·kee teeyeh·neh mee tahr·kheh·tah_ |

For Business Travel, see page 143.

## Weather

| What's the forecast? | **¿Cuál es el pronóstico del tiempo?** _kwahl ehs ehl proh·nohs·tee·koh dehl teeyehm·poh_ |
|---|---|
| What beautiful/ terrible weather! | **¡Qué tiempo más bonito/feo hace!** _keh teeyehm·poh mahs boh·nee·toh/feh·oh ah·seh_ |
| It's cool/warm. | **Hace frío/calor.** _ah·seh free·oh/kah·lohr_ |
| It's rainy/sunny. | **Está lluvioso/soleado.** _ehs·tah yoo·beeyoh·soh/soh·leh·ah·doh_ |
| It's snowy/icy. | **Hay nieve/hielo.** _aye neeyeh·beh/eeyeh·loh_ |
| Do I need a jacket/ an umbrella? | **¿Necesito una chaqueta/un paraguas?** _neh·seh·see·toh oo·nah chah·keh·tah/oon pah·rah·gwahs_ |

For Temperature, see page 177.

## ESSENTIAL

| | |
|---|---|
| Would you like to go out for a drink/dinner? | **¿Le gustaría salir a tomar una copa/cenar?** *leh goos•tah•ree•ah sah•leer ah toh•mahr oo•nah koh•pah/seh•nahr* |
| What are your plans for tonight/tomorrow? | **¿Qué planes tiene para esta noche/mañana?** *keh plah•nehs teeyeh•neh pah•rah ehs•tah noh•cheh/mah•nyah•nah* |
| Can I have your number? | **¿Puede darme su número?** *pweh•deh dahr•meh soo noo•meh•roh* |
| Can I join you? | **¿Puedo acompañarlo m/acompañarla f?** *pweh•doh ah•kohm•pah•nyahr•loh/ah•kohm•pah•nyahr•lah* |
| Can I buy you a drink? | **¿Puedo invitarle una copa?** *pweh•doh een•bee•tahr•leh oo•nah koh•pah* |
| I like you. | **Me gustas.** *meh goos•tahs* |
| I love you. | **Te quiero.** *teh keeyeh•roh* |

## The Dating Game

| | |
|---|---|
| Would you like to go out for…? | **¿Le gustaría ir…?** *leh goos•tah•ree•ah eer…* |
| coffee | **a tomar un café** *ah toh•mahr oon kah•feh* |
| a drink | **a tomar una copa** *ah toh•mahr oo•nah koh•pah* |
| dinner | **a cenar** *ah seh•nahr* |
| What are your plans for…? | **¿Qué planes tiene para…?** *keh plahn•ehs teeyeh•neh pah•rah…* |
| today | **hoy** *ohy* |
| tonight | **esta noche** *ehs•tah noh•cheh* |
| tomorrow | **mañana** *mah•nyah•nah* |
| this weekend | **este fin de semana** *ehs•teh feen deh seh•mah•nah* |

| | |
|---|---|
| Where would you like to go? | **¿Adónde le gustaría ir?** |
| | *ah dohn·deh leh goos·tah·ree·ah eer* |
| I'd like to go to... | **Me gustaría ir a...** *meh goos·tah·ree·ah eer ah...* |
| Do you like...? | **¿Le gusta...?** *leh goos·tah...* |
| Can I have your number/e-mail? | **¿Puede darme su número/dirección de correo electrónico?** *pweh·deh dahr·meh soo noo·meh·roh/dee·rehk·seeyohn deh koh·rreh·oh eh·lehk·troh·nee·koh* |
| Are you on Facebook/Twitter? | **¿Estás en Facebook/Twitter?** |
| | *ehs·tahs ehn fays·book/twee·tehr* |
| Can I join you? | **¿Puedo acompañarlo m/acompañarla f?** |
| | *pweh·doh ah·kohm·pah·nyahr·loh/ ah·kohm·pah·nyahr·lah* |
| You're very attractive. | **Eres muy apuesto m/bonita f.** |
| | *eh·rehs mooy ah·pwehs·toh/boh·nee·tah* |
| Let's go somewhere quieter. | **Vayamos a un sitio más tranquilo.** |
| | *bah·yah·mohs ah oon see·teeyoh mahs trahn·kee·loh* |

For Communications, see page 50.

## Accepting & Rejecting

| | |
|---|---|
| I'd love to. | **Me encantaría.** *meh ehn·kahn·tah·ree·yah* |
| Where should we meet? | **¿Dónde nos encontramos?** |
| | *dohn·deh nohs en·kohn·trah·mohs* |
| I'll meet you at the bar/your hotel. | **Nos encontramos en el bar/su hotel.** |
| | *nohs en·kohn·trah·mohs ehn ehl bahr/soo oh·tehl* |
| I'll come by at... | **Pasaré a recogerlo m/recogerla f a las...** |
| | *pah·sah·reh ah reh·koh·khehr·loh/ reh·koh·khehr·lah ah lahs...* |
| What is your address? | **¿Cuál es su dirección?** *kwahl ehs soo dee·rehk·seeyohn* |
| I'm busy. | **Estoy ocupado m/ocupada f.** |
| | *ehs·toy oh·koo·pah·doh/oh·koo·pah·dah* |

| | |
|---|---|
| I'm not interested. | **No me interesa.** *noh meh een·teh·<u>reh</u>·sah* |
| Leave me alone. | **Déjeme en paz.** <u>*deh*</u>·*kheh·meh ehn pahs* |
| Stop bothering me! | **¡Deje de molestarme!** *deh·kheh <u>deh</u> moh·lehs·<u>tahr</u>·meh* |

For Time, see page 173.

## Getting Intimate

| | |
|---|---|
| Can I hug/kiss you? | **¿Puedo abrazarte/besarte?** |
| | <u>*pweh*</u>·*doh ah·brah·<u>sahr</u>·teh/beh·<u>sahr</u>·teh* |
| Yes. | **Sí.** *see* |
| No. | **No.** *noh* |
| Stop! | **¡Basta!** <u>*bahs*</u>·*tah* |
| I love you. | **Te quiero.** *teh <u>keeyeh</u>·roh* |

## Sexual Preferences

| | |
|---|---|
| Are you gay? | **¿Eres gay?** <u>*eh*</u>·*rehs gay* |
| I'm... | **Soy...** *soy...* |
| heterosexual | **heterosexual** *eh·teh·roh·sehks·<u>wahl</u>* |
| homosexual | **homosexual** *oh·moh·sehks·<u>wahl</u>* |
| bisexual | **bisexual** *bee·sehks·<u>wahl</u>* |
| Do you like | **¿Te gustan los hombres/las mujeres?** |
| men/women? | *teh <u>goos</u>·tahn lohs <u>ohm</u>·brehs/lahs moo·<u>kheh</u>·rehs* |

For Grammar, see page 166.

# Leisure Time

# Sightseeing

## ESSENTIAL

| | |
|---|---|
| Where's the tourist information office? | **¿Dónde está la oficina de turismo?** *dohn·deh ehs·tah lah oh·fee·see·nah deh too·reez·moh* |
| What are the main attractions? | **¿Dónde están los principales sitios de interés?** *dohn·deh ehs·tahn lohs preen·see·pah·lehs see·teeyohs deh een·teh·rehs* |
| Do you have tours in English? | **¿Hay visitas en inglés?** *aye bee·see·tahs ehn een·glehs* |
| Can I have a map/guide? | **¿Puede darme un mapa/una guía?** *pweh·deh dahr·meh oon mah·pah/oo·nah gee·ah* |

## Tourist Information

| | |
|---|---|
| Do you have information on…? | **¿Tiene información sobre…?** *teeyeh·neh een·fohr·mah·seeyohn soh·breh…* |
| Can you recommend…? | **¿Puede recomendarme…?** *pweh·deh reh·koh·mehn·dahr·meh…* |
|   a bus tour | **un recorrido en autobús** *oon reh·koh·rree·doh ehn awtoh·boos* |
|   an excursion to… | **una excursión a…** *oo·nah ehx·koor·seeyohn ah…* |
|   a sightseeing tour of… | **un recorrido turístico de …** *oon reh·koh·rree·doh too·rees·tee·koh deh* |

Tourist offices are located in major Latin American cities and in many of the smaller towns that are popular tourist attractions. Ask at your hotel or check online to find the nearest office.

## On Tour

| | |
|---|---|
| I'd like to go on the excursion to... | **Quiero ir a la visita de...** |
| | _keeyeh·roh eer ah lah bee·see·tah deh..._ |
| When's the next tour? | **¿Cuándo es la próxima visita?** |
| | _kwahn·doh ehs lah proh·xee·mah bee·see·tah_ |
| Are there tours in English? | **¿Hay visitas en inglés?** |
| | _aye bee·see·tahs ehn een·glehs_ |
| Is there an English guide book/audio guide? | **¿Hay una guía/audioguía en inglés?** |
| | _aye oo·nah gee·ah/awoo·deeyoh·gee·ah ehn een·glehs_ |
| What time do we leave/return? | **¿A qué hora salimos/volvemos?** |
| | _ah keh oh·rah sah·lee·mohs/bohl·beh·mohs_ |
| We'd like to see... | **Queremos ver...** _keh·reh·mohs behr..._ |
| Can we stop here...? | **¿Podemos parar aquí...?** |
| | _poh·deh·mohs pah·rahr ah·kee..._ |
| to take photos | **para tomar fotos** _pah·rah toh·mahr foh·tohs_ |
| for souvenirs | **para comprar recuerdos** |
| | _pah·rah kohm·prahr reh·kwehr·dohs_ |
| for the restroom [toilet] | **para ir al servicio** |
| | _pah·rah eer ahl sehr·bee· seeyoh_ |
| Is it handicapped [disabled]-accessible? | **¿Tiene acceso para discapacitados?** |
| | _teeyeh·neh ahk·seh·soh pah·rah dees·kah·pah·see·tah·dohs_ |

For Tickets, see page 20.

## Seeing the Sights

| | |
|---|---|
| Where is/are...? | **¿Dónde está/están...?** |
| | _dohn·deh ehs·tah/ehs·tahn..._ |
| the battleground | **el campo de batalla** _ehl kahm·poh dch bah·tah·yah_ |
| the botanical garden | **el jardín botánico** |
| | _ehl khahr·deen boh·tah·nee·koh_ |

| the battleground | **el campo de batalla?** |
| | *ehl kahm·poh deh bah·tah·yah* |
| the castle | **el castillo** *ehl kahs·tee·yoh* |
| the downtown area | **el centro** *ehl sehn·troh* |
| the fountain | **la fuente** *lah fwehn·teh* |
| the library | **la biblioteca** *lah bee·bleeyoh·teh·kah* |
| the market | **el mercado** *ehl mehr·kah·doh* |
| the museum | **el museo** *ehl moo·seh·oh* |
| the old town | **el casco antiguo** |
| | *ehl kahs·koh ahn·tee·gwoh* |
| the palace | **el palacio** *ehl pah·lah·seeyoh* |
| the park | **el parque** *ehl pahr·keh* |
| the ruins | **las ruinas** *lahs rwee·nahs* |
| the shopping area | **la zona comercial** *lahs soh·nah koh·mehr·seeyahl* |
| the town square | **la plaza** *lah plah·sah* |
| Can you show me on the map? | **¿Puede indicármelo en el mapa?** *pweh·deh een·dee·kahr·meh·loh ehn ehl mah·pah* |
| It's... | **Es...** *ehs...* |
| amazing | **increíble** *een·kreh·ee·bleh* |
| beautiful | **precioso** *preh·seeyoh·soh* |
| boring | **aburrido** *ah·boo·rree·doh* |

| | |
|---|---|
| interesting | **interesante** een·teh·reh·*sahn*·teh |
| magnificent | **magnífico** mahg·*nee*·fee·koh |
| romantic | **romántico** roh·*mahn*·tee·koh |
| strange | **extraño** ex·*trah*·nyoh |
| stunning | **impresionante** eem·preh·seeyoh·*nahn*·teh |
| terrible | **horrible** oh·*rree*·bleh |
| ugly | **feo** *feh*·oh |
| I (don't) like it. | **(No) Me gusta.** (noh) meh *goo*·stah |

For Asking Directions, see page 35.

## Religious Sites

| | |
|---|---|
| Where is…? | **¿Dónde está…?** *dohn*·deh ehs·*tah*… |
| the cathedral | **la catedral** lah kah·teh·*drahl* |
| the Catholic/ Protestant church | **la iglesia católica/protestante** lah ee·*gleh*·seeyah kah·*toh*·lee·kah/ proh·tehs·*tahn*·teh |
| the mosque | **la mezquita** lah mehs·*kee*·tah |
| the shrine | **el santuario** ehl sahn·*twah*·reeyoh |
| the synagogue | **la sinagoga** lah see·nah·*goh*·gah |
| the temple | **el templo** ehl *tehm*·ploh |
| What time is mass/the service? | **¿A qué hora es la misa/el culto?** ah keh *oh*·rah ehs lah *mee*·sah/ehl *kool*·toh |

## ESSENTIAL

| | |
|---|---|
| Where's the market/ mall [shopping centre]? | **¿Dónde está el mercado/centro comercial?** _dohn_•deh ehs•_tah_ ehl mehr•_kah_•doh/_sen_•troh koh•mehr•_seeyahl_ |
| I'm just looking. | **Sólo estoy mirando.** _soh_•loh ehs•_toy_ mee•_rahn_•doh |
| Can you help me? | **¿Puede ayudarme?** _pweh_•deh ah•yoo•_dahr_•meh |
| I'm being helped. | **Ya me atienden.** yah meh ah•_teeyehn_•dehn |
| How much? | **¿Cuánto es?** _kwahn_•toh ehs |
| That one, please. | **Ése m/Ésa f, por favor.** _eh_•she/_eh_•sah pohr fah•bohr |
| That's all. | **Eso es todo.** _eh_•soh ehs _toh_•doh |
| Where can I pay? | **¿Dónde se paga?** _dohn_•deh seh pah•gah |
| I'll pay in cash/by credit card. | **Voy a pagar en efectivo/con tarjeta de crédito.** boy ah pah•_gahr_ ehn eh•_fehk_•tee•_bee_•boh/kohn tahr•_kheh_•tah deh _kreh_•dee•toh |
| A receipt, please. | **Un recibo, por favor.** oon reh•_see_•boh pohr fah•_bohr_ |

There are many types of markets in the towns of Latin America. You can find a wide variety of goods at these markets, including fruit and vegetables, antiques, souvenirs, and regional specialty items. Your hotel or local tourist office should be able to provide information on the markets for your area. Most permanent markets are open daily from early morning until late afternoon; traveling market times vary by location.

## YOU MAY SEE...

| | |
|---|---|
| **HORARIO DE APERTURA** | Opening hours |
| **CERRADO POR HORARIO DE COMIDA** | Closed for lunch |
| **PROBADORES** | Fitting room |
| **CAJERO/CAJERA** | Cashier |
| **SOLO EFECTIVO** | Cash only |
| **SE ACEPTAN TARJETAS DE CRÉDITO** | Credit cards accepted |

## At the Shops

| Where is/are...? | **¿Dónde está/están...?** _dohn·deh ehs·tah/ehs·tahn._ |
|---|---|
| the antiques store | **la tienda de antigüedades** _lah teeyehn·dah deh ahn·tee·gweh·dah·dehs_ |
| the bakery | **la panadería** _lah pah·nah·deh·ree·ah_ |
| the bank | **el banco** _ehl bahn·koh_ |
| the bookstore | **la librería** _lah lee·breh·ree·ah_ |
| the clothing store | **la tienda de ropa** _lah teeyehn·dah deh roh·pah_ |
| the delicatessen | **la charcutería** _lah chahr·koo·teh·ree·ah_ |
| the department store | **los grandes almacenes** _lohs grahn·dehs ahl·mah·seh·nehs_ |
| the gift shop | **la tienda de regalos** _lah teeyehn·dah deh reh·gah·lohs_ |
| the health food store | **la tienda de alimentos naturales** _lah teeyehn·dah deh ah·lee·mehn·tohs nah·too·rahl·ehs_ |
| the jeweler | **la joyería** _lah khoh·yeh·ree·ah_ |
| the liquor store [off-licence] | **la tienda de bebidas alcohólicas** _lah teeyehn·dah deh beh·bee·dahs ahl·koh·oh·lee·kahs_ |
| the market | **el mercado** _ehl mehr·kah·doh_ |
| the music store | **la tienda de música?** _lah teeyehn·dah deh moo·see·kah?_ |

| | | |
|---|---|---|
| the pastry shop | **la pastelería** | *lah pahs•teh•leh•ree•ah* |
| the pharmacy | **la farmacia** | *lah fahr•mah•seeyah* |
| the produce | **la tienda de frutas y verduras** | *lah* |
| [grocery] store | | *teeyehn•dah deh froo•tahs ee behr•doo•rahs* |
| the shoe store | **la zapatería** | *lah sah•pah•teh•ree•ah* |
| the shopping mall | **el centro comercial** | *ehl sehn•troh koh•mehr•seeyahl* |
| the souvenir store | **la tienda de recuerdos** | |
| | | *lah teeyehn•dah deh reh•kwehr•dohs* |
| the supermarket | **el supermercado** | *ehl soo•pehr•mehr•kah•doh* |
| the tobacconist | **la tabaquería** | *lah tah•bah•keh•ree•ah* |
| the toy store | **la juguetería** | *lah khoo•geh•teh•ree•ah* |

## Ask an Assistant

| | | |
|---|---|---|
| When do you open/close ? | **¿A qué hora abren/cierran?** | *ah keh oh•rah ah•brehn/seeyeh•rrahn* |
| Where is/are...? | **¿Dónde está/están...?** | *dohn•deh ehs•tah/ehs•tahn...* |
| the cashier | **la caja** *lah kah•khah* | |
| the escalators | **las escaleras mecánicas** | |
| | *lahs ehs•kah•leh•rahs meh•kah•nee•kahs* | |
| the elevator [lift] | **el ascensor** *ehl ahs•sehn•sohr* | |
| the fitting room | **el probador** *ehl proh•bah•dohr* | |
| the store directory | **la guía de tiendas** *lah gee•ah deh teeyehn•dahs* | |
| Can you help me? | **¿Puede ayudarme?** *pweh•deh ah•yoo•dahr•meh* | |
| I'm just looking. | **Sólo estoy mirando.** *soh•loh ehs•toy mee•rahn•doh* | |
| I'm being helped. | **Ya me atienden.** *yah meh ah•teeyehn•dehn* | |
| Do you have...? | **¿Tienen...?** *teeyeh•nehn...* | |
| Can you show me...? | **¿Podría enseñarme...?** | |
| | *poh•dree•ah ehn•seh•nyahr•meh...* | |
| Can you ship/ wrap it? | **¿Pueden hacer un envío/envolverlo?** | |
| | *pweh•dehn ah•sehr oon ehn•bee•oh/ehn•bohl•behr•loh* | |

| How much? | **¿Cuánto es?** _kwahn•toh ehs_ |
| That's all. | **Eso es todo.** _eh•soh ehs toh•doh_ |

For Meals & Cooking, see page 67.

For Souvenirs, see page 130.

## YOU MAY HEAR...

**¿Necesita ayuda?**
_neh•seh•see•tah ah•yoo•dah_

Can I help you?

**Un momento.** _oon moh•mehn•toh_

One moment.

**¿Qué desea?** _keh deh•seh•ah_

What would you like?

**¿Algo más?** _ahl•goh mahs_

Anything else?

## Personal Preferences

| I'd like something... | **Quiero algo...** _keeyeh•roh ahl•goh..._ |
| cheap/expensive | **barato/caro** _bah•rah•toh/kah•roh_ |
| larger/smaller | **más grande/más pequeño** |
| | _mahs grahn•deh/mahs peh•keh•nyoh_ |
| from this region | **de esta región** _deh ehs•tah reh•kheeyohn_ |
| Around...pesos. | **Alrededor de los...pesos.** |
| | _ahl•reh•deh•dohr deh lohs...peh•sohs_ |
| Is it real? | **¿Es auténtico _m_ / auténtica _f_?** |
| | _ehs awoo•tehn•tee•koh/awoo•tehn•tee•kah_ |
| Can you show me | **¿Puede mostrarme esto/eso?** |
| this/that? | _pweh•deh mohs•trahr•meh ehs•toh/eh•soh_ |
| That's not quite what | **Eso no es realmente lo que busco.** _eh•soh_ |
| I want. | _noh ehs reh•ahl•mehn•teh loh keh boos•koh_ |
| No, I don't like it. | **No, no me gusta.** _noh noh meh goos•tah_ |
| It's too expensive. | **Es demasiado caro.** _ehs deh•mah•seeyah•doh kah•ro_ |

| | | |
|---|---|---|
| I have to think about it. | **Quiero pensarlo.** | _keeyeh·roh pehn·sahr·loh_ |
| I'll take it. | **Me lo llevo.** | _meh loh yeh·boh_ |

## Paying & Bargaining

| | | |
|---|---|---|
| How much? | **¿Cuánto es?** | _kwahn·toh ehs_ |
| I'll pay... | **Voy a pagar...** | _boy ah pah·gahr..._ |
| in cash | **en efectivo** | _ehn eh·fehk·tee·boh_ |
| by credit card | **con tarjeta de crédito** | |
| | _kohn tahr·kheh·tah deh kreh·dee·toh_ | |
| by traveler's | **con cheque de viajero** | |
| check [cheque] | _kohn cheh·keh deh beeyah·kheh·roh_ | |
| A receipt, please. | **Un recibo, por favor.** | _oon reh·see·boh pohr fah·bohr_ |
| That's too much. | **Eso es demasiado.** | _eh·soh ehs deh·mah·seeyah·doh_ |
| I'll give you... | **Le doy...** | _leh doy..._ |
| I have only... pesos. | **Sólo tengo... pesos.** | _soh·loh tehn·goh... peh·sohs_ |
| Is that your best price? | **¿Es el mejor precio que me puede hacer?** | _ehs ehl meh·khohr preh·seeyoh keh meh pweh·deh ah·sehr_ |
| Can you give me a discount? | **¿Puede hacerme un descuento?** | _pweh·deh ah·sehr·meh oon dehs·kwehn·toh_ |

For Numbers, see page 171.

Credit cards are widely accepted throughout Latin America; you will need to show ID when using a credit card. Mastercard™ and Visa™ are the most commonly used; American Express® is accepted in most places. Debit cards are also commonly used; these are usually accepted if backed by Visa™ or Mastercard™. Traveler's checks cannot be used everywhere. Cash is always accepted — some places, such as newsstands, tobacconists, flower shops and market or street stands, take cash only.

## YOU MAY HEAR...

**¿Cómo va a pagar?**
*koh•moh bah ah pah•gahr*

How are you paying?

**Su tarjeta ha sido rechazada.** *soo tahr•kheh•tah ah see•doh reh•chah•sah•dah*

Your credit card has been declined.

**Su documento de identidad, por favor.** *soo doh•koo•mehn•toh deh ee•dehn•tee•dahd pohr fah•bohr*

ID, please.

**No aceptamos tarjetas de crédito.** *noh ah•sehp•tah•mohs tahr•kheh•tahs deh kreh•dee•toh*

We don't accept credit cards.

**Sólo en efectivo, por favor.** *soh•loh ehn eh•fehk•tee•boh pohr fah•bohr*

Cash only, please.

**¿Tiene cambio/billetes más pequeños?** *teeyeh•neh kahm•beeyoh/bee•yeh•tehs mahs peh•keh•nyohs*

Do you have change/small bills [notes]?

Latin America produces a wide range of souvenirs, from typical
tourist T-shirts to high-quality regional crafts. Mexican tapestries
and Chilean wine, among others, are popular gifts. Specialty regional
goods include copperware, earthenware, leather goods, jewelry, lace,
porcelain and wood carvings. To find a good representation of the
specialty goods in each Latin American country at reasonable prices,
visit the markets in each town.

Throughout Latin America you can find quality gold and silver jewelry,
especially in Peru and Mexico. Quality jewelry can be purchased
in jewelry stores, but for a more personal approach, visit the local
markets. These, along with small specialty stores in rural villages and
towns, are a great source for handmade jewelry.

## Making a Complaint

| | |
|---|---|
| I'd like... | **Quiero...** _keeyeh_·roh... |
| to exchange this | **cambiar esto por otro** |
| | kahm·_beeyahr_ ehs·toh pohr _oh_·troh |
| to return this | **devolver esto** deh·bohl·_behr_ ehs·toh |
| a refund | **que me devuelvan el dinero** |
| | keh meh deh·_bwehl_·bahn ehl dee·_neh_·roh |
| to speak to the | **hablar con el encargado** |
| manager | ah·_blahr_ kohn ehl ehn·kahr·_gah_·doh |

## Services

| | |
|---|---|
| Can you | **¿Puede recomendarme...?** |
| recommend...? | _pweh_·deh reh·koh·mehn·_dahr_·meh... |
| a barber | **una peluquería de caballeros** |
| | _oo_·nah peh·loo·keh·_ree_·ah deh kah·bah·_yeh_·rohs |
| a dry cleaner | **una lavandería** _oo_·nah lah·bahn·deh·_ree_·ah |

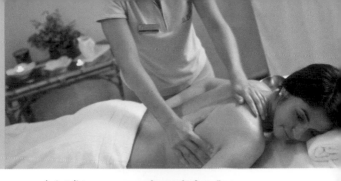

| | |
|---|---|
| a hairstylist | **una peluquería de señoras** |
| | _oo_•nah peh•loo•keh•_ree_•ah deh seh•_nyoh_•rahs |
| a laundromat | **un autoservicio de lavandería** _oon_ |
| [launderette] | ahoo•toh•sehr•_bee_•seeyoh deh lah•bahn•deh•_ree_•ah |
| a nail salon | **un salón de manicura** |
| | oon sah•_lohn_ deh mah•nee•_koo_•rah |
| a spa | **un centro de salud y belleza** |
| | oon _sen_•troh deh sah•_lood_ ee beh•_yeh_•sah |
| Can you…this? | **¿Puede…esto?** _pweh_•deh…_ehs_•toh |
| alter | **hacerle un arreglo a** ah•_sehr_•leh oon ah•_rreh_•gloh a|
| clean | **limpiar** leem•_peeyahr_ |
| fix [mend] | **zurcir** soor•_seer_ |
| press | **planchar** plahn•_chahr_ |
| When will it be ready? | **¿Cuándo estará listo?** _kwahn_•doh ehs•tah•_rah_ lees•t|

## Hair & Beauty

| | |
|---|---|
| I'd like… | **Quiero…** _keeyeh_•roh… |
| an appointment for | **pedir cita para hoy/mañana** |
| today/tomorrow | peh•_deer_ see•tah _pah_•rah oy/mah•_nyah_•nah |
| some color | **teñirme el pelo** teh•_nyeer_•meh ehl peh•_loh_ |
| an eyebrow/ | **depilarme las cejas/ingles** |
| bikini wax | deh•pee•_lahr_•meh lahs _seh_•khahs/_een_•glehs |

| | | |
|---|---|---|
| a facial | **hacerme una limpieza de cutis** | |
| | *ah·sehr·meh oo·nah leem·peeyeh·sah deh koo·tees* | |
| some highlights | **hacerme mechas** *ah·sehr·meh meh·chahs* | |
| my hair styled | **hacerme un peinado** *ah·sehr·meh oon peyee·nah·doh* | |
| a haircut | **cortarme el pelo** *kohr·tahr·meh ehl peh·loh* | |
| a manicure/ | **hacerme la manicura/pedicura** | |
| pedicure | *ah·sehr·meh lah mah·nee·koo·rah/peh·dee·koo·rah* | |
| a (sports) massage | **un masaje (deportivo)** | |
| | *oon mah·sah·kheh (deh·pohr·tee·boh)* | |
| a trim | **cortarme las puntas** *kohr·tahr·meh lahs poon·tahs* | |
| Not too short. | **No me lo corte demasiado.** | |
| | *noh meh loh kohr·teh deh·mah·seeyah·doh* | |
| Shorter here. | **Quíteme más de aquí.** *kee·teh·meh mahs deh ah·kee* | |
| Do you do…? | **¿Hacen…?** *ah·sehn…* | |
| acupuncture | **acupuntura** *ah·koo·poon·too·rah* | |
| aromatherapy | **aromaterapia** *ah·roh·mah·teh·rah·peeyah* | |
| oxygen treatment | **oxígenoterapia** *oh·xee·kheh·noh·teh·rah·peeyah* | |
| Do you have a sauna? | **¿Tienen una sauna?** *teeyehn·ehn oo·nah sawoo·nah* | |

With its variety of landscapes, Latin America has spas, wellness centers and health-based resorts. These facilities offer a wide selection of treatments, including relaxation therapies and herbal remedies. Spas can be found in Mexico, Chile, Argentina, Venezuela, Uruguay, Peru and other Latin American countries. Resort and overnight spas often offer individual services to those not staying there. Many of these also offer other relaxation activities such as horseback riding, guided tours, golf and swimming. Some spas and resorts do not allow children, so check before booking if you are traveling with kids.

## Antiques

| | |
|---|---|
| How old is it? | **¿Qué antigüedad tiene?** |
| | *keh ahn·tee·gweh·dahd teeyeh·neh* |
| Do you have anything from the…period? | **¿Tiene algo de la época…?** |
| | *teeyeh·neh ahl·goh deh lah eh·poh·kah…* |
| Do I have to fill out any forms? | **¿Tengo que completar algún formulario?** |
| | *tehn·goh keh cohm·pleh·tahr ahl·goon fohr·moo·lah·reeoh* |
| Is there a certificate of authenticity? | **¿Tiene el certificado de autenticidad?** |
| | *teeyeh·neh ehl sehr·tee·fee·kah·doh deh awoo·tehn·tee·see·dahd* |

## Clothing

| | |
|---|---|
| I'd like… | **Quiero…** *keeyeh·roh…* |
| Can I try this on? | **¿Puedo probarme esto?** |
| | *pweh·doh proh·bahr·meh ehs·toh* |
| It doesn't fit. | **No me queda bien.** *noh meh keh·dah beeyehn* |
| It's too… | **Me queda demasiado…** |
| | *meh keh·dah deh·mah·seeyah·doh…* |
| big | **grande** *grahn·deh* |
| small | **pequeño** *m*/**pequeña** *f peh·keh·nyoh/peh·keh·nyah* |
| short | **corto** *m*/**corta** *f kohr·toh/kohr·tah* |
| tight | **apretado** *ah·preh·tah·doh* |
| loose | **flojo** *floh·khoh* |
| long | **largo** *m*/**larga** *f lahr·goh/lahr·gah* |
| Do you have this in size…? | **¿Tiene esto en la talla…?** *teeyeh·neh ehs·toh ehn lah tah·yah…* |
| Do you have this in a bigger/ smaller size? | **¿Tiene esto en una talla más grande/pequeña?** *teeyeh·nch ehs·toh ehn oo·nah tah·yah mahs grahn·deh/peh·keh·nyah* |

For Numbers, see page 171.

## YOU MAY HEAR...

**Se le ve muy bien.**      That looks great on you.
*seh leh beh mooy beeyehn*

**¿Cómo le queda?** *koh·moh leh keh·dah*    How does it fit?
**No tenemos su talla.**     We don't have your size.
*noh teh·neh·mohs soo tah·yah*

## YOU MAY SEE...

| | |
|---|---|
| **CABALLEROS** | men's |
| **DAMAS** | women's |
| **NIÑOS** | children's |

## Colors

| | |
|---|---|
| I'd like something... | **Busco algo...** *boos·koh ahl·goh...* |
| beige | **beige** *beh·eesh* |
| black | **negro** *neh·groh* |
| blue | **azul** *ah·sool* |
| brown | **marrón** *mah·rrohn* |
| green | **verde** *behr·deh* |
| gray | **gris** *grees* |
| orange | **naranja** *nah·rahn·khah* |
| pink | **rosa** *roh·sah* |
| purple | **morado** *moh·rah·doh* |
| red | **rojo** *roh·khoh* |
| white | **blanco** *blahn·koh* |
| yellow | **amarillo** *ah·mah·ree·yoh* |

## Clothes & Accessories

| | | |
|---|---|---|
| backpack | **la mochila** | *lah moh•chee•lah* |
| belt | **el cinturón** | *ehl seen•too•rohn* |
| bikini | **el bikini** | *ehl bee•kee•nee* |
| blouse | **la blusa** | *lah bloo•sah* |
| bra | **el sujetador** | *ehl soo•kheh•tah•dohr* |
| briefs [underpants] | **los calzoncillos** | *lohs kahl•sohn•see•yohs* |
| coat | **el abrigo** | *ehl ah•bree•goh* |
| dress | **el vestido** | *ehl behs•tee•doh* |
| hat | **el sombrero** | *ehl sohm•breh•roh* |
| jacket | **la chaqueta** | *lah chah•keh•tah* |
| jeans | **los vaqueros** | *lohs bah•keh•rohs* |
| pajamas | **el pijama** | *ehl pee•khah•mah* |
| pants [trousers] | **los pantalones** | *lohs pahn•tah•loh•nehs* |
| panties (women's underwear) | **calzones** | *kahl•soh•nehs* |
| pantyhose [tights] | **las medias** | *lahs meh•deeyahs* |
| purse [handbag] | **el bolso** | *ehl bohl•soh* |
| raincoat | **el impermeable** | *ehl eem•pehr•meh•ah•bleh* |
| scarf | **la bufanda** | *lah boo•fahn•dah* |
| shirt | **la camisa** | *lah kah•mee•sah* |
| shorts | **los pantalones cortos** | *lohs pahn•tah•loh•nehs kohr•tohs* |
| skirt | **la falda** | *lah fahl•dah* |
| socks | **los calcetines** | *lohs kahl•seh•tee•nehs* |
| suit | **el traje** | *ehl trah•kheh* |
| sunglasses | **los anteojos de sol** | *lahs anh•teh•oh•khos deh sohl* |
| sweater | **el suéter** | *ehl soo•eh•tehr* |
| sweatshirt | **la sudadera** | *lah soo•dah•deh•rah* |
| swimsuit | **el traje de baño** | *ehl trah•kheh deh bah•nyoh* |

| | |
|---|---|
| T-shirt | **la camiseta** *lah kah•mee•seh•tah* |
| tie | **la corbata** *lah kohr•bah•tah* |
| underwear | **la ropa interior** *lah roh•pah een•teh•reeyohr* |
| underpants (men's underwear) | **calzoncillos** *kahl•sohn•see•yohs* |

## Fabric

| | |
|---|---|
| I'd like... | **Quiero...** *keeyeh•roh...* |
| cotton | **algodón** *ahl•goh•dohn* |
| denim | **tela vaquera** *teh•lah bah•keh•rah* |
| lace | **encaje** *ehn•kah•kheh* |
| leather | **cuero** *kweh•roh* |
| linen | **lino** *lee•noh* |
| silk | **seda** *seh•dah* |
| wool | **lana** *lah•nah* |
| Is it machine washable? | **¿Se puede lavar a máquina?** *seh pweh•deh lah•bahr ah mah•kee•nah* |

## Shoes

| | |
|---|---|
| I'd like... | **Quiero...** *keeyeh•roh...* |
| high-heeled/flat shoes | **zapatos de tacón/planos** *sah•pah•tohs deh tah•kohn/plah•nohs* |

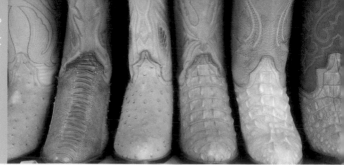

| | |
|---|---|
| boots | **botas** <u>boh</u>•tahs |
| loafers | **mocasines** moh•kah•<u>see</u>•nehs |
| sandals | **sandalias** sahn•<u>dah</u>•leeyahs |
| shoes | **zapatos** sah•<u>pah</u>•tohs |
| slippers | **pantuflas** pahn•<u>too</u>•flahs |
| sneakers | **zapatillas de deporte** |
| | sah•pah•<u>tee</u>•yahs deh deh•<u>pohr</u>•teh |
| In size… | **En la talla…** ehn lah <u>tah</u>•yah… |

For Numbers, see page 171.

## Sizes

| | |
|---|---|
| small (S) | **pequeña (S)** peh•<u>keh</u>•nyah (<u>eh</u>•seh) |
| medium (M) | **mediana (M)** meh•<u>deeyah</u>•nah (<u>eh</u>•meh) |
| large (L) | **grande (L)** <u>grahn</u>•deh (<u>eh</u>•leh) |
| extra large (XL) | **XL** <u>eh</u>•kees <u>eh</u>•leh |
| petite | **tallas pequeñas** <u>tah</u>•yahs peh•<u>keh</u>•nyahs |
| plus size | **tallas grandes** <u>tah</u>•yahs <u>grahn</u>•dehs |

## Newsagent & Tobacconist

| | |
|---|---|
| Do you sell English-language newspapers? | **¿Venden periódicos en inglés?** <u>behn</u>•dehn peh•<u>reeyoh</u>•dee•kohs ehn een•<u>glehs</u> |
| I'd like… | **Quiero…** <u>keeyeh</u>•roh… |

| candy [sweets] | **caramelos** _kah·rah·meh·lohs_ |
| chewing gum | **chicle** _chee·kleh_ |
| a chocolate bar | **un chocolate** _oon choh·koh·lah·teh_ |
| a cigar | **un puro** _oon poo·roh_ |
| a pack/carton of | **un paquete/cartón** _de tabaco oon_ |
| cigarettes | _pah·keh·teh/kahr·tohn deh tah·bah·koh_ |
| a lighter | **un encendedor** _oon ehn·sehn·deh·dohr_ |
| a magazine | **una revista** _oo·nah reh·bees·tah_ |
| matches | **fósforos** _fohs·foh·rohs_ |
| a newspaper | **un periódico** _oon peh·reeyoh·dee·koh_ |
| a pen | **un bolígrafo** _oon boh·lee·grah·foh_ |
| a postcard | **una postal** _oo·nah pohs·tahl_ |
| a road/town | **un mapa de las carreteras/plano de...** |
| map of... | _oon mah·pah deh lahs kah·rreh·teh·rahs/_ |
| | _plah·noh deh..._ |
| stamps | **estampillas** _esh·tam·pee·yahs_ |

## Photography

| I'd like a/an... | **Quiero una cámara...** |
| | _keeyeh·roh oo·nah camera.kah·mah·rah..._ |
| automatic | **automática** _awoo·toh·mah·tee·kah_ |
| digital | **digital** _dee·khee·tahl_ |
| disposable | **desechable** _deh·seh·chah·bleh_ |
| I'd like... | **Quiero...** _keeyeh·roh..._ |
| a battery | **una pila** _oo·nah pee·lah_ |
| digital prints | **fotos digitales** _foh·tohs dee·khee·tah·lehs_ |
| a memory card | **una tarjeta de memoria** |
| | _oo·nah tahr·kheh·tah deh meh·moh·reeyah_ |
| Can I print digital | **¿Puedo imprimir aquí fotos digitales?** |
| photos here? | _pweh·doh eem·pree·meer ah·kee foh·tohs_ |
| | _dee·khee·tah·lehs_ |

## Souvenirs

| | |
|---|---|
| bottle of wine | **la botella de vino** *lah boh•teh•yah deh bee•noh* |
| box of chocolates | **la caja de bombones** *lah kah•khah deh bohm•boh•neh* |
| doll | **la muñeca** *lah moo•nyeh•kah* |
| fan (wooden) | **el abanico de madera** *ehl ah•bah•nee•koh deh mah•deh•rah* |
| key ring | **el llavero** *ehl yah•beh•roh* |
| mug | **la taza** *lah tah•sah* |
| postcard | **la postal** *lah pohs•tahl* |
| pottery | **la cerámica** *lah seh•rah•mee•kah* |
| serrano ham | **el jamón serrano** *ehl khah•mohn seh•rrah•noh* |
| T-shirt | **la camiseta** *lah kah•mee•seh•tah* |
| toy | **el juguete** *ehl khoo•geh•teh* |
| wine | **el vino** *ehl bee•noh* |
| Can I see this/that? | **¿Puedo ver esto/eso?** *pweh•doh behr ehs•toh/eh•soh* |
| It's in the window/ display case. | **Está en el escaparate/la vitrina.** *ehs•tah ehn ehl ehs•kah•pah•rah•teh/lah bee•tree•nah* |
| I'd like... | **Quiero...** *keeyeh•roh...* |
| a battery | **una pila** *oo•nah pee•lah* |
| a bracelet | **una pulsera** *oo•nah pool•seh•rah* |
| a brooch | **un broche** *oon broh•cheh* |

| earrings | **unos pendientes** _oo_·nohs pehn·_deeyehn_·tehs |
| a necklace | **un collar** oon koh·_yahr_ |
| a ring | **un anillo** oon ah·_nee_·yoh |
| a watch | **un reloj de pulsera** oon reh·_lohkh_ deh pool·_seh_·rah |
| I'd like... | **Quiero...** _keeyeh_·roh... |
| copper | **cobre** _koh_·breh |
| crystal | **cristal** krees·_tahl_ |
| diamonds | **diamantes** deeyah·_mahn_·tehs |
| white/yellow gold | **oro blanco/amarillo** _oh_·roh _blahn_·koh/ah·mah·_ree_·yoh |
| pearls | **perlas** _pehr_·lahs |
| pewter | **peltre** _pehl_·treh |
| platinum | **platino** plah·_tee_·noh |
| sterling silver | **plata esterlina** _plah_·tah ehs·tehr·_lee_·nah |
| Is this real? | **¿Es auténtico?** ehs awoo·_tehn_·tee·koh |
| Can you engrave it? | **¿Puede grabármelo?** _pweh_·deh grah·_bahr_·meh·loh |

# Sport & Leisure

## ESSENTIAL

| When's the game? | **¿Cuándo empieza el partido?** |
| | _kwahn_·doh ehm·_peeyeh_·sah ehl pahr·_tee_·doh |
| Where's...? | **¿Dónde está...?** _dohn_·deh ehs·_tah_... |
| the beach | **la playa** lah _plah_·yah |
| the park | **el parque** ehl _pahr_·keh |
| the pool | **la piscina** lah pees·_see_·nah |
| Is it safe to swim here? | **¿Es seguro nadar aquí?** ehs seh·_goo_·roh |
| | nah·_dahr_ ah·_kee_ |
| Can I rent [hire] golf clubs? | **¿Puedo alquilar palos de golf?** |
| | _pweh_·doh ahl·kee·_lahr_ _pah_·lohs deh golf |

| How much per hour? | **¿Cuánto cuesta por hora?** |
| | *kwahn•toh kwehs•tah pohr oh•rah* |
| How far is it to…? | **¿A qué distancia está…?** |
| | *ah keh dees•tahn•seeyah ehs•tah…* |
| Can you show me on the map, please? | **¿Puede indicármelo en el mapa, por favor?** |
| | *pweh•deh een•dee•kahr•meh•loh ehn ehl mah•pah* |
| | *pohr fah•bohr* |

## Watching Sport

| When's…? | **¿Cuándo empieza…?** *kwahn•doh ehm•peeyeh•sah…* |
| the baseball game | **el juego de béisbol?** *ehl khooeh•goh deh behys•bohl* |
| the basketball game | **el partido de baloncesto** |
| | *ehl pahr•tee•doh deh bah•lohn•sehs•toh* |
| the boxing match | **la pelea de boxeo** *lah peh•leh•ah deh bohks•eh•oh* |
| cricket game | **juego de críquet** *khweh•goh deh kree•keht* |
| the cycling race | **la carrera de bicicletas** |
| | *lah kha•rreh•rah deh bee•see•kleh•tahs* |
| the golf tournament | **el torneo de golf** *ehl tohr•neh•oh deh golf* |
| the soccer [football] game | **el partido de fútbol** |
| | *ehl pahr•tee•doh deh foot•bohl* |
| the tennis match | **el partido de tenis** *ehl pahr•tee•doh deh teh•nees* |
| the volleyball game | **el partido de voleibol** *ehl pahr•tee•doh deh* |
| | *boh•leyee•bohl* |
| Who's playing? | **¿Quiénes juegan?** *keeyeh•nehs khweh•gahn* |
| Where is…? | **¿Dónde está…?** *dohn•deh ehs•tah…* |
| the horsetrack | **el hipódromo** *ehl ee•poh•droh•moh* |
| the racetrack | **el circuito de carreras** *ehl seer•kwee•toh* |
| | *de kah•rreh•rahs* |
| the stadium | **el estadio** *ehl ehs•tah•deeyoh* |
| Where can I place a bet? | **¿Dónde puedo hacer una apuesta?** |
| | *dohn•deh pweh•doh ah•sehr oo•nah ah•pwehs•tah* |

**Fútbol** (soccer) is the most popular sport in Latin America; most of the countries in Latin America have their own professional teams with a large fan base. Note that fans are extremely dedicated, so be sure not to insult the team.
Other popular sports include basketball, tennis, auto racing and golf.

## Playing Sport

| | |
|---|---|
| Where is/are…? | **¿Dónde está/están…?** _dohn_·deh ehs·_tah_/ehs·_tahn_… |
| the golf course | **el campo de golf** ehl _kahm_·poh deh golf |
| the gym | **el gimnasio** ehl kheem·_nah_·seeyoh |
| the park | **el parque** ehl _pahr_·keh |
| the tennis courts | **las canchas de tenis** lahs _kahn_·chahs deh _teh_·nees |
| How much per…? | **¿Cuánto cuesta por…?** _kwahn_·toh _kwehs_·tah pohr… |
| day | **día** _dee_·ah |
| hour | **hora** _oh_·rah |
| game | **partido** pahr·_tee_·doh |
| round | **juego** _khweh_·goh |
| Can I rent [hire]…? | **¿Puedo alquilar…?** _pweh_·doh ahl·kee·_lahr_… |
| golf clubs | **palos de golf** _pah_·lohs deh golf |
| equipment | **equipo** eh·_kee_·poh |
| a racket | **una raqueta** _oo_·nah rah·_keh_·tah |

## At the Beach/Pool

| | |
|---|---|
| Where's the beach/pool? | **¿Dónde está la playa/piscina?** _dohn_·deh ehs·_tah_ lah _plah_·yah/pees·_see_·nah |
| Is there…? | **¿Hay…?** aye… |
| a kiddie pool | **una piscina infantil** _oo_·nah pees·_see_·nah een·fahn·_teel_ |
| an indoor/outdoor pool | **una piscina cubierta/exterior** _oo_·nah pees·_see_·nah koo·_beeyehr_·tah/ehx·teh·_reeyohr_ |

| | | |
|---|---|---|
| a lifeguard | **un socorrista** | oon soh•koh•_rrees_•tah |
| Is it safe…? | **¿Es seguro…?** | ehs seh•_goo_•roh… |
| to swim | **nadar** | nah•_dahr_ |
| to dive | **tirarse de cabeza** | tee•_rahr_•seh deh kah•_beh_•sah |
| for children | **para los niños** | _pah_•rah lohs _nee_•nyohs |
| I'd like to rent [hire]… | **Quiero alquilar…** | _keeyeh_•roh ahl•kee•_lahr_… |
| a deck chair | **una tumbona** | _oo_•nah toom•_boh_•nah |
| diving equipment | **equipo de buceo** | eh•_kee_•poh deh boo•_seh_•oh |
| a jet ski | **una moto acuática** | _oo_•nah _moh_•toh ah•_kwah_•tee•ka |
| a motorboat | **una lancha motora** | _oo_•nah _lahn_•chah moh•_toh_•rah |
| a rowboat | **un bote a remos** | oon _boh_•teh ah _reh_•mohs |
| snorkeling equipment | **equipo de esnórquel** | eh•_kee_•poh deh ehz•_nohr_•kehl |
| a surfboard | **una tabla de surf** | _oo_•nah _tah_•blah deh soorf |
| a towel | **una toalla** | _oo_•nah toh•_ah_•yah |
| an umbrella | **una sombrilla** | _oo_•nah sohm•_bree_•yah |
| water skis | **unos esquís acuáticos** | _oo_•nohs ehs•_kees_ ah•_kwah_•tee•kohs |
| a windsurfer | **una tabla de windsurf** | _oo_•nah _tah_•blah deh _weend_•soorf |
| For…hours. | **Por…horas.** | pohr…_oh_•rahs |

Coastal countries in Latin America have many miles of coastline
and beaches. The Dominican Republic, on the Caribbean Sea,
boasts some of the most beautiful beaches in the world. Cuba,
Venezuela, Mexico and Colombia also have world-famous beaches. If
you decide to go for a swim, check the safety flags at each beach. Green
flags indicate the water is safe, yellow flags indicate that you should use
caution and red flags indicate that the water is unsafe for swimming.

## Winter Sports

| | |
|---|---|
| A lift pass for a day/five days, please. | **Un pase de un día/cinco días de acceso a los medios de elevación.** *oon pah·seh deh oon dee·ah/seen·koh dee·ahs deh ahk·seh·soh ah lohs meh·deeohs deh eh·le·va·see·ohn* |
| I'd like to rent [hire]... | **Quiero alquilar...** *keeyeh·roh ahl·kee·lahr...* |
| boots | **botas** *boh·tahs* |
| a helmet | **un casco** *oon kahs·koh* |
| poles | **bastones** *bahs·toh·nehs* |
| skis | **esquís** *ehs·kees* |
| a snowboard | **una tabla de snowboard** *oo·nah tah·blah deh znoh·bohrd* |
| snowshoes | **raquetas de nieve** *rah·keh·tahs deh neeyeh·beh* |
| These are too big/small. | **Me quedan demasiado grandes/pequeños.** *meh keh·dahn deh·mah·seeyah·doh grahn·dehs/peh·keh·nyohs* |
| Are there lessons? | **¿Dan clases?** *dahn klah·schs* |
| I'm a beginner. | **Soy principiante.** *soy preen·see·peeyahn·teh* |
| I'm experienced. | **Tengo experiencia.** *tehn·goh ehx·peh·reeyehn·seeyah* |
| A trail [piste] map, please. | **Un mapa de las pistas, por favor.** *oon mah·pah deh lahs pees·tahs pohr fah·bohr* |

There is no shortage of great skiing in Latin America. The Andes in South America is the longest mountain range in the world, forming a continuous chain along the west. It is over 4,400 miles (7,000 km) long. The mountains extend over seven countries: Argentina, Bolivia, Chile, Colombia, Ecuador, Peru and Venezuela. The highest peak in the Andes is the Aconcagua in Argentina which reaches 22,841 feet (6,962 m).

## Out in the Country

| | | |
|---|---|---|
| A map of..., please. | **Un mapa de..., por favor.** | *oon mah•pah deh... pohr fah•bohr* |
| this region | **esta región** | *ehs•tah reh•kheeyohn* |
| the walking routes | **las rutas de senderismo** | *lahs roo•tahs deh sehn•deh•reez•moh* |
| the bike routes | **los senderos para bicicletas** | *lohs sehn•deh•rohs pah•rah bee•see•kleh•tahs* |
| the trails | **los senderos** | *lohs sehn•deh•rohs* |
| Is it easy/difficult? | **¿Es fácil/difícil?** | *ehs fah•seel/dee•fee•seel* |
| Is it far/steep? | **¿Está lejos/empinado?** | *ehs•tah leh•khohs/ehm•pee•nah•doh* |
| How far is it to...? | **¿A qué distancia está...?** | *ah keh dees•tahn•seeyah ehs•tah...* |
| Can you show me on the map, please? | **¿Puede indicármelo en el mapa, por favor?** | *pweh•deh een•dee•kahr•meh•loh ehn ehl mah•pah pohr fah•bohr* |
| I'm lost. | **Me he perdido.** | *meh eh pehr•dee•doh* |
| Where is...? | **¿Dónde está...?** | *dohn•deh ehs•tah...* |
| the bridge | **el puente** | *ehl pwehn•teh* |
| the cave | **la cueva** | *lah kweh•bah* |
| the cliff | **el acantilado** | *ehl ah•kahn•tee•lah•doh* |

| the desert | **el desierto** *ehl deh·seeyehr·toh* |
| the farm | **la granja** *lah grahn·khah* |
| the field | **el campo** *ehl kahm·poh* |
| the forest | **el bosque** *ehl bohs·keh* |
| the hill | **la colina** *lah koh·lee·nah* |
| the lake | **el lago** *ehl lah·goh* |
| the mountain | **la montaña** *lah mohn·tah·nyah* |
| the nature preserve | **la reserva natural** *lah reh·sehr·bah nah·too·rahl* |
| the overlook [viewpoint] | **el mirador** *ehl mee·rah·dohr* |
| the park | **el parque** *ehl pahr·keh* |
| the path | **el camino** *ehl kah·mee·noh* |
| the peak | **el pico** *ehl pee·koh* |
| the picnic area | **la zona de picnic** *lah soh·nah deh peek·neek* |
| the pond | **el estanque** *ehl ehs·tahn·keh* |
| the river | **el río** *ehl ree·oh* |
| the sea | **el mar** *ehl mahr* |
| the (thermal) spring | **el manantial (de aguas termales)** *ehl muh·nahn·teeyahl (deh ah·gwahs tehr·mah·lehs)* |
| the stream | **el arroyo** *ehl ah·rroh·yoh* |
| the valley | **el valle** *ehl bah·yeh* |

## YOU MAY SEE…

| | |
| --- | --- |
| **TELESQUÍ** | drag lift |
| **TELEFÉRICO** | cable car |
| **TELESILLA** | chair lift |
| **PRINCIPIANTE** | novice |
| **NIVEL INTERMEDIO** | intermediate |
| **EXPERTO** | expert |
| **PISTA CERRADA** | trail [piste] closed |

| the vineyard | **el viñedo** *ehl bee·nyeh·doh* |
| the waterfall | **la cascada** *lah kahs·kah·dah* |

## Going Out

### ESSENTIAL

| What's there to do at night? | **¿Qué se puede hacer por las noches?** *keh seh pweh·deh ah·sehr pohr lahs noh·chehs* |
| Do you have a program of events? | **¿Tiene un programa de espectáculos?** *teeyeh·neh oon proh·grah·mah deh ehs·pehk·tah·koo·lohs* |
| What's playing tonight? | **¿Qué hay en cartelera esta noche?** *keh aye ehn kahr·teh·leh·rah ehs·tah noh·cheh* |
| Where's…? | **¿Dónde está…?** *dohn·deh ehs·tah…* |
| the arcade? | **la galería?** *lah gah·leh·ree·ah* |
| the downtown area | **el centro** *ehl sehn·troh* |
| the bar | **el bar** *ehl bahr* |
| the dance club | **la discoteca** *lah dees·koh·teh·kah* |
| Is there a cover charge? | **¿Hay que pagar entrada?** *aye keh pah·gahr ehn·trah·dah* |

**Cinco de Mayo** (the fifth of May) is primarily a regional, and not a federal, holiday in Mexico; the date is observed in the United States and other locations around the world as a celebration of Mexican heritage and pride. It commemorates an initial victory of Mexican forces led by General Ignacio Zaragoza Seguín over French forces in the Battle of Puebla on May 5, 1862.

Each country in Latin America has its own celebrations. Many are religious celebrations such as Holy Week (**Semana Santa**), which is characterized by elaborate religious processions. This takes place the week before Easter (**la Pascua**) in many countries. Other important celebrations are the ones to commemorate important battles or to celebrate the independence day of each country. See page 175 for more on Holidays.

## Entertainment

| | |
|---|---|
| Can you recommend...? | **¿Puede recomendarme...?** _pweh·deh reh·koh·mehn·dahr·meh..._ |
| a concert | **un concierto** _oon kohn·seeyehr·toh_ |
| a movie | **una película** _oo·nah peh·lee·koo·lah_ |
| an opera | **una ópera** _oo·nah oh·peh·rah_ |
| a play | **una obra de teatro** _oo·nah oh·brah deh tch·ah·troh_ |
| When does it start/end? | **¿A qué hora empieza/termina?** _ah keh oh·rah ehm·peeyeh·sah/tehr·mee·nah_ |
| What's the dress code? | **¿Cómo hay que ir vestido _m_/ vestida _f_?** _koh·moh aye keh eer behs·tee·doh/behs·tee·dah_ |
| I like... | **Me gusta...** _meh goos·tah..._ |
| classical music | **la música clásica** _lah moo·see·kah klah·see·kah_ |
| folk music | **la música folk** _lah moo·see·kah folk_ |
| jazz | **el jazz** _ehl jazz_ |
| pop music | **la música pop** _lah moo·see·kah pop_ |
| rap | **el rap** _ehl rap_ |

For Tickets, see page 20.

**YOU MAY HEAR...**

**Por favor apaguen sus celulares.**
*pohr fah·bohr ah·pah·gehn soos sehl·yoo·lah·rehs*

Turn off your cell [mobile] phones, please.

There are many casinos throughout Latin America. Minimum entrance and gaming age is 18; ID is required and the dress code is business casual.

## Nightlife

| | |
|---|---|
| What's there to do at night? | **¿Qué se puede hacer por las noches?** *keh seh pweh·deh ah·sehr pohr lahs noh·chehs* |
| Is this area safe at night? | **¿Esta área es segura en la noche?** *ehs·tah ah·rehah ehs seh·goo·rah ehn lah noh·cheh* |
| Can you recommend...? | **¿Puede recomendarme...?** *pweh·deh reh·koh·mehn·dahr·meh...* |
| a bar | **un bar** *oon bahr* |
| a casino | **un casino** *oon kah·see·noh* |
| a cabaret | **un cabaret** *oon kah·bah·reht* |
| a club with .... | **Music un club con .... música** *oon kloob kohn moo·see·kah* |
| a dance club | **una discoteca** *oo·nah dees·koh·teh·kah* |
| a tango performance | **un espectáculo de tango** *oon ehs·pehk·tah·koo·loh deh tahn·goh* |
| a gay club | **una discoteca gay** *oo·nah dees·koh·teh·kah gay* |
| a jazz club | **un club de jazz** *oon kloob deh jazz* |

| | |
|---|---|
| a club with typical music | **un bar con música típica** <br> *oon bahr kohn <u>moo</u>•see•kah <u>tee</u>•pee•kah* |
| Is there live music? | **¿Hay música en vivo?** *aye <u>moo</u>•see•kah ehn <u>bee</u>•boh* |
| How do I get there? | **¿Cómo se llega allí?** *<u>koh</u>•moh seh <u>yeh</u>•gah ah•<u>yee</u>* |
| Is there a cover charge? | **¿Hay que pagar entrada?** *aye keh pah•<u>gahr</u> ehn•<u>trah</u>•dah* |
| Let's go dancing. | **Vamos a bailar.** *<u>bah</u>•mohs ah <u>bayee</u>•luhr* |

One of Argentina's greatest cultural achievements is the tango. Tango is a social dance that originated in Buenos Aires in Argentina. The musical styles that evolved together with the dance are also known as 'tango'.

Music and dance elements of tango are also popular in activities related to dancing such as figure skating and synchronized swimming because of its dramatic expression and its cultural associations with romance and love.

In Argentina, you may want to visit one of the many tango clubs, and you can even learn how to dance.

# Special
# Requirements

## ESSENTIAL

| | |
|---|---|
| I'm here on business. | **Estoy aquí en viaje de negocios.** |
| | *ehs•toy ah•kee ehn beeyah•kheh deh neh•goh•seeyohs* |
| Here's my business card. | **Aquí tiene mi tarjeta.** |
| | *ah•kee teeyeh•neh mee tahr•kheh•tah* |
| Can I have your card? | **¿Puede darme su tarjeta?** |
| | *pweh•deh dahr•meh soo tahr•kheh•tah* |
| I have a meeting with... | **Tengo una reunión con...** |
| | *tehn•goh oo•nah rewoo•neeyohn kohn...* |
| Where's...? | **¿Dónde está...?** *dohn•deh ehs•tah...* |
| the business center | **el centro de negocios** |
| | *ehl sehn•troh deh neh•goh•seeyohs* |
| the convention hall | **el salón de congresos** |
| | *ehl sah•lohn deh kohn•greh•sohs* |
| the meeting room | **la sala de reuniones** |
| | *lah sah•lah deh rewoo•neeyohn•ehs* |

---

It is common to greet colleagues with **buenos días** (good day).
Shake hands if it is the first time you are meeting someone in a
professional setting, or if it is someone you haven't seen in a while.
When leaving, simply say **adiós, gracias** (goodbye, thank you).

## On Business

| | |
|---|---|
| I'm here to attend... | **Estoy aquí para asistir...** |
| | *ehs-toy ah-kee pah-rah ah-sees-teer...* |
| a seminar | **a un seminario** *ah oon seh-mee-nah-reeyoh* |
| a conference | **a una conferencia** *ah oo-nah* |
| | *kohn-feh-rehn-seeyah* |
| a meeting | **a una reunión** *ah oo-nah rewoo-neeyohn* |
| My name is... | **Me llamo...** *meh yah-moh...* |
| May I introduce my | **Le presento a mi compañero m/** |
| colleague... | **compañera f de trabajo...** |
| | *leh preh-sehn-toh ah mee kohm-pah-nyeh-roh/* |
| | *kohm-pah-nyeh-rah deh trah-bah-khoh...* |
| I have a meeting/an | **Tengo una reunión/cita con...** |
| appointment with... | *tehn-goh oo-nah rewoo-neeyohn/see-tah kohn...* |
| I'm sorry I'm late. | **Perdone que haya llegado tarde.** |
| | *pehr-doh-neh keh ah-yah yeh-gah-doh tahr-deh* |
| I need an interpreter. | **Necesito un intérprete.** |
| | *neh-seh-see-toh oon een-tehr-preh-teh* |
| You can reach me | **Puede contactarme en el Hotel...** |
| at the...Hotel. | *pweh-deh kohn-tahk-tahr-meh ehn ehl oh-tehl...* |
| I'm here until... | **Estaré aquí hasta...** *ehs-tah-reh ah-kee ahs-tah...* |
| I need to... | **Necesito...** *neh-seh-see-toh...* |
| make a call | **hacer una llamada** *ah-sehr oo-nah yah-mah-dah* |
| make a photocopy | **hacer una fotocopia** |
| | *ah-sehr oo-nah foh-toh-koh-peeyah* |
| send an email | **enviar un correo electrónico** |
| | *ehn-beeyahr oon koh-rreh-oh ee-lehk-troh-nee-koh* |
| send a fax | **enviar un fax** *ehn-beeyahr oon fahx* |
| send a package | **enviar un paquete (para entrega el día** |
| (overnight) | **siguiente)** *ehn-beeyahr oon pah-keh-teh (pah-rah* |
| | *ehn-treh-gah ehl dee-ah see-geeyehn-teh)* |

| It was a pleasure to meet you. | **Ha sido un placer conocerlo _m_/ conocerla _f._** _ah <u>see</u>•doh oon plah•<u>sehr</u> koh•noh•<u>sehr</u>•loh/koh•noh•<u>sehr</u>•lah_ |
|---|---|

For Communications, see page 50.

For Social Media, see page 52.

## YOU MAY HEAR…

**¿Tiene cita?**
_<u>teeyeh</u>•neh <u>see</u>•tah_
**¿Con quién?** _kohn keeyehn_
**Está en una reunión.**
_ehs•<u>tah</u> ehn <u>oo</u>•nah rewoo•<u>neeyohn</u>_
**Un momento, por favor.**
_oon moh•<u>mehn</u>•toh pohr fah•<u>bohr</u>_
**Siéntese.** _<u>seeyehn</u>•teh•seh_
**¿Quiere algo de beber?** _keeyeh•reh_
_<u>ahl</u>•goh deh beh•<u>behr</u>_
**Gracias por su visita.** _<u>grah</u>•seeyahs_
_pohr soo bee•<u>see</u>•tah_

Do you have
an appointment?
With whom?
He/She is in
a meeting.
One moment,
please.
Have a seat.
Would you like
something to drink?
Thank you for
coming.

## Traveling with Children

### ESSENTIAL

| | |
|---|---|
| Is there a discount for children? | **¿Hacen descuento a niños?** _ah_·sen dehs·_kwehn_·toh ah _nee_·nyohs |
| Can you recommend a babysitter? | **¿Puede recomendarme una niñera?** _pweh_·deh reh·koh·mehn·_dahr_·meh _oo_·nah neeh·_nyeh_·rah |
| Do you have a child's seat/ highchair? | **¿Tienen una silla para niños/alta?** _teeyeh_·nehn _oo_·nah _see_·yah _pah_·rah _nee_·nyohs/_ahl_·tah |
| Where can I change the baby? | **¿Dónde puedo cambiar al bebé?** _dohn_·deh _pweh_·doh kahm·_beeyahr_ ahl beh·_beh_ |

### Out & About

| | |
|---|---|
| Can you recommend something for kids? | **¿Puede recomendarme algo para los niños?** _pweh_·deh reh·koh·mehn·_dahr_·meh _ahl_·goh _pah_·rah lohs _nee_·nyohs |
| Where's…? | **¿Dónde está…?** _dohn_·deh ehs·_tah_… |
| the amusement park | **el parque de atracciones** ehl _pahr_·keh deh ah·trahk·_seeyoh_·nehs |
| the arcade | **el salón de juegos recreativos** ehl sah·_lohn_ deh _khweh_·gohs reh·kreh·ah·_tee_·bohs |
| the kiddie [paddling] pool | **la piscina infantil** lah pees·_see_·nah een·fahn·_teel_ |
| the park | **el parque** ehl _pahr_·keh |
| the playground | **el parque infantil** ehl _pahr_·keh een·fahn·_teel_ |
| the zoo | **el zoológico** ehl soh·oh·_loh_·khee·koh |

| | |
|---|---|
| Are kids allowed? | **¿Se permite la entrada a niños?** |
| | *seh pehr•mee•teh lah ehn•trah•dah ah nee•nyohs* |
| Is it safe for kids? | **¿Es seguro para niños?** |
| | *ehs seh•goo•roh pah•rah nee•nyohs* |
| Is it suitable for… | **¿Es apto para niños de…años?** |
| year olds? | *ehs ahp•toh pah•rah nee•nyohs deh… ah•nyohs* |

For Numbers, see page 171.

## YOU MAY HEAR…

| | |
|---|---|
| **¡Qué bonito?/bonita/!** | How cute! |
| *keh boh•nih•toh/boh•nih•tah* | |
| **¿Cómo se llama?** | What's his/her |
| *koh•moh seh yah•mah* | name? |
| **¿Qué edad tiene?** | How old is he/she? |
| *keh eh•dahd teeyeh•neh* | |

## Baby Essentials

| | | |
|---|---|---|
| Do you have…? | **¿Tiene…?** _teeyeh•neh…_ | |
| a baby bottle | **un biberón** | |
| | _oon bee•beh•rohn_ | |
| baby wipes | **toallitas** _toh•ah•yee•tahs_ | |
| a car seat | **un asiento para niños** | |
| | _oon ah•seeyehn•toh pah•rah nee•nyohs_ | |
| a children's menu/portion | **un menú/una ración para niños** | |
| | _oon meh•noo/oo•nah rah•seeyohn pah•rah nee•nyohs_ | |
| a child's seat/ highchair | **una silla para niños/alta** | |
| | _oo•nah see•yah pah•rah nee•nyohs/ahl•tah_ | |
| a crib/cot | **una cuna/un catre** | |
| | _oo•nah koo•nah/oon kah•treh_ | |
| diapers [nappies] | **pañales** | |
| | _pah•nyah•lehs_ | |
| formula | **fórmula infantil** | |
| | _fohr•moo•lah een•fahn•teel_ | |
| a pacifier [soother] | **un chupete** _oon choo•peh•teh_ | |
| a playpen | **un parque** _oon pahr•keh_ | |
| a stroller [pushchair] | **un coche** _oon koh•cheh_ | |

| Can I breastfeed the baby here? | **¿Puedo darle de lactar al bebé aquí?** |
| | *pweh•doh dahr•leh deh lahk•tahr ahl beh•beh ah•kee* |
| Where can I change the baby? | **¿Dónde puedo cambiar al bebé?** |
| | *dohn•deh pweh•doh kahm•beeyahr ahl beh•beh* |

## Babysitting

| Can you recommend a babysitter? | **¿Puede recomendarme una niñera?** |
| | *pweh•deh reh•koh•mehn•dahr•meh oo•nah neeh•nyeh•rah* |
| What's the charge? | **¿Cuánto cuesta?** |
| | *kwahn•toh kwehs•tah* |
| I'll be back by. . . | **Vuelvo a la/las. . .** *bwehl•boh ah lah/lahs. . .* |
| I can be reached at. . . | **Puede contactarme en el. . .** |
| | *pweh•deh kohn•tahk•tahr•meh ehn ehl. . .* |

For Grammar, see page 166.

For Time, see page 173.

## Health & Emergency

| Can you recommend a pediatrician? | **¿Puede recomendarme un pediatra?** |
| | *pweh•deh reh•koh•mehn•dahr•meh oon peh•deeyah•trah* |
| My child is allergic to. . . | **Mi hijo m/hija f es alérgico m/alérgica f a. . .** |
| | *mee ee•khoh/ee•khah/ehs ah•lehr•khee•koh/ah•lehr•khee•kah ah. . .* |
| My child is missing. | **Mi hijo m/hija f ha desaparecido.** |
| | *mee ee•khoh/ee•khah ah deh•sah•pah•reh•see•doh* |
| Have you seen a boy/girl? | **¿Ha visto a un niño m/una niña f** |
| | *ah bees•toh ah oon nee•nyoh/oo•nah nee•nyah* |

For Police, see page 154.

# Disabled Travelers

## ESSENTIAL

| | |
|---|---|
| Is there…? | **¿Hay…?** *aye…* |
| access for the disabled | **acceso para los discapacitados** *ahk•seh•soh pah•rah lohs dees•kah•pah•see•tah•dohs* |
| a wheelchair ramp | **una rampa para sillas de ruedas** *oo•nah rahm•pah pah•rah see•yahs deh rweh•dahs* |
| a handicapped [disabled] accessible toilet | **un baño con acceso para discapacitados** *oon bah•nyoh kohn ahk•seh•soh pah•rah dees•kah•pah•see•tah•dohs* |
| I need… | **Necesito…** *neh•seh•see•toh…* |
| assistance | **ayuda** *ah•yoo•dah* |
| an elevator [a lift] | **un ascensor** *oon ah•sehn•sohr* |
| a ground floor room | **una habitación** en la planta baja *oo•nah ah•bee•tah•seeyohn ehn lah plahn•tah bah•khah* |

## Asking for Assistance

| | |
|---|---|
| I'm disabled. | **Soy discapacitado m/discapacitada f.** *soy dees•kah•pah•see•tah•doh/ dees•kah•pah•see•tah•dah* |
| I'm deaf. | **Soy sordo m/sorda f.** *soy sohr•doh/sohr•dah* |
| I'm visually/hearing impaired. | **Tengo discapacidad visual/auditiva.** *tehn•goh dees•kah•pah•see•dahd bee•swahl/ awoo•dee•tee•bah* |
| I'm unable to walk far/use the stairs. | **No puedo caminar muy lejos/subir las escaleras** *noh pweh•doh kah•mee•nahr mooy leh•khohs/soo•beer lahs ehs•kah•leh•rahs* |

| | |
|---|---|
| Can I bring my wheelchair? | **¿Puedo traer la silla de ruedas?** |
| | *pweh•doh trah•ehr lah see•yah deh rweh•dahs* |
| Are guide dogs permitted? | **¿Permiten a perros guía?** |
| | *pehr•mee•tehn ah peh•rrohs gee•ah* |
| Can you help me? | **¿Puede ayudarme?** *pweh•deh ah•yoo•dahr•meh* |
| Please open/hold the door. | **Por favor, abra/sostenga la puerta.** |
| | *pohr fah•bohr ah•brah/sohs•tehn•gah lah pwehr•tah* |

For Emergencies, see page 153.

# In an
# Emergency

# Emergencies

## ESSENTIAL

| | | |
|---|---|---|
| Help! | **¡Socorro!** | *soh·koh·rroh* |
| Go away! | **¡Váyase!** | *bah·yah·seh* |
| Stop, thief! | **¡Deténgase, ladrón!** | *deh·tehn·gah·seh lah·drohn* |
| Get a doctor! | **¡Llame a un médico!** | *yah·meh ah oon meh·dee·koh* |
| Fire! | **¡Fuego!** | *fweh·goh* |
| I'm lost. | **Me he perdido.** | *meh eh pehr·dee·doh* |
| Can you help me? | **¿Puede ayudarme?** | *pweh·deh ah·yoo·dahr·meh* |

## YOU MAY HEAR...

**Rellene este formulario.**
*reh·yeh·neh ehs·teh fohr·mooh·lah·reeoh*

Fill out this form.

**Su documento de identidad, por favor.**
*soo doh·koo·mehn·toh deh
ee·dehn·tee·dahd pohr fah·bohr*

Your identification, please.

**¿Cuándo/Dónde ocurrió?**
*kwahn·doh·dohn·deh oh·koo·rreeyoh*

**¿Puede describirlo m/describirla f?**
*pweh·deh dehs·kree·beer·loh/
dehs·kree·beer·lah*

When/Where did it happen?
What does he/she look like?

## Police

### ESSENTIAL

| | |
|---|---|
| Call the police! | **¡Llame a la policía!** _yah•meh ah lah poh•lee•see•ah_ |
| Where's the police station? | **¿Dónde está la comisaría?** _dohn•deh ehs•tah lah koh•mee•sah•ree•ah_ |
| There was an accident/attack. | **Hubo un accidente/asalto.** _ooh•boh oon ahk•see•dehn•teh/ah•sahl•toh_ |
| My son/daughter is missing. | **Mi hijo m/hija f desapareció.** _mee ee•khoh/ee•khah deh•sah•pah•reh•seeoh_ |
| I need... | **Necesito...** _neh•seh•see•toh..._ |
| an interpreter | **un intérprete** _oon een•tehr•preh•teh_ |
| to contact my lawyer | **ponerme en contacto** con mi abogado _poh•nehr•meh ehn kohn•tahk•toh kohn mee ah•boh•gah•doh_ |
| to make a phone call | **hacer una llamada** _ah•sehr oo•nah yah•mah•dah_ |
| I'm innocent. | **Soy inocente.** _soy ee•noh•sehn•teh_ |

---

> Contact your consulate, ask the concierge at your hotel or ask the tourist information office for telephone numbers of the local ambulance, emergency services and police.

## Crime & Lost Property

| | |
|---|---|
| I'd like to report... | **Quiero denunciar...** _keeyeh•roh deh•noon•seeyahr..._ |
| a mugging | **un asalto** _oon ah•sahl•toh_ |
| a rape | **una violación** _oo•nah beeyoh•lah•seeyohn_ |
| a theft | **un robo** _oon roh•boh_ |

| | |
|---|---|
| I was mugged/robbed. | **Me asaltaron/atracaron.** *meh ah•sahl•tah•rohn/ah•trah•kah•rohn* |
| I lost my... | **Perdí mi...** *pehr•dee mee...* |
| My...was stolen. | **Me robaron...** *meh roh•bah•rohn...* |
| backpack | **la mochila** *lah moh•chee•lah* |
| bicycle | **la bicicleta** *lah bee•see•kleh•tah* |
| camera | **la cámara** *lah kah•mah•rah* |
| (rental [hire]) car | **el auto (de alquiler)** *ehl awoo•toh (deh ahl•kee•lehr)* |
| computer | **la computadora** *lah kohm•poo•tah•doh•rah* |
| credit card | **la tarjeta de crédito** *lah tahr•kheh•tah deh kreh•dee•toh* |
| jewelry | **las joyas** *lahs khoh•yahs* |
| money | **el dinero** *ehl dee•neh•roh* |
| passport | **el pasaporte** *ehl pah•sah•pohr•teh* |
| purse [handbag] | **el bolso** *ehl bohl•soh* |
| traveler's checks [cheques] | **los cheques de viajero** *lohs cheh•kehs deh beeyah•kheh•roh* |
| wallet | **la cartera** *lah kahr•teh•rah* |

| I need a police report. | **Necesito un certificado de la policía.** *neh·seh·<u>see</u>·toh oon sehr·tee·fee·<u>kah</u>·doh deh lah poh·lee·<u>see</u>·ah* |
| Where is the British /American/Irish embassy? | **¿Dónde está la embajada británica/americana/irlandesa?** *dohn·deh ehs·tah lah ehm·bah·khah·dah bree·tah·nee·kah/ah·meh·ree·kah·nah/eer·lahn·deh·sah.* |

## Health

### ESSENTIAL

| I'm sick. | **Me siento mal.** *meh <u>seeyehn</u>·toh mahl* |
| I need an English-speaking doctor. | **Necesito un médico que hable inglés.** *neh·seh·<u>see</u>·toh oon <u>meh</u>·dee·koh keh <u>ah</u>·bleh een·<u>glehs</u>* |
| It hurts here. | **Me duele aquí.** *meh <u>dweh</u>·leh ah·<u>kee</u>* |
| I have a stomachache. | **Tengo dolor de estómago.** *<u>tehn</u>·goh doh·<u>lohr</u> deh ehs·<u>toh</u>·mah·goh* |

## Finding a Doctor

| Can you recommend a doctor/dentist? | **¿Puede recomendarme un médico/dentista?** *<u>pweh</u>·deh reh·koh·mehn·<u>dahr</u>·meh oon <u>meh</u>·dee·koh/dehn·<u>tees</u>·tah* |
| Can the doctor come here? | **¿Podría el médico venir aquí?** *poh·<u>dree</u>·ah ehl <u>meh</u>·dee·koh beh·<u>neer</u> ah·<u>kee</u>* |
| I need an English-speaking doctor. | **Necesito un médico que hable inglés.** *neh·seh·<u>see</u>·toh oon <u>meh</u>·dee·koh keh <u>ah</u>·bleh een·<u>glehs</u>* |
| What are the office hours? | **¿Cuáles son las horas de consulta?** *<u>kwah</u>·lehs sohn lahs <u>oh</u>·rahs deh kohn·<u>sool</u>·tah* |
| I'd like an appointment… | **Quiero una cita…** *<u>keeyeh</u>·roh <u>oo</u>·nah <u>see</u>·tah…* |

| | | |
|---|---|---|
| for today | **para hoy** _pah_·rah ohy | |
| for tomorrow | **para mañana** _pah_·rah mah·_nyah_·nah | |
| as soon as possible | **lo antes posible** loh _ahn_·tehs poh·_see_·bleh | |
| It's urgent. | **Es urgente.** ehs oor·_kheh_n·teh | |

## Symptoms

| | |
|---|---|
| I'm... | **Estoy...** ehs·_toy_... |
| bleeding | **sangrando** sahn·_grahn_·doh |
| constipated | **estreñido?/estreñida** ehs·treh·_nyee_·doh?/ehs·treh·_nyee_·dah |
| dizzy | **mareado** _m_/**mareada** _f_ mah·reh·_ah_·doh/mah·reh·_ah_·dah |
| I'm nauseous/ vomiting. | **Tengo náuseas/vómitos.** _tehn_·goh _naw_·seh·ahs/_boh_·mee·tohs |
| It hurts here. | **Me duele aquí.** meh _dweh_·leh ah·_kee_ |
| I have... | **Tengo...** _tehn_·goh... |
| an allergic reaction | **una reacción alérgica** _oo_·nah reh·ahk·_seeyohn_ ah·_lehr_·khee·kah |
| chest pain | **dolor de pecho** doh·_lohr_ deh _peh_·choh |
| an earache | **dolor de oído** doh·_lohr_ deh oh·_ee_·doh |
| a fever | **fiebre** _fee_eyeh·breh |
| pain | **dolor** doh·_lohr_ |
| a rash | **una erupción cutánea** _oo_·nah ch·roop·_seeyohn_ koo·_tah_·nec·ah |
| a sprain | **un esguince** oon ehz·_geen_·seh |
| some swelling | **una hinchazón** _oo_·nah een·chah·_sohn_ |
| a stomach ache | **dolor de estómago** doh·_lohr_ deh ehs·_toh_·mah·goh |
| sunstroke | **una insolación** _oo_·nah een·soh·lah·_seeyohn_ |
| I've been sick [ill] for...days. | **Hace...días que me siento mal.** _ah_·seh..._dee_·ahs keh meh seeh·_ehn_·toh mahl |

For Numbers, see page 171.

## Conditions

| I'm... | **Soy...** |
|---|---|
| anemic | **anemic** *m*/**anémica** *f* |
| | *ah·neh·mee·koh/ah·neh·mee·kah* |
| asthmatic | **asmático** *m*/**asmática** *f* |
| | *ahz·mah·tee·koh?/ahz·mah·tee·kah* |
| diabetic | **diabetic** *m*/**diabetic** *f* |
| | *deeyah·beh·tee·koh/deeyah·beh·tee·kah* |

| I'm epileptic. | **Tengo epilepsia.** *tehn·goh eh·pee·lehp·seeya* |
|---|---|
| I'm allergic to antibiotics/penicillin. | **Soy alérgico** *m*/**alérgica** *f* **a los antibióticos/la penicilina.** |
| | *soy ah·lehr·khee·koh/ah·lehr·khee·kah ah lohs* |
| | *ahn·tee·beeyoh·tee·kohs/lah peh·nee·see·lee·na* |
| I have arthritis. | **Tengo artritis.** *tehn·goh ahr·tree·tees* |
| I have high/low blood pressure. | **Tengo la presión alta/baja.** |
| | *tehn·goh lah preh·seeyohn ahl·tah/bah·khah* |
| I have a heart condition. | **Sufro del corazón.** |
| | *soo·froh dehl koh·rah·son* |
| I'm on... | **Estoy tomando...** |
| | *ehs·toy toh·mahn·doh...* |

For Meals & Cooking, see page 67.

## Treatment

| Do I need a prescription /medicine? | **¿Necesito una receta/medicina?** |
|---|---|
| | *neh·seh·see·toh oo·nah reh·seh·tah]* |
| | */meh·dee·see·nah* |
| Can you prescribe a generic drug [unbranded medication]? | **¿Me puede recetar un medicamento genérico [medicina sin marca]?** |
| | *meh pweh·deh reh·seh·tahr oon* |
| | *meh·dee·kah·mehn·toh kheh·neh·ree·coh* |
| | *(meh·dee·see·nah seen mahr·kah)* |

## YOU MAY HEAR...

**¿Qué le pasa?** *keh leh pah·sah* — What's wrong?

**¿Dónde le duele?** *dohn·deh leh dweh·leh* — Where does it hurt?

**¿Le duele aquí?** *leh dweh·leh ah·kee* — Does it hurt here?

**¿Está tomando algún medicamento?**
*ehs·tah toh·mahn·doh ahl·goon*
*meh·dee·kah·mehn·toh* — Are you on medication?

**¿Es alérgico m/alérgica f a algo?**
*ehs ah·lehr·khee·koh/ah·lehr·khee·kah*
*ah ahl·goh* — Are you allergic to anything?

**Abra la boca.** *ah·brah lah boh·kah* — Open your mouth.

**Respire hondo.** *rehs·pee·reh ohn·doh* — Breathe deeply.

**Tiene que ir al hospital.**
*teeyeh·neh keh eer ahl ohs·pee·tahl* — Go to the hospital.

Where can I get it? **¿Dónde lo puedo conseguir?**
*dohn·deh loh pweh·doh kohn·seh·geer*

For Pharmacy, see page 162.

## Hospital

| | |
|---|---|
| Notify my family, please. | **Por favor, avise a mi familia.** *pohr fah-bohr ah-bee-seh ah mee fah-mee-leeyah* |
| I'm in pain. | **Tengo dolor.** *tehn-goh doh-lohr* |
| I need a doctor/nurse. | **Necesito un médico/una enfermera.** *neh-seh-see-toh oon meh-dee-koh/oo-nah ehn-fehr-meh-rah* |
| When are visiting hours? | **¿Qué horario de visita tienen?** *keh oh-rah-ree-oh deh bee-see-tah teeyeh-nehn* |
| I'm visiting... | **Vengo a hacer una visita a...** *behn-goh ah ah-sehr oo-nah bee-see-tah ah...* |

## Dentist

| | |
|---|---|
| I've broken a tooth/lost a filling. | **Se me ha roto un diente/caído un empaste.** *seh meh ah roh-toh oon deeyehn-teh/kah-ee-doh oon ehm-pahs-teh* |
| I have a toothache. | **Tengo dolor de muelas.** *tehn-goh doh-lohr deh mweh-lahs* |
| Can you fix this denture? | **¿Puede arreglarme la dentadura postiza?** *pweh-deh ah-rreh-glahr-meh lah dehn-tah-doo-rah pohs-tee-sah* |

## Gynecologist

| | |
|---|---|
| I have menstrual cramps/a vaginal infection. | **Tengo dolores menstruales/una infección vaginal.** *tehn-goh doh-loh-rehs mehns-trwah-lehs/oo-nah een-fehk-seeyohn bah-khee-nahl* |
| I missed my period. | **No me ha venido la regla.** *noh meh ah beh-nee-doh lah reh-glah* |
| I'm on the Pill. | **Tomo la píldora.** *toh-moh lah peel-doh-rah* |

| I'm (...months) pregnant. | **Estoy embarazada de.... meses.** |
| | *ehs•toy ehm•bah•rah•sah•dah deh... meh•sehs* |
| I'm (not) pregnant. | (No) **Estoy embarazada. (noh)** |
| | *ehs•toy ehm•bah•rah•sah•dah* |
| My last period was... | **La última vez que me vino la regla fue...** |
| | *lah ool•tee•mah behs keh meh bee•noh lah* |
| | *reh•glah fweh...* |

For Numbers, see page 171.

## Optician

| I lost... | **He perdido...** *eh pehr•dee•doh...* |
| a contact lens | **un lente de contacto** |
| | *oon lehn•teh deh kohn•tuhk•toh* |
| my glasses | **los anteojos** |
| | *lohs ahn•teh•oh•khos* |
| a lens | **una lente** *oo•nah lehn•teh* |

## Payment & Insurance

| How much? | **¿Cuánto es?** *kwahn•toh ehs* |
| Can I pay by credit card? | **¿Puedo pagar con tarjeta de crédito?** |
| | *pweh•doh pah•gahr kohn tahr•kheh•tah deh* |
| | *kreh•dee•toh* |
| I have insurance. | **Tengo seguro médico.** |
| | *tehn•goh seh•goo•roh meh•dee•koh* |
| I need a receipt for my insurance. | **Necesito una factura para el seguro médico.** |
| | *neh•seh•see•toh oo•nah fahk•too•rah pah•rah ehl* |
| | *seh•goo•roh meh•dee•koh* |

## Pharmacy

### ESSENTIAL

| | |
|---|---|
| Where's the pharmacy [chemist]? | **¿Dónde está la farmacia?** <br> _dohn·deh ehs·tah lah fahr·mah·seeyah_ |
| What time does it open/close? | **¿A qué hora abre/cierra?** _ah keh_ <br> _oh·rah ah·breh/seeyeh·rrah_ |
| What would you recommend for…? | **¿Qué me recomienda para…?** _keh meh_ <br> _reh·koh·meeyehn·dah pah·rah…_ |
| How much do I take? | **¿Qué dosis tomo?** _keh doh·sees toh·moh_ |
| Can you fill [make up] this prescription? | **¿Puede darme este medicamento?** <br> _pweh·deh dahr·meh ehs·teh_ <br> _meh·dee·kah·mehn·toh_ |
| I'm allergic to… | **Soy alérgico _m_/alérgica _f_ a…** <br> _soy ah·lehr·khee·koh/ah·lehr·khee·kah ah…_ |

## What to Take

| | |
|---|---|
| How much do I Take? | **¿Qué dosis tomo?** _keh doh·sees toh·moh_ |
| How often? | **¿Con qué frecuencia?** _kohn keh freh·kwehn·seeyah_ |
| Is it safe for children? | **¿Está indicado para niños?** _ehs·tah_ <br> _een·dee·kah·doh pah·rah nee·nyohs_ |

There is a wide variety of pharmacies in Latin America. Hours are generally from 9:00 a.m. until 7:00 p.m. In smaller towns they may close for lunch. 24-hour pharmacies can be found in larger cities.

| | | |
|---|---|---|
| I'm taking... | **Estoy tomando...** | *ehs·toy toh·mahn·doh...* |
| I need something for... | **Necesito algo para...** | *neh·seh·see·toh ahl·goh pah·rah...* |
| a cold | **el resfrío** | *ehl rehs·free·oh* |
| a cough | **la tos** | *lah tohs* |
| diarrhea | **la diarrea** | *lah deeyah·rreh·ah* |
| a headache | **dolor de cabeza** | *doh·lohr deh kah·beh·sah* |
| insect bites | **las picaduras de insecto** | *lahs pee·kah·doo·rahs deh een·sehk·toh* |
| motion [travel] sickness | **la cinetosis** | *lah see·neh·toh·sees* |
| a sore throat | **las anginas** | *lahs ahn·khee·nahs* |
| sunburn | **la quemadura solar** | *lah keh·mah·doo·rah   soh·lahr* |
| a toothache | **dolor de dientes** | *doh·lohr deh dee·ehn·tehs* |
| an upset stomach | **el malestar estomacal** | *ehl mah·lehs·tahr ehs·toh·mah·kahl* |
| Are there side effects? | **¿Tiene algún efecto secundario?** | *teeyeh·neh ahl·goon eh·fehk·toh seh·koon·dah·reeyoh* |

## Basic Supplies

| | | |
|---|---|---|
| I'd like... | **Quiero...** | *keeyeh·roh...* |
| acetaminophen [paracetamol] | **paracetamol** | *pah·rah·seh·tah·mohl* |
| antiseptic cream | **crema antiséptica** | *kreh·mah ahn·tee·sehp·tee·kah* |
| aspirin | **aspirinas** | *ahs·pee·ree·nahs* |

**YOU MAY SEE...**

| | |
|---|---|
| **UNA VEZ/TRES VECES AL DÍA** | once/three times a day |
| **COMPRIMIDO** | tablet |
| **GOTA** | drop |
| **CUCHARADITA** | teaspoon |
| **DESPUÉS DE/ANTES DE/ CON LAS COMIDAS** | after/before/with meals |
| **CON EL ESTÓMAGO VACÍO** | on an empty stomach |
| **TRAGUE EL COMPRIMIDO ENTERO** | swallow whole |
| **PUEDE CAUSAR SOMNOLENCIA** | may cause drowsiness |
| **DE USO TÓPICO SOLAMENTE** | for external use only |
| **NO INGERIR** | do not ingest |

| | |
|---|---|
| bandages | **curitas** koo·_ree_·tahs |
| a comb | **un peine** oon _peyee_·neh |
| condoms | **preservativos** preh·sehr·bah·_tee_·bohs |
| contact lens solution | **líquido para lentes de contacto** _lee_·kee·doh pah·rah _lehn_·tehs deh kohn·_tahk_·toh |
| deodorant | **desodorante** deh·soh·doh·_rahn_·teh |
| a hairbrush | **un cepillo de pelo** oon seh·_pee_·yoh deh _peh_·loh |
| hairspray | **fijador de cabello** fee·khah·dohr deh kah·beh·yoh |
| I'd like... | **Quiero...** _keeyeh_·roh... |
| ibuprofen | **ibuprofeno** ee·boo·proh·_feh_·noh |
| insect repellent | **repelente de insectos** reh·peh·_lehn_·teh deh een·_sehk_·tohs |
| lotion | **crema hidratante** _kreh_·mah ee·drah·_tahn_·teh |

| | | |
|---|---|---|
| a nail file | **una lima para uñas** | |
| | *oo•na lee•mah pah•rah oo•nyas* | |
| a razor | **una cuchilla** <u>oo</u>•nah koo•<u>chee</u>•yah | |
| razor blades | **hojas de afeitar** | |
| | <u>oh</u>•khahs deh ah•feyee•<u>tahr</u> | |
| sanitary napkins | **toallas higiénicas** | |
| [pads] | *toh•<u>ah</u>•yas ee•<u>khye</u>•<u>nee</u>•cahs* | |
| a scissors | **tijeras** *tee•kheh•rahs* | |
| shampoo/ | **champú/acondicionador** *chahm•<u>poo</u>/* | |
| conditioner | *ah•kohn•dee•seeoh•nah•<u>dohr</u>* | |
| soap | **jabón** *khah•<u>bohn</u>* | |
| sunscreen | **protector solar** *proh•tehk•<u>tohr</u> soh•<u>lahr</u>* | |
| tampons | **tampones** *tahm•<u>poh</u>•nehs* | |
| tissues | **pañuelos de papel** | |
| | *pah•<u>nyweh</u>•lohs deh pah•<u>pehl</u>* | |
| toilet paper | **papel higiénico** | |
| | *pah•<u>pehl</u> ee•<u>kheeyeh</u>•nee•koh* | |
| a toothbrush | **un cepillo de dientes** | |
| | *oon seh•<u>pee</u>•yoh deh <u>deeyehn</u>•tehs* | |
| toothpaste | **pasta de dientes** | |
| | *<u>pahs</u>•tah deh <u>deeyehn</u>•tehs* | |

For Baby Essentials, see page 148.

165

# The Basics

## Grammar

In Latin American Spanish, there are a number of forms for 'you' (taking different verb forms): **tú** (singular) is informal, and used when talking to relatives, close friends and children; **usted** (singular) is used in all other cases If in doubt, use **usted**. For 'you plural' **ustedes** is always used. The following abbreviations are used in this section: **Ud. = Usted; Uds. = Ustedes;** sing. = singular; pl. = plural; inf. = informal; for. = formal.

## Regular Verbs

There are three verb types that follow a regular conjugation pattern. These verbs end in **ar, er** and **ir.** Following are the present, past and future forms of the verbs **hablar** (to speak), **comer** (to eat) and **vivir** (to live). The different conjugation endings are in bold.

| HABLAR | | Present | Past | Future |
|---|---|---|---|---|
| I | yo | habl**o** | habl**é** | hablar**é** |
| you (sing.) | tú | habl**as** | habl**aste** | hablar**ás** |
| he/she/you | él/ella/Ud. | habl**a** | habl**ó** | hablar**á** |
| we | nosotros | habl**amos** | habl**amos** | hablar**emos** |
| they/you (pl.) | ellos/ellas /Uds. | habl**an** | habl**aron** | hablar**án** |

| COMER | | Present | Past | Future |
|---|---|---|---|---|
| I | yo | com**o** | com**í** | comer**é** |
| you (sing.) | tú | com**es** | com**iste** | comer**ás** |
| he/she/you | él/ella/Ud. | com**e** | com**ió** | comer**á** |
| we | nosotros | com**emos** | com**imos** | comer**emos** |
| they/you (pl.) | ellos/ellas /Uds. | com**en** | com**ieron** | comer**án** |

| VIVIR | | Present | Past | Future |
|---|---|---|---|---|
| I | yo | viv**o** | viv**í** | vivir**é** |
| you (sing.) | tú | viv**es** | viv**iste** | vivir**ás** |
| he/she/you | él/ella/Ud. | viv**e** | viv**ió** | vivir**á** |
| we | nosotros | viv**imos** | viv**imos** | vivir**emos** |
| they/you (pl.) | ellos/ellas /Uds. | viv**en** | viv**ieron** | vivir**án** |

## Irregular Verbs

In Spanish, there are many different irregular verbs; these aren't conjugated by following the normal rules. The two most commonly used, and confused, irregular verbs are **ser** and **estar**. Both verbs mean 'to be'. Following is the past, present and future tenses of **ser** and **estar** for easy reference.

| SER | Present | Past | Future |
|---|---|---|---|
| yo | soy | fui | seré |
| tú | eres | fuiste | serás |
| él/ella/Ud. | es | fue | será |
| nosotros | somos | fuimos | seremos |
| ellos/ellas/Uds. | son | fueron | serán |

| ESTAR | Present | Past | Future |
|---|---|---|---|
| yo | estoy | estuve | estaré |
| tú | estás | estuviste | estarás |
| él/ella/Ud. | está | estuvo | estará |
| nosotros | estamos | estuvimos | estaremos |
| ellos/ellas/Uds. | están | estuvieron | estarán |

**Ser** is used to describe a fixed quality or characteristic. It is also used to tell time and dates. Example: **Yo soy estadounidense.** I am American.
Here **ser** is used because it is a permanent characteristic.
**Estar** is used when describing a physical location or a temporary condition.

Example: **Estoy cansado.** I am tired.
Here **estar** is used because being tired is a temporary condition, i.e. you won't always be tired.

## Nouns & Articles

Nouns are either masculine or feminine. Masculine nouns usually end in **o**, and feminine nouns usually end in **a**. Nouns become plural by adding an **s**, or **es** to nouns not ending in **o** or **a** (e.g. **tren** becomes **trenes**). Nouns in Spanish get an indefinite or definite article. An article must agree with the noun to which i refers in gender and number. Indefinite articles are the equivalent of 'a', 'an' or 'some' in English, while definite articles are the equivalent of 'the'.
Indefinite examples: **un tren** *m* (a train); **unos trenes** *f pl* (some trains); **una mesa** *f* (a table); **unas mesas** *f pl* (some tables)

Definite examples: **el libro** *m* (the book); **los libros** *m pl* (the books); **la casa** *f* (the house); **las casas** *f pl* (the houses)

A possessive adjective relates to the gender of the noun that follows and must agree in number and gender.

|  | Singular | Plural |
|---|---|---|
| my | mi | **mis** |
| your (inf.) | tu | **tus** |
| his/her/its/your (form.) | su | **sus** |
| our | nuestro *m*/nuestra *f* | **nuestros** *m*/**nuestras** *f* |
| their/your | su | **sus** |

Examples: **¿Dónde está tu chaqueta?** Where is your jacket?
**Su vuelo sale a las ocho.** Your flight leaves at eight.

## Word Order

In Spanish, the conjugated verb comes after the subject.

Example: **Yo trabajo en Bogotá.** I work in Bogota.

To ask a question, reverse the order of the subject and verb, change your intonation or use key question words such as **cuándo** (when).

Examples: **¿Cuándo cierra el banco?** When does the bank close?

Literally translates to: 'When closes the bank?' Notice the order of the subject and verb is reversed; a question word also begins the sentence.

**¿El hotel es viejo?** Is the hotel old?

Literally: The hotel is old. This statement becomes a question by raising the pitch of the last syllable of the sentence.

## Negation

To form a negative sentence, add **no** (not) before the verb.

Example: **Fumamos.** We smoke.

**No fumamos.** We don't smoke.

## Imperatives

Imperative sentences, or sentences that are commands, are formed by adding the appropriate ending to the stem of the verb (i.e. the verb in the infinitive without the **-ar, -er, -ir** ending).

Example: Speak!

| you (sing.) (inf.) | tú | **¡Habla!** |
| you (sing.) (for.) | Ud. | **¡Hable!** |
| we | nosotros | **¡Hablemos!** |
| you (pl.) (for.) | Uds. | **¡Hablen!** |

## Comparative & Superlative

The comparative is usually formed by adding **más** (more) or **menos** (less) before the adjective or noun. The superlative is formed by adding the appropriate definite article **(la/las, el/los)** and **más** (the most) or **menos** (the least) before the adjective or noun.

Example:

| | | |
|---|---|---|
| **grande** | **más grande** | **el** *m*/**la** *f* **más grande** |
| big | bigger | biggest |
| **caro** *m*/**cara** *f* | **menos caro** *m*/**cara** *f* | **el** *m*/**la** *f* **menos caro** *m*/**cara** |
| expensive | less expensive | least expensive |

## Possessive Pronouns

Pronouns serve as substitutes for specific nouns and must agree with the noun in gender and number.

| | Singular | Plural |
|---|---|---|
| mine | mío *m*/mía *f* | **míos** *m*/**mías** *f* |
| yours (inf.) | tuyo *m*/tuya *f* | **tuyos** *m*/**tuyas** *f* |
| yours | suyo *m*/suya *f* | **suyos** *m*/**suyas** *f* |
| his/her/its | suyo *m*/suya *f* | **suyos** *m*/**suyas** *f* |
| ours | nuestro *m*/nuestra *f* | **nuestros** *m*/**nuestras** *f* |
| theirs | suyo *m*/suya *f* | **suyos** *m*/**suyas** *f* |

Example: **Ese asiento es mío.** That seat is mine.

## Adjectives

Adjectives describe nouns and must agree with the noun in gender and number. In Spanish, adjectives usually come after the noun. Masculine adjectives generally end in **o**, feminine adjectives in **a**. If the masculine form ends in **e** or with a consonant, the feminine form is generally the same. Most adjectives form their plurals the same way as nouns.

Examples:
**Su hijo** *m*/**hija** *f* **es simpático** *m*/**simpática** *f*. Your son/daughter is nice.

**El mar** *m*/**La flor** *f* **es azul.** The ocean/The flower is blue.

## Adverbs & Adverbial Expressions

Adverbs are used to describe verbs. Some adverbs are formed by adding
**-mente** to the adjective.

Example: **Roberto conduce lentamente.** Robert drives slowly.

The following are some common adverbial time expressions:

| | |
|---|---|
| **actualmente** | presently |
| **todavía** | no not yet |
| **todavía** | still |
| **ya no** | not anymore |

## Numbers

### ESSENTIAL

| | | |
|---|---|---|
| 0 | **cero** | <u>seh</u>·roh |
| 1 | **uno** | <u>oo</u>·noh |
| 2 | **dos** | dohs |
| 3 | **tres** | trehs |
| 4 | **cuatro** | <u>kwah</u>·troh |
| 5 | **cinco** | <u>seen</u>·koh |
| 6 | **seis** | seyees |
| 7 | **siete** | <u>seeyeh</u>·teh |
| 8 | **ocho** | <u>oh</u>·choh |
| 9 | **nueve** | <u>nweh</u>·beh |
| 10 | **diez** | deeyehs |
| 11 | **once** | <u>ohn</u>·seh |
| 12 | **doce** | <u>doh</u>·seh |
| 13 | **trece** | <u>treh</u>·seh |
| 14 | **catorce** | kah·<u>tohr</u>·seh |
| 15 | **quince** | <u>keen</u>·seh |
| 16 | **dieciséis** | deeyeh·see·<u>seyees</u> |

| 17 | **diecisiete** *deeyeh•see•seeyeh•teh* |
| 18 | **dieciocho** *deeyeh•see•oh•choh* |
| 19 | **diecinueve** *deeyeh•see•nweh•beh* |
| 20 | **veinte** *beyeen•teh* |
| 21 | **veintiuno** *beyeen•tee•oo•noh* |
| 22 | **veintidós** *beyeen•tee•dohs* |
| 30 | **treinta** *treyeen•tah* |
| 31 | **treinta y uno** *treyeen•tah ee oo•noh* |
| 40 | **cuarenta** *kwah•rehn•tah* |
| 50 | **cincuenta** *seen•kwehn•tah* |
| 60 | **sesenta** *seh•sehn•tah* |
| 70 | **setenta** *seh•tehn•tah* |
| 80 | **ochenta** *oh•chehn•tah* |
| 90 | **noventa** *noh•behn•tah* |
| 100 | **cien** *seeyehn* |
| 101 | **ciento uno** *seeyehn•toh oo•noh* |
| 200 | **doscientos** *dohs•seeyehn•tohs* |
| 500 | **quinientos** *kee•neeyehn•tohs* |
| 1,000 | **mil** *meel* |
| 10,000 | **diez mil** *deeyehs meel* |
| 1,000,000 | **un millón** *oon mee•yohn* |

## Ordinal Numbers

| first | **primero** *m*/**primera** *f* |
| | *pree•meh•roh/pree•meh•rah* |
| second | **segundo** *m*/**segunda** *f* |
| | *seh•goon•doh/seh•goon•dah* |
| third | **tercero** *m*/**tercera** *f* |
| | *tehr•seh•roh/tehr•seh•rah* |

| fourth | **cuarto m/cuarta f** |
| | _kwahr•toh/kwahr•tah_ |
| fifth | **quinto m/quinta f** |
| | _keen•toh/keen•lah_ |
| once | **una vez** _oo•nah behs_ |
| twice | **dos veces** _dohs beh•ses_ |
| three times | **tres veces** _trehs beh•ses_ |

Large numbers are read as in English. Example: 1,234,567 would be **un millón, doscientos treinta y cuatro mil, quinientos sesenta y siete** (one million, two hundred thirty-four thousand, five hundred sixty-seven). Notice the use of y (and) between tens and units for numbers between 31 (**treinta y uno**; literally, thirty and one) and 99 (**noventa y nueve**; literally, ninety and nine).

## Time

### ESSENTIAL

| What time is it? | **¿Qué hora es?** _keh oh•rah ehs_ |
| It's noon [midday]. | **Son las doce del mediodía.** _sohn lahs_ |
| | _doh•seh dehl meh•deeyoh•dee•ah_ |
| At midnight. | **A medianoche.** _ah meh•deeyah•noh•cheh_ |
| From one o'clock | **De una a dos en punto.** |
| to two o'clock. | _deh oo•nah ah dohs ehn poon•toh_ |
| Five after three. | **Las tres y cinco.** _lahs trehs ee seen•koh_ |
| A quarter to five. | **Las cinco menos cuarto.** |
| | _lahs seen•koh meh•nohs kwahr•toh_ |
| 5:30 a.m./p.m. | **Las cinco y media de la mañana/tarde.** _lahs_ |
| | _seen•koh ee meh•deeyah deh lah mah•nyah•nah/tahr•deh_ |

Latin Americans use the 24-hour clock when writing time, especially in schedules. The morning hours from 1:00 a.m. to noon are the same as in English. After that, just add 12 to the time: 1:00 p.m. would be 13:00, 5:00 p.m. would be 17:00 and so on.

## Days

### ESSENTIAL

| | |
|---|---|
| Monday | **lunes** _loo_•nehs |
| Tuesday | **martes** _mahr_•tehs |
| Wednesday | **miércoles** _meeyehr_•koh•lehs |
| Thursday | **jueves** _khweh_•behs |
| Friday | **viernes** _beeyehr_•nehs |
| Saturday | **sábado** _sah_•bah•doh |
| Sunday | **domingo** doh•_meen_•goh |

In Latin America, the week begins on Monday and ends on Sunday. This distinction is especially apparent when looking at calendars where Monday will be the first column and not Sunday.

## Dates

| | |
|---|---|
| yesterday | **ayer** ah•_yehr_ |
| today | **hoy** oy |
| tomorrow | **mañana** mah•_nyah_•nah |
| day | **día** _dee_•ah |
| week | **semana** seh•_mah_•nah |

| month | **mes** *mehs* |
| year | **año** <u>*ah*</u>*·nyoh* |

## Months

| January | **enero** *eh·*<u>*neh*</u>*·roh* |
| February | **febrero** *feh·*<u>*breh*</u>*·roh* |
| March | **marzo** <u>*mahr*</u>*·soh* |
| April | **abril** *ah·*<u>*breel*</u> |
| May | **mayo** <u>*mah*</u>*·yoh* |
| June | **junio** <u>*khoo*</u>*·neeyoh* |
| July | **julio** <u>*khoo*</u>*·leeyoh* |
| August | **agosto** *ah·*<u>*gohs*</u>*·toh* |
| September | **septiembre** *sehp·*<u>*teeyehm*</u>*·breh* |
| October | **octubre** *ohk·*<u>*too*</u>*·breh* |
| November | **noviembre** *noh·*<u>*beeyehm*</u>*·breh* |
| December | **diciembre** *dee·*<u>*seeyehm*</u>*·breh* |

## Seasons

| the spring | **la primavera** *lah pree·mah·*<u>*beh*</u>*·rah* |
| the summer | **el verano** *ehl beh·*<u>*rah*</u>*·noh* |
| the fall [autumn] | **el otoño** *ehl oh·*<u>*toh*</u>*·nyoh* |
| the winter | **el invierno** *ehl een·*<u>*beeyehr*</u>*·noh* |

## Holidays

| January 1: New Year's Day | **Año Nuevo** |
| January 6: Epiphany | **Epifanía** |
| May 1: Labor Day | **Día del Trabajo** |
| May 5: Feast of Mexican heritage | **Cinco de Mayo** |
| July 9: Argentina's Independence Day | **Día de la Independencia** |
| July 28: Peru's Independence Day | **Día de la Independencia** |
| August 6: Bolivia's Independence Day | **Día de la Independencia** |
| August 15: Feast of the Assumption | **Asunción** |

September 16: Mexico's Independence Day **Día de la Independencia**
October 12: Colombus Day **Día de la Raza**
November 1: All Saint's Day **Todos los Santos**
December 8: Feast of the Immaculate Conception **Inmaculada Concepción**
December 25: Christmas **Navidad**

Easter festivities take place on different dates each year since this holiday is traditionally celebrated on the first Sunday after the first full moon on or after the spring equinox.

## Conversion Tables

| When you know | Multiply by | To find |
|---|---|---|
| ounces | 28.3 | grams |
| pounds | 0.45 | kilograms |
| inches | 2.54 | centimeters |
| feet | 0.3 | meters |
| miles | 1.61 | kilometers |
| square inches | 6.45 | sq. centimeters |
| square feet | 0.09 | sq. meters |
| square miles | 2.59 | sq. kilometers |
| pints (U.S./Brit) | 0.47/0.56 | liters |
| gallons (U.S./Brit) | 3.8/4.5 | liters |
| Fahrenheit | 5/9, after 32 | Centigrade |
| Centigrade | 9/5, then +32 | Fahrenheit |

### Kilometers to Miles Conversions

| | |
|---|---|
| 1 km - 0.62 mi | 20 km - 12.4 mi |
| 5 km - 3.10 mi | 50 km - 31.0 mi |
| 10 km - 6.20 mi | 100 km - 61.0 mi |

## Measurement

| | | |
|---|---|---|
| 1 gram | **un gramo** *oon grah·moh* | = 0.035 oz. |
| 1 kilogram (kg) | **un kilogramo** *oon kee·loh·grah·moh* | = 2.2 lb |
| 1 liter (l) Brit. quarts | **un litro** *oon lee·troh* | = 1.06 U.S./0.88 |
| 1 centimeter (cm) | **un centímetro** *oon sehn·tee·meh·troh* | = 0.4 inch |
| 1 meter (m) | **un metro** *oon meh·troh* | = 3.28 ft. |
| 1 kilometer (km) | **un kilómetro** *oon kee·loh·meh·troh* | = 0.62 mile |

## Temperature

| | | |
|---|---|---|
| -40° C -40° F | -1° C 30° F | 20° C 68° F |
| -30° C -22° F | 0° C 32° F | 25° C 77° F |
| -20° C -4° F | 5° C 41° F | 30° C 86° F |
| -10° C 14° F | 10° C 50° F | 35° C 95° F |
| -5° C 23° F | 15° C 59° F | |

## Oven Temperature

| | | | |
|---|---|---|---|
| 100° C | 212° F | 177° C | 350° F |
| 121° C | 250° F | 204° C | 400° F |
| 149° C | 300° F | 260° C | 500° F |

Latin America follows a day-month-year format:
Examples: **el 25 de agosto de 2008** = August 25, 2008
**25.8.08** = 8/25/2008

# Dictionary

*m* Rpl gaucho
*f* (sea)gull
adj gay **2** *m* gay (man)
cho *m* gazpacho (cold soup made
omatoes, peppers, garlic etc)
gel *f* gelatin(e); GASTR Jell-O®, Br jel-

adj icy
*f* gem
io **1** adj twin atr; **hermano gemelo**
brother **2** *mpl* **gemelos** twins; (gemelos

geometría *f* geometría
geométrico adj geométri
geranio *m* BOT geranio
gerente *m/f* manager
geriatría *f* geriatrics sg
germen *m* germ
germinar ⟨1a⟩ v/i tb fig g
gerundio *m* GRAM gerun
gestación *f* gestation
gesticular ⟨1a⟩ v/i gest
gestión *f* managemen
(trámites) formalities
gestionar ⟨1a⟩ v/t tr
negociar manage
gesto *m* movimient

## A

**abbey** la abadía
**abbey** la abadía
**accept** v aceptar
**access** el acceso
**accident** el accidente
**accommodation** el alojamiento
**account** la cuenta
**acupuncture** la acupuntura
**adapter** el adaptador
**address** la dirección
**admission** la entrada
**after** después; **~noon** la tarde;
 **~shave** la loción para después
 de afeitar
**age** la edad
**agency** la agencia
**AIDS** el sida
**air** el aire; **~ conditioning**
el aire acondicionado; **~ pump**
el aire; **~line** la compañía aérea;
 **~mail** el correo aéreo; **~plane**
el avión; **~port** el aeropuerto
**aisle** el pasillo; **~ seat** el asiento
 de pasillo
**allergic** alérgico; **~ reaction**

la reacción alérgica
**allow** v permitir
**alone** solo
**alter v (clothing)** hacer un arreglo
**alternate route** el otro camino
**aluminum foil** el papel de aluminio
**amazing** increíble
**ambulance** la ambulancia
**American** estadounidense
**amusement park** el parque de
 atracciones
**anemic** anémico
**anesthesia** la anestesia
**animal** el animal
**ankle** el tobillo
**antibiotic** el antibiótico
**antiques store** la tienda de
 -antigüedades
**antiseptic cream** la crema
 antiséptica
**anything** algo
**apartment** el apartamento
**appendix (body part)** el apéndice
**appetizer** el aperitivo
**appointment** la cita
**arcade** el salón de juegos

| | | |
|---|---|---|
| **adj** adjective | **BE** British English | **prep** preposition |
| **adv** adverb | **n** noun | **v** verb |

recreativos

**area code** el prefijo

**arm** el brazo

**aromatherapy** la aromaterapia

**around (the corner)** doblando (la esquina)

**arrivals (airport)** las llegadas

**arrive** v llegar

**artery** la arteria

**arthritis** la artritis

**arts** las letras

**Asian** asiático

**aspirin** la aspirina

**asthmatic** asmático

**ATM** el cajero automático

**attack** el asalto

**attend** v asistir

**attraction (place)** el sitio de interés

**attractive** guapo

**Australia** Australia

**Australian** australiano

**automatic** automático; ~ **car** auto/carro automático

**available** disponible

# B

**baby** el bebé; ~ **bottle** el biberón; ~ **wipe** la toallita; **~sitter** el/la niñero/a

**back** la espalda; **~ache** el dolor de espalda; **~pack** la mochila

**bag** la maleta

**baggage** el equipaje; ~ **claim** el reclamo de equipaje; ~ **ticket** el talón de equipaje

**bakery** la panadería

**ballet** el ballet

**bandage** la curita

**bank** el banco

**bar** el bar

**barbecue** la barbacoa

**barber** la peluquería de caballeros

**baseball** el béisbol

**basket (grocery store)** la cesta

**basketball** el baloncesto

**bathroom** el baño

**battery (car)** la batería

**battery** la pila

**battleground** el campo de batalla

**be** v ser/estar

**beach** la playa

**beautiful** precioso

**bed** la cama; ~ **and breakfast** la pensión

**begin** v empezar

**before** antes de

**beginner** principiante

**behind** detrás de

**beige** beis

**belt** el cinturón

**berth** la litera

**best** el/la mejor

**better** mejor

**bicycle** la bicicleta

**big** grande

**bigger** más grande
**bike route** el sendero para bicicletas
**bikini** el biquini; **~ wax** la depilación de las ingles
**bill v (charge)** cobrar; **~ n (money)** el billete; **~ n (of sale)** el recibo
**bird** el pájaro
**birthday** el cumpleaños
**black** negro
**bladder** la vejiga
**bland** soso
**blanket** la manta
**bleed** v sangrar
**blood** la sangre; **~ pressure** la tensión arterial
**blouse** la blusa
**blue** azul
**board** v embarcar
**boarding pass** la tarjeta de embarque
**boat** el barco
**bone** el hueso
**book** el libro; **~store** la librería
**boots** las botas
**boring** aburrido
**botanical garden** el jardín botánico
**bother** v molestar
**bottle** la botella; **~ opener** el abrebotellas
**bowl** el bol

**box** la caja
**boxing match** la pelea de boxeo
**boy** el niño; **~friend** el novio
**bra** el sujetador
**bracelet** la pulsera
**brakes (car)** los frenos
**break** v romper
**break-in (burglary)** el allanamiento de morada
**breakdown** la avería
**breakfast** el desayuno
**breast** el seno; **~feed** dar de lactar
**breathe** v respirar
**bridge** el puente
**briefs (clothing)** los calzoncillos
**bring** v traer
**British** británico
**broken** roto
**brooch** el broche
**broom** la escoba
**brother** el hermano
**brown** marrón
**bug** el insecto
**building** el edificio
**burn** v quemar
**bus** el autobús; **~ station** la estación de autobuses; **~ stop** la parada de autobús; **~ ticket** el boleto de autobús; **~ tour** el recorrido en autobús
**business** los negocios; **~ card** la tarjeta de negocios;

~ **center** el centro de negocios;
~ **class** la clase preferente;
~ **hours** el horario de atención al
público
**butcher** el carnicero
**buttocks** las nalgas
**buy** *v* comprar
**bye** adiós

## C

**cabaret** el cabaré
**cabin (house)** la cabaña;
~ **(ship)** el camarote
**cable car** el teleférico
**cafe** la cafetería
**call** *v* llamar; *n* la llamada
**calories** las calorías
**camera** la cámara;
**digital** ~ la cámara digital;
~ **case** la funda para la cámara;
~ **store** la tienda de fotografía
**camp** *v* acampar; ~ **stove**
el hornillo; **~site** el cámping
**can opener** el abrelatas
**Canada** Canadá
**Canadian** canadiense
**cancel** *v* cancelar
**candy** el caramelo
**canned goods** las conservas
**canyon** el cañón
**car** el auto; ~ **hire [BE]**
el alquiler de autos; ~ **park**
[BE] el estacionamiento;

~ **rental** el alquiler de autos;
~ **seat** el asiento de niño
**carafe** la jarra
**card** la tarjeta; **ATM** ~ la tarjeta de
cajero automático;
**credit** ~ la tarjeta de crédito;
**debit** ~ la tarjeta de débito;
**phone** ~ la tarjeta telefónica
**carry-on (piece of hand
luggage)** el equipaje de mano
**cart (grocery store)** el carrito;
~ **(luggage)** el carrito para el
equipaje
**carton el cartón;** ~ **of
cigarettes** el cartón de tabaco
**case (amount)** la caja
**cash** *v* cobrar; *n* el efectivo;
~ **advance** sacar dinero de la
tarjeta
**cashier el cajero**
**casino** el casino
**castle** el castillo
**cathedral** la catedral
**cave** la cueva
**CD** el CD
**cell phone** el teléfono celular
**Celsius** el grado centígrado
**centimeter** el centímetro
**certificate** el certificado
**chair** la silla; ~ **lift** la telesilla
**change** *v* **(buses)** cambiar;
~ *n* **(money)** el cambio
**charcoal** el carbón

**charge** v (credit card) cobrar;
~ n (cost) el precio
**cheap** barato
**cheaper** más barato
**check** v (on something) revisar;
~ v (luggage) registrar;
~ n (payment) el cheque;
~-in (airport) el preembarque;
~-in (hotel) el registro;
~ing account la cuenta corriente;
~-out (hotel) la salida
**Cheers!** ¡Salud!
**chemical toilet** el inodoro químico
**chemist [BE]** la farmacia
**cheque [BE]** el cheque
**chest (body part)** el pecho;
~ pain el dolor de pecho
**chewing gum** el chicle
**child** el niño; ~ seat la silla para
niños
**children's menu** el menú para
niños
**children's portion** la ración para
niños
**Chinese** chino
**chopsticks** los palillos chinos
**church** la iglesia
**cigar** el puro
**cigarette** el cigarrillo
**class** la clase; **business ~** la clase
preferente; **economy ~** la clase
económica; **first ~** la primera clase
**classical music** la música clásica

**clean** v limpiar; adj limpio; ~ing
**product** el producto de limpieza;
~ing supplies los productos de
limpieza
**clear** v (on an ATM) borrar
**cliff** el acantilado
**cling film [BE]** el film transparente
**close** v (a shop) cerrar
**closed** cerrado
**clothing** la ropa; ~ store la tienda
de ropa
**club** la discoteca
**coat** el abrigo
**coffee shop** la cafetería
**coin** la moneda
**colander** el escurridor
**cold** n (sickness) el resfriado;
~ adj (temperature) frío
**colleague** el compañero de trabajo
**cologne** la colonia
**color** el color
**comb** el peine
**come** v venir
**complaint** la queja
**computer** la computadora
**concert** el concierto; ~ hall la sala
de conciertos
**condition (medical)** el estado de
salud
**conditioner** el acondicionador
**condom** el preservativo
**conference** la conferencia
**confirm** v confirmar

**congestion** la congestión
**connect** *v* **(internet)** conectarse
**connection (internet)** la conexión;
  ~ **(flight)** la conexión de vuelo
**constipated** estreñido
**consulate** el consulado
**consultant** el consultor
**contact** *v* ponerse en contacto con
**contact lens** el lente de contacto;
  ~ **solution** el líquido de lentes de
  contacto
**contagious** contagioso
**convention hall** el salón de
  congresos
**conveyor belt** la cinta transportadora
**cook** *v* cocinar
**cooking gas** el gas butano
**cool (temperature)** frío
**copper** el cobre
**corkscrew** el sacacorchos
**cost** *v* costar
**cot** el catre
**cotton** el algodón
**cough** *v* toser; ~ *n* la tos
**country code** el código de país
**cover charge** la entrada
**crash** *v* **(car)** estrellarse
**cream (ointment)** la pomada
**credit card** la tarjeta de crédito
**crew neck** el cuello redondo
**crib** la cuna
**crystal** el cristal
**cup** la taza

**currency** la moneda; ~ **exchange**
  el cambio de divisas; ~ **exchange**
  **office** la casa de cambio
**current account [BE]** la cuenta
  corriente
**customs** las aduanas
**cut** *v* **(hair)** cortar; ~ *n* **(injury)** el
  corte
**cute** bonito
**cycling** el ciclismo

## D

**damage** *v* causar daño
**damaged** ha sufrido daños
**dance** *v* bailar; ~ **club** la discoteca
**dangerous** peligroso
**dark** oscuro
**date (calendar)** la fecha
**day** el día
**deaf** sordo
**debit card** la tarjeta de débito
**deck chair** la tumbona
**declare** *v* declarar
**decline** *v* **(credit card)** rechazar
**deeply** hondo
**degrees (temperature)** los grados
**delay** *v* retrasarse
**delete** *v* **(computer)** borrar
**delicatessen** la charcutería
**delicious** delicioso
**denim** tela vaquera
**dentist** el dentista
**denture** la dentadura

**deodorant** el desodorante

**department store** los grandes almacenes

**departures (airport)** las salidas

**deposit** v depositar; ~ n **(bank)** el depósito bancario; ~ n **(reserve a room)** la fianza

**desert** el desierto

**dessert** el postre

**detergent** el detergente

**develop** v **(film)** revelar

**diabetic** diabético

**dial** v marcar

**diamond** el diamante

**diaper** el pañal

**diarrhea** la diarrea

**diesel** el diésel

**difficult** difícil

**digital** digital; ~ **camera** la cámara digital; ~ **photos** las fotos digitales; ~ **prints** las fotos digitales

**dining room** el comedor

**dinner** la cena

**direction** la dirección

**dirty** sucio

**disabled** discapacitado

**discharge (bodily fluid)** la secreción

**disconnect (computer)** desconectar

**discount** el descuento

**dish (kitchen)** el plato; ~**washer** el lavavajillas; ~**washing liquid** el líquido lavavajillas

**display** v mostrar; ~ **case** la vitrina

**disposable** desechable; ~ **razor** la cuchilla desechable

**dive** v bucear

**diving equipment** el equipo de buceo

**divorce** v divorciar

**dizzy** mareado

**doctor** el médico

**doll** la muñeca

**dollar (U.S.)** el dólar

**domestic** nacional; ~ **flight** el vuelo nacional

**door** la puerta

**dormitory** el dormitorio

**double bed** la cama matrimonial

**downtown** el centro

**dozen** la docena

**drag lift** el telesquí

**dress (piece of clothing)** el vestido; ~ **code** las normas de vestuario

**drink** v beber; ~ n la bebida; ~ **menu** la carta de bebidas; ~**ing water** el agua potable

**drive** v conducir

**driver's license number** el número de permiso de conducir

**drop (medicine)** la gota

**drowsiness** la somnolencia

**dry cleaner** la tintorería

**dubbed** doblada
**during** durante
**duty (tax)** el impuesto;
　**~-free** libre de impuestos
**DVD** el DVD

# E

**ear** la oreja; ~*ache* el dolor de oído
**earlier** más temprano
**early** temprano
**earrings** los pendientes
**east** el este
**easy** fácil
**eat** *v* comer
**economy class** la clase económica
**elbow** el codo
**electric outlet** el enchufe eléctrico
**elevator** el ascensor
**e-mail** *v* enviar un correo
　electrónico; ~ n el correo
　electrónico; **~ address** la
　dirección de correo electrónico
**emergency** la emergencia;
　**~ exit** la salida de emergencia
**empty** *v* vaciar
**enamel (jewelry)** el esmalte
**end** *v* terminar
**English** el inglés
**engrave** *v* grabar
**enjoy** *v* disfrutar
**enter** *v* entrar
**entertainment** el entretenimiento
**entrance** la entrada

**envelope** el sobre
**equipment** el equipo
**escalators** las escaleras mecánicas
**e-ticket** el billete electrónico
**EU resident** el/la residente de la UE
**euro** el euro
**evening** la noche
**excess** el exceso
**exchange** *v* **(money)** cambiar;
　**~** *v* **(goods)** devolver;
　**~** *n* **(place)** la casa de cambio;
　**~ rate** el tipo de cambio
**excursion** la excursión
**excuse** *v* **(to get past)** pedir
　perdón; **~** *v* **(to get
　attention)** disculparse
**exhausted** agotado
**exit** *v* salir; ~ n la salida
**expensive** caro
**expert (skill level)** experto
**exposure (film)** la foto
**express** rápido; **~ bus** el autobús
　rápido; **~ train** el tren rápido
**extension (phone)** la extensión
**extra** adicional; **~ large** equis
　ele **(XL)**
**extract** *v* **(tooth)** extraer
**eye** el ojo
**eyebrow wax** la depilación de cejas

# F

**face** la cara
**facial** la limpieza de cutis

**family** la familia
**fan (appliance)** el ventilador;
~ **(souvenir)** el abanico
**far** lejos; ~**-sighted** hipermétrope
**farm** la granja
**fast** rápido; ~ **food** la comida
rápida
**faster** más rápido
**fat free** sin grasa
**father** el padre
**fax** v enviar un fax; ~ n el fax;
~ **number** el número de fax
**fee** la tasa
**feed** v alimentar
**ferry** el ferry
**fever** la fiebre
**field (sports)** el campo
**fill** v llenar ; ~ **out** v
**(form)** rellenar
**filling (tooth)** el empaste
**film (camera)** el carrete
**fine (fee for breaking law)** la
multa
**finger** el dedo; ~**nail** la uña del
dedo
**fire** fuego; ~ **department** los
bomberos; ~ **door** la puerta de
incendios
**first** primero; ~ **class** la primera
clase
**fit (clothing)** quedar bien
**fitting room** el probador
**fix** v **(repair)** reparar

**flashlight** la linterna
**flight** el vuelo
**floor** el suelo
**flower** la flor
**folk music** la música folk
**food** la comida
**foot** el pie
**football** [BE] el fútbol
**for** para/por
**forecast** el pronóstico
**forest** el bosque
**fork** el tenedor
**form** el formulario
**formula (baby)** la fórmula infantil
**fort** el fuerte
**fountain** la fuente
**free** gratuito
**freezer** el congelador
**fresh** fresco
**friend** el amigo
**frying pan** la sartén
**full** completo;
~**-service** el servicio completo;
~**-time** a tiempo completo

# G

**game** el partido
**garage (parking)** el garaje;
~ **(repair)** el taller
**garbage bag** la bolsa de basura
**gas** la gasolina; ~ **station** la
gasolinera
**gate (airport)** la puerta

**gay** gay; ~ **bar** el bar gay;
~ **club** la discoteca gay
**gel (hair)** la gomina
**get to** v ir a
**get off** v (a train/bus/
subway) bajarse
**gift** el regalo; ~ **shop** la tienda de
regalos
**girl** la niña; ~**friend** la novia
**give** v dar
**glass (drinking)** el vaso;
~ **(material)** el vidrio
**glasses** las gafas
**go** v **(somewhere)** ir a
**gold** el oro
**golf** golf; ~ **course** el campo de
golf; ~ **tournament** el torneo
de golf
**good** n el producto; ~ adj bueno;
~ **afternoon** buenas tardes;
~ **evening** buenas noches;
~ **morning** buenos días;
~**bye** adiós
**gram** el gramo
**grandchild** el nieto
**grandparent** el abuelo
**gray** gris
**green** verde
**grocery store** el supermercado
**ground** la tierra; ~ **floor** la
planta baja; ~**cloth** la tela
impermeable
**group** el grupo

**guide** el guía; ~ **book** la guía;
~ **dog** el perro guía
**gym** el gimnasio
**gynecologist** el ginecólogo

## H

**hair** el pelo; ~ **dryer** el secador
de pelo; ~ **salon** la peluquería;
~**brush** el cepillo de pelo;
~**cut** el corte de pelo; ~**spray** la
laca; ~**style** el peinado;
~**stylist** el estilista
**half** medio; ~ **hour** la media hora;
~-**kilo** el medio kilo
**hammer** el martillo
**hand** la mano; ~ **luggage [BE]** el
equipaje de mano; ~**bag [BE]** el
bolso
**handicapped** discapacitado
**hangover** la resaca
**happy** feliz
**hat** el sombrero
**have** v tener
**head (body part)** la cabeza;
~**ache** el dolor de cabeza;
~**phones** los cascos
**health** la salud; ~ **food store**
la tienda de alimentos naturales
**heart** el corazón; ~ **condition**
padecer del corazón
**heat** v calentar; ~ n el calor
**heater [heating BE]** la calefacción
**hello** hola

**helmet** el casco
**help** v ayudar; ~ n la ayuda
**here** aquí
**hi** hola
**high** alto; ~**chair** la silla alta;
~**way** la autopista
**hiking boots** las botas de
montaña
**hill** la colina
**hire** v [BE] alquilar; ~ **car** [BE]
el coche de alquiler
**hitchhike** v hacer autostop
**hockey** el hockey
**holiday** [BE] las vacaciones
**horse track** el hipódromo
**hospital** el hospital
**hostel** el albergue
**hot (temperature)** caliente;
~ **(spicy)** picante; ~ **spring** el
agua termal; ~ **water** el agua
caliente
**hotel** el hotel
**hour** la hora
**house** la casa; ~**hold goods**
los artículos para el hogar;
~**keeping services** el servicio de
limpieza de habitaciones
**how (question)** cómo; ~ **much
(question)** cuánto cuesta
**hug** v abrazar
**hungry** hambriento
**hurt** v **(have pain)** tener dolor
**husband** el marido

**I**

**ibuprofen** el ibuprofeno
**ice** el hielo; ~ **hockey** el hockey
sobre hielo
**icy** helado
**identification** el documento de
identidad
**ill** v **(to feel)** encontrarse mal
**in** dentro
**include** v incluir
**indoor pool** la piscina cubierta
**inexpensive** barato
**infected** infectado
**information (phone)** el número
de teléfono de información; ~
**desk** el mostrador de información
**insect** el insecto; ~ **bite**
la picadura de insecto; ~ **repellent**
el repelente de insectos
**insert** v introducir
**insomnia** el insomnio
**instant message** el mensaje
instantáneo
**insulin** la insulina
**insurance** el seguro; ~ **card**
la tarjeta de seguro; ~ **company**
la compañía de seguros
**interesting** interesante
**intermediate** el nivel intermedio
**international (airport area)**
internacional; ~ **flight** el vuelo
internacional; ~ **student card** la
tarjeta internacional de estudiante

**internet** la internet; ~ **cafe** el cibercafé; ~ **service** el servicio de internet; **wireless** ~ el acceso inalámbrico
**interpreter** el/la intérprete
**intersection** el cruce
**intestine** el intestino
**introduce** v presentar
**invoice [BE]** la factura
**Ireland** Irlanda
**Irish** irlandés
**iron** n la plancha; ~ v (**clothes**) planchar
**Italian** italiano

## J

**jacket** la chaqueta
**jar** el bote
**jaw** la mandíbula
**jazz** el jazz; ~ **club** el club de jazz
**jeans** los vaqueros
**jet ski** la moto acuática
**jeweler** la joyería
**jewelry** las joyas
**join** v acompañar a
**joint (body part)** la articulación

## K

**key** la llave; ~ **card** la llave electrónica; ~ **ring** el llavero
**kiddie pool** la piscina infantil
**kidney (body part)** el riñón
**kilo** el kilo; ~**gram** el kilogramo; ~**meter** el kilómetro
**kiss** v besar
**kitchen** la cocina; ~ **foil [BE]** el papel de aluminio
**knee** la rodilla
**knife** el cuchillo

## L

**lace** el encaje
**lactose intolerant** intolerante a la lactosa
**lake** el lago
**large** grande; ~**er** más grande
**last** último
**late (time)** tarde; ~er más tarde
**launderette [BE]** la lavandería
**laundromat** el autoservicio de lavandería
**laundry** lavar ropa; ~ **facility** la lavandería; ~ **service** el servicio de lavandería
**lawyer** el abogado
**leather** el cuero
**to leave** v salir
**left (direction)** la izquierda
**leg** la pierna
**lens** el lente
**less** menos
**lesson** la lección
**letter** la carta
**library** la biblioteca
**life** la vida; ~ **jacket** el chaleco salvavidas; ~**guard** el socorrista

**lift** n [BE] el ascensor; ~ v **(to give a ride)** llevar en auto; ~ **pass** el pase de acceso a los remontes

**light** n **(overhead)** la luz; ~ v **(cigarette)** encender un cigarrillo; **~bulb** la bombilla

**lighter** el encendedor

**like** v gustar; I like me gusta

**line (train)** la línea

**linen** el lino

**lip** el labio

**liquor store** la tienda de bebidas alcohólicas

**liter** el litro

**little** pequeño

**live** v vivir

**liver (body part)** el hígado

**loafers** los mocasines

**local** de la zona

**lock** v cerrar; ~ n el cerrojo

**locker** el casillero

**log on** v **(computer)** iniciar sesión

**log off** v **(computer)** cerrar sesión

**long** largo; ~ **sleeves** las mangas largas; **~-sighted** [BE] hipermétrope

**look** v mirar

**lose** v **(something)** perder

**lost** perdido; ~ **and found** la oficina de objetos perdidos

**lotion** la crema hidratante

**louder** más alto

**love** v querer; ~ n el amor

**low** bajo; **~er** más bajo

**luggage** el equipaje; ~ **cart** el carrito de equipaje; ~ **locker** el casillero automático; ~ **ticket** el talón de equipaje; **hand ~** [BE] el equipaje de mano

**lunch** la comida

**lung** el pulmón

# M

**magazine** la revista

**magnificent** magnífico

**mail** v enviar por correo; ~ n el correo; **~box** el buzón de correo

**main** principal; ~ **attractions** los principales sitios de interés; ~ **course** el plato principal

**make up a prescription** v [BE] despachar medicamentos

**mall** el centro comercial

**man** el hombre

**manager** el gerente

**manicure** la manicura

**manual car** el auto/carro con transmisión manual

**map** el mapa

**market** el mercado

**married** casado

**marry** v casarse

**mass (church service)** la misa

**massage** el masaje

**match** el fósforo

**meal** la comida

**easure** *v* **(someone)** medir
**measuring cup** la taza medidora
**measuring spoon** la cuchara
  medidora
**mechanic** el mecánico
**medicine** el medicamento
**medium (size)** mediano
**meet** *v* **(someone)** conocer
**meeting** la reunión; **~ room**
la sala de reuniones
**membership card** la tarjeta de socio
**memorial (place)** el monumento
  conmemorativo
**memory card** la tarjeta de memoria
**mend** *v* zurcir
**menstrual cramps** los dolores
  menstruales
**menu** la carta
**message** el mensaje
**meter (parking)** el parquímetro
**microwave** el microondas
**midday [BE]** el mediodía
**midnight** la medianoche
**mileage** el kilometraje
**mini-bar** el minibar
**minute** el minuto
**missing** desaparecido
**mistake** el error
**mobile** móvil; **~ home** la
  caravana; **~ phone [BE]** el
  teléfono celular
**mobility** la movilidad
**money** el dinero

**month** el mes
**mop** el trapeador
**moped** el ciclomotor
**more** más
**morning** la mañana
**mosque** la mezquita
**mother** la madre
**motion sickness** el mareo
**motor** el motor; **~ boat** la lancha
  motora; **~cycle** la motocicleta;
  **~way [BE]** la autopista
**mountain** la montaña; **~ bike**
  la bicicleta de montaña
**mousse (hair)** la espuma para el pelo
**mouth** la boca
**movie** la película; **~ theater** el cine
**mug** *v* asaltar
**muscle (body part)** el músculo
**museum** el museo
**music** la música; **~ store** la tienda
  de música

## N

**nail** la uña; **~ file** la lima de uñas
**~ salon** el salón de manicura
**name** el nombre
**napkin** la servilleta
**nappy [BE]** el pañal
**nationality** la nacionalidad
**nature preserve** la reserva natural
**(be) nauseous** *v* tener náuseas
**near** cerca; **~-sighted** miope;
  **~by** cerca de aquí

**neck** el cuello
**necklace** el collar
**need** *v* necesitar
**newspaper** el periódico
**newsstand** el quiosco
**next** próximo
**nice** amable
**night** la noche; **~club** la discoteca
**no** no
**non** sin; **~-alcoholic** sin alcohol;
  **~-smoking** para no fumadores
**noon** el mediodía
**north** el norte
**nose** la nariz
**note [BE]** el billete
**nothing** nada
**notify** *v* avisar
**novice (skill level)** principiante
**now** ahora
**number** el número
**nurse** el enfermero/la enfermera

**O**

**office** la oficina; **~ hours**
  **(doctor's)** las horas de consulta; **~**
  **hours (other offices)** el horario
  de oficina
**off-licence [BE]** la tienda de
  bebidas alcohólicas
**oil** el aceite
**OK** de acuerdo
**old** viejo
**on the corner** en la esquina

**once** una vez
**one** uno; **~-way ticket** el billete
  de ida; **~-way street** la calle de
  sentido único
**only** solamente
**open** *v* abrir; ~ *adj* abierto
**opera** la ópera; **~ house** el teatro
  de la ópera
**opposite** frente a
**optician** el oculista
**orange (color)** naranja
**orchestra** la orquesta
**order** *v* pedir
**outdoor pool** la piscina exterior
**outside** fuera
**over** sobre; **~ the counter**
  **(medication)** sin receta; **~look**
  **(scenic place)** el mirador;
  **~night** por la noche
**oxygen treatment** la oxígenoterapia

**P**

**p.m.** de la tarde
**pacifier** el chupete
**pack** *v* hacer las maletas
**package** el paquete
**paddling pool [BE]** la piscina
  infantil
**pad [BE]** la toalla higiénica
**pain** el dolor
**pajamas** los pijamas
**palace** el palacio
**pants** los pantalones

**pantyhose** las medias
**paper** el papel; **~ towel** el papel de cocina
**paracetamol [BE]** el paracetamol
**park** v aparcar; ~n el parque; **~ing garage** el párking; **~ing lot** el estacionamiento
**parliament building** el palacio de las cortes
**part (for car)** la pieza; **~-time** a tiempo parcial
**pass through** v estar de paso
**passenger** el pasajero
**passport** el pasaporte; **~ control** el control de pasaportes
**password** la contraseña
**pastry shop** la pastelería
**path** el camino
**pay** v pagar; **~ phone** el teléfono público
**peak (of a mountain)** la cima
**pearl** la perla
**pedestrian** el peatón
**pediatrician** el pediatra
**pedicure** la pedicura
**pen** el bolígrafo
**penicillin** la penicilina
**penis** el pene
**per** por; **~ day** por día; **~ hour** por hora; **~ night** por noche; **~ week** por semana
**perfume** el perfume
**period (menstrual)** la regla;

**~ (of time)** la época
**permit** v permitir
**petite** las tallas pequeñas
**petrol** la gasolina; **~ station** la gasolinera
**pewter** el peltre
**pharmacy** la farmacia
**phone** v hacer una llamada; **~** n el teléfono; **~ call** la llamada de teléfono; **~ card** la tarjeta telefónica; **~ number** el número de teléfono
**photo** la foto; **~copy** la fotocopia; **~graphy** la fotografía
**pick up** v **(something)** recoger
**picnic area** la zona para picnic
**piece** el trozo
**pill (birth control)** la píldora
**pillow** la almohada
**personal identification number (PIN)** la clave
**pink** rosa
**piste [BE]** la pista; **~ map [BE]** el mapa de pistas
**pizzeria** la pizzería
**place** v **(a bet)** hacer una apuesta
**plane** el avión
**plastic wrap** el film transparente
**plate** el plato
**platform [BE] (train)** el andén
**platinum** el platino
**play** v jugar; ~ n **(theater)** la obra de teatro; **~ground** el patio de

recreo; **~pen** el parque
**please** por favor
**pleasure** el placer
**plunger** el desatascador
**plus size** la talla grande
**pocket** el bolsillo
**poison** el veneno
**poles (skiing)** los bastones
**police** la policía; **~ report** el certificado de la policía; **~ station** la comisaría
**pond** el estanque
**pool** la piscina
**pop music** la música pop
**portion** la ración
**post [BE]** el correo; **~ office** la oficina de correos; **~box [BE]** el buzón de correos; **~card** la tarjeta postal
**pot** la olla
**pottery** la cerámica
**pounds (British sterling)** las libras esterlinas
**pregnant** embarazada
**prescribe** v recetar
**prescription** la receta
**press** v **(clothing)** planchar
**price** el precio
**print** v imprimir
**problem** el problema
**produce** las frutas y verduras; **~ store** la frutería y verdulería
**prohibit** v prohibir

**pronounce** v pronunciar
**public** el público
**pull** v **(door sign)** tirar
**purple** morado
**purse** el bolso
**push** v **(door sign)** empujar; **~chair [BE]** el coche de niño

## Q

**quality** la calidad
**question** la pregunta
**quiet** tranquilo

## R

**racetrack** el circuito de carreras
**racket (sports)** la raqueta
**railway station [BE]** la estación de trenes
**rain** la lluvia; **~coat** el chubasquero; **~forest** el bosque pluvial; **~y** lluvioso
**rap (music)** el rap
**rape** v violar; **~** n la violación
**rash** la erupción cutánea
**razor blade** la hoja de afeitar
**reach** v localizar
**ready** listo
**real** auténtico
**receipt** el recibo
**receive** v recibir
**reception** la recepción
**recharge** v recargar
**recommend** v recomendar

**recommendation** la recomendación
**recycle** v reciclar
**red** rojo
**refrigerator** el refrigerador
**region** la región
**registered mail** el correo certificado
**regular** normal
**relationship** la relación
**rent** v alquilar
**rental car** el auto de alquiler
**repair** v arreglar
**repeat** v repetir
**reservation** la reserva; ~ **desk** la taquilla
**reserve** v reservar
**restaurant** el restaurante
**restroom** el servicio
**retired** jubilado
**return** v **(something)** devolver; ~ n **[BE]** la ida y vuelta
**rib (body part)** la costilla
**right (direction)** derecha; ~ **of way** prioridad de paso
**ring** el anillo
**river** el río
**road map** el mapa de carreteras
**rob** v atracar
**robbed** atracado
**romantic** romántico
**room** la habitación; ~ **key** la llave de habitación; ~ **service** el servicio de habitaciones

**round-trip** ida y vuelta
**route** la ruta
**rowboat** la barca de remos
**rubbish [BE]** la basura; ~ *bag* **[BE]** la bolsa de basura
**rugby** el rubgy
**ruins** las ruinas
**rush** la prisa

## S

**sad** triste
**safe** n la caja fuerte; ~ *adj* seguro
**sales tax** el IVA
**same** mismo
**sandals** las sandalias
**sanitary napkin** la toalla higiénica
**saucepan** el cazo
**sauna** la sauna
**save** v **(computer)** guardar
**savings (account)** la cuenta de ahorro
**scanner** el escáner
**scarf** la bufanda
**schedule** v programar; ~ *n* el horario
**school** el colegio
**science** la ciencia
**scissors** las tijeras
**sea** el mar
**seat** el asiento
**security** la seguridad
**see** v ver
**self-service** el autoservicio

**sell** v vender
**seminar** el seminario
**send** v enviar
**senior citizen** jubilado
**separated (marriage)** -separado
**serious** serio
**service (in a restaurant)** el servicio
**sexually transmitted disease
(STD)** la enfermedad de
transmisión sexual
**shampoo** el champú
**sharp** afilado
**shaving cream** la crema de afeitar
**sheet** la sábana
**ship** v enviar
**shirt** la camisa
**shoe store** la zapatería
**shoes** los zapatos
**shop** v comprar
**shopping** ir de compras;
~ **area** la zona de compras;
~ **centre [BE]** el centro comercial;
~ **mall** el centro comercial
**short** corto; ~ **sleeves** las mangas
cortas; ~**s** los pantalones cortos;
~**-sighted [BE]** miope
**shoulder** el hombro
**show** v enseñar
**shower** la ducha
**shrine** el santuario
**sick** enfermo
**side** el lado; ~ **dish** la guarnición;
~ **effect** el efecto secundario;

~ **order** la guarnición
**sightsee** v hacer turismo
**sightseeing tour** el recorrido
turístico
**sign** v **(name)** firmar
**silk** la seda
**silver** la plata
**single (unmarried)** soltero; ~
**bed** la cama; ~ **prints** una copia;
~ **room** una habitación individual
**sink** el lavabo
**sister** la hermana
**sit** v sentarse
**size** la talla
**skin** la piel
**skirt** la falda
**ski** v esquiar; ~ n el esquí;
~ **lift** el telesquí
**sleep** v dormir; ~**er car** el coche
cama; ~**ing bag** el saco de dormir
**slice** v cortar en rodajas
**slippers** las pantuflas
**slower** más despacio
**slowly** despacio
**small** pequeño
**smaller** más pequeño
**smoke** v fumar
**smoking (area)** la zona de
fumadores
**snack bar** la cafetería
**sneakers** las zapatillas de deporte
**snorkeling equipment** el equipo
de esnórquel

**snow** la nieve; **~board** la tabla de snowboard; **~shoe** la raqueta de nieve; **~y** nevado

**soap** el jabón

**soccer** el fútbol

**sock** el calcetín

**some** alguno

**soother** [BE] el chupete

**sore throat** las anginas

**sorry** lo siento

**south** el sur

**souvenir** el recuerdo; **~ store** la tienda de recuerdos

**spa** el centro de salud y belleza

**Spain** España

**Spanish** el español

**spatula** la espátula

**speak** v hablar

**special (food)** la especialidad de la casa

**specialist (doctor)** el especialista

**specimen** el ejemplar

**speeding** el exceso de velocidad

**spell** v deletrear

**spicy** picante

**spine (body part)** la columna vertebral

**spoon** la cuchara

**sports** los deportes; **~ massage** el masaje deportivo

**sporting goods store** la tienda de deportes

**sprain** el esguince

**square** cuadrado; **~ kilometer** el kilómetro cuadrado; **~ meter** el metro cuadrado

**stadium** el estadio

**stairs** las escaleras

**stamp** v (a ticket) picar; **~ n (postage)** el sello

**start** v empezar

**starter** [BE] el aperitivo

**station** la estación; **bus ~** la estación de autobuses; **gas ~** la gasolinera; **muster ~** [BE] el punto de reunión; **petrol ~** [BE] la gasolinera; **subway ~** el metro; **train ~** la estación de tren

**statue** la estatua

**stay** v quedarse

**steal** v robar

**steep** empinado

**sterling silver** la plata esterlina

**sting** el escozor

**stolen** robado

**stomach** el estómago; **~ache** el dolor de estómago

**stop** v pararse; **~ n** la parada

**store directory** la guía de tiendas

**storey** [BE] la planta

**stove** el horno

**straight** recto

**strange** extraño

**stream** el arroyo

**stroller** el coche

**student** el estudiante

**study** *v* estudiar
**studying** estudiando
**stunning** impresionante
**subtitle** el subtítulo
**subway** el metro; **~ station** la estación de metro
**suit** el traje
**suitcase** la maleta
**sun** el sol; **~block** el protector solar total; **~burn** la quemadura solar; **~glasses** las gafas de sol; **~ny** soleado, **~screen** el protector solar; **~stroke** la insolación
**super (fuel)** súper; **~market** el supermercado
**surfboard** la tabla de surf
**surgical spirit [BE]** el alcohol etílico
**swallow** *v* tragar
**sweater** el jersey
**sweatshirt** la sudadera
**sweet (taste)** dulce; **~s [BE]** los caramelos
**swelling** la hinchazón
**swim** *v* nadar; **~suit** el bañador
**symbol (keyboard)** el símbolo
**synagogue** la sinagoga

**T**

**table** la mesa
**tablet (medicine)** la tableta
**take** *v* llevar; **~ away [BE]** para llevar

**tampon** el tampón
**taste** *v* probar
**taxi** el taxi
**team** el equipo
**teaspoon** la cucharadita
**telephone** el teléfono
**temple (religious)** el templo
**temporary** provisional
**tennis** el tenis
**tent** la tienda de campaña; **~ peg** la estaca; **~ pole** el mástil
**terminal (airport)** la terminal
**terracotta** la terracota
**terrible** terrible
**text** *v* **(send a message)** enviar un mensaje de texto; **~ n (message)** el texto
**thank** *v* dar las gracias a; **~ you** gracias
**that** eso
**theater** el teatro
**theft** el robo
**there** ahí
**thief** el ladrón
**thigh** el muslo
**thirsty** sediento
**this** esto
**throat** la garganta
**ticket** el boleto; **~ office** el despacho de boletos; **~ed passenger** el pasajero con boleto
**tie (clothing)** la corbata
**time** el tiempo; **~table [BE]**

el horario
**tire** la rueda
**tired** cansado
**tissue** el pañuelo de papel
**tobacconist** el estanco
**today** hoy
**toe** el dedo del pie; **~nail** la uña del pie
**toilet [BE]** el servicio; **~ paper** el papel higiénico
**tomorrow** mañana
**tongue** la lengua
**tonight** esta noche
**too** demasiado
**tooth** el diente; **~brush** el cepillo de dientes; **~paste** la pasta de dientes
**total (amount)** el total
**tough (food)** duro
**tourist** el turista; **~ information office** la oficina de turismo
**tour** el recorrido turístico
**tow truck** la grúa
**towel** la toalla
**tower** la torre
**town** la ciudad; **~ hall** la municipalidad; **~ map** el mapa de ciudad; **~ square** la plaza
**toy** el juguete; **~ store** la tienda de juguetes
**track (train)** el andén
**traditional** tradicional
**traffic light** el semáforo

**trail** la pista; **~ map** el mapa de la pista
**trailer** el remolque
**train** el tren; **~ station** la estación de tren
**transfer** v cambiar
**translate** v traducir
**trash** la basura
**travel** v viajar; **~ agency** la agencia de viajes; **~ sickness** el mareo; **~er's check [cheque BE]** el cheque de viajero
**tree** el árbol
**trim (hair cut)** v cortarse las puntas
**trip** el viaje
**trolley [BE]** el carrito
**trousers [BE]** los pantalones
**T-shirt** la camiseta
**turn off** v apagar
**turn on** v encender
**TV** la televisión
**type** v escribir a máquina
**tyre [BE]** la rueda

## U

**United Kingdom (U.K.)** el Reino Unido
**United States (U.S.)** los Estados Unidos
**ugly** feo
**umbrella** el paraguas
**unattended** desatendido
**unbranded medication [BE]**

el fármaco genérico
**unconscious** inconsciente
**underground [BE]** el metro;
**~ station [BE]** la estación de metro
**underpants [BE]** los calzoncillos
**understand** v entender
**underwear** la ropa interior
**university** la universidad
**unleaded (gas)** la gasolina sin plomo
**upper** superior
**urgent** urgente
**use** v usar
**username** el nombre de usuario
**utensil** el cubierto

## V

**vacancy** la habitación libre
**vacation** las vacaciones
**vaccination** la vacuna
**vacuum cleaner** la aspiradora
**vagina** la vagina
**vaginal infection** la infección
vaginal
**validity** validez
**valley** el valle
**valuable** valioso
**value** el valor
**VAT [BE]** el IVA
**vegetarian** vegetariano
**vehicle registration** el registro
del auto
**viewpoint [BE]** el mirador
**village** el pueblo

**vineyard** la viña
**visa (passport document)** la visa
**visit** v visitar; **~ing hours**
el horario de visita
**visually impaired** la persona con
discapacidad visual
**vitamin** la vitamina
**V-neck** el cuello en V
**volleyball game** el partido de
voleibol
**vomit** v vomitar

## W

**wait** v esperar; **~** n la espera;
**~ing room** la sala de espera
**waiter** el camarero
**waitress** la camarera
**wake** v despertarse; **~-up call**
la llamada despertador
**walk** v caminar; **~** n la caminata;
**~ing route** la ruta de senderismo
**wall clock** el reloj de pared
**wallet** la cartera
**warm** v **(something)** calentar;
**~** adj **(temperature)** calor
**washing machine** la lavadora
**watch** el reloj
**water skis** los esquís acuáticos
**waterfall** la cascada
**weather** el tiempo
**week** la semana; **~end** el fin de
semana; **~ly** semanal
**welcome** v acoger; **~** bienvenido

**well** bien; **~-rested** descansado
**west** el oeste
**what (question)** qué
**wheelchair** la silla de ruedas; **~ ramp** la rampa para silla de ruedas
**when (question)** cuándo
**where (question)** dónde
**white** blanco; **~ gold** el oro blanco
**who (question)** quién
**widowed** viudo
**wife** la mujer
**window** la ventana; **~ case** el escaparate
**windsurfer** el surfista
**wine list** la carta de vinos
**wireless** inalámbrico; **~ internet** el acceso inalámbrico a internet; **~ internet service** el servicio inalámbrico a internet; **~ phone** el teléfono móvil
**with** con

**withdraw** v retirar; **~al (bank)** retirar fondos
**without** sin
**woman** la mujer
**wool** la lana
**work** v trabajar
**wrap** v envolver
**wrist** la muñeca
**write** v escribir

## Y

**year** el año
**yellow** amarillo; **~ gold** el oro amarillo
**yes** sí
**yesterday** ayer
**young** joven
**youth hostel** el albergue juvenil

## Z

**zoo** el zoológico

## Spanish–English

## A

**a tiempo completo** full-time
**a tiempo parcial** part-time
**la abadía** abbey
**el abanico** fan (souvenir)
**abierto** *adj* open
**el abogado** lawyer
**abrazar** v hug

**el abrebotellas** bottle opener
**el abrelatas** can opener
**el abrigo** coat
**abrir** v open
**el abuelo** grandparent
**aburrido** boring
**acampar** v camp
**el acantilado** cliff

**el acceso** access; **~ inalámbrico a internet** wireless internet; **~ para discapacitados** handicapped-[disabled- BE] accessible

**el accidente** accident

**el aceite** oil

**aceptar** v accept

**acoger** v welcome

**acompañar a** v join

**el acondicionador** conditioner

**la acupuntura** acupuncture

**el adaptador** adapter

**adicional** extra

**adiós** goodbye

**las aduanas** customs

**el aeropuerto** airport

**afilado** sharp

**la agencia** agency; **~ de viajes** travel agency

**agotado** exhausted

**el agua** water; **~ caliente** hot water; **~ potable** drinking water

**las aguas termales** hot spring

**ahí** there

**ahora** now

**el aire** air, air pump; **~ acondicionado** air conditioning

**el albergue** hostel; **~ juvenil** youth hostel

**alérgico** allergic; **~ a la lactosa** lactose intolerant

**algo** anything

**el algodón** cotton

**alguno** some

**alimentar** v feed

**el allanamiento de morada** break-in (burglary)

**la almohada** pillow

**el alojamiento** accommodation

**alquilar** v rent [hire BE]; **el ~ de autos** car rental [hire BE]

**alto** high

**amable** nice

**amarillo** yellow

**la ambulancia** ambulance

**el amigo** friend

**el amor** n love

**el andén** track [platform BE] (train)

**anémico** anemic

**la anestesia** anesthesia

**las anginas** sore throat

**el anillo** ring

**el animal** animal

**antes de** before

**el antibiótico** antibiotic

**el año** year

**apagar** v turn off

**el aparcamiento** parking lot [car park BE]

**el apartamento** apartment

**el apéndice** appendix (body part)

**el aperitivo** appetizer [starter BE]

**aquí** here

**el árbol** tree

**la aromaterapia** aromatherapy

**arreglar** v repair

**el arroyo** stream
**la arteria** artery
**la articulación** joint (body part)
**los artículos** goods; **~ para el hogar** household good
**la artritis** arthritis
**asaltar** v mug
**el asalto** attack
**el ascensor** elevator [lift BE]
**asiático** Asian
**el asiento** seat; **~ de niño** car seat; **~ de pasillo** aisle seat
**asistir** v attend
**asmático** asthmatic
**la aspiradora** vacuum cleaner
**la aspirina** aspirin
**atracado** robbed
**atracar** v rob
**los audífonos** headphones
**Australia** Australia
**australiano** Australian
**auténtico** real
**el auto** car; **~ de alquiler** rental [hire BE] car; **~ automático** automatic car; **~ cama** sleeper [sleeping BE] car; **~ con transmisión manual** manual car **el autobús** bus; **~ rápido** express bus
**automático** automatic
**la autopista** highway [motorway BE]
**el autoservicio** self-service

**la avería** breakdown
**el avión** airplane, plane
**avisar** v notify
**ayer** yesterday
**la ayuda** n help
**ayudar** v help
**el ayuntamiento** town hall
**azul** blue

**B**

**bailar** v dance
**bajarse** v get off (a train, bus, subway)
**bajo** low
**el ballet** ballet
**el baloncesto** basketball
**el banco** bank
**el baño** bathroom
**el bar** bar; **~ gay** gay bar
**barato** cheap, inexpensive
**la barbacoa** barbecue
**la barca de remos** rowboat
**el barco** boat
**los bastones** poles (skiing)
**la basura** trash [rubbish BE]
**la batería** battery (car)
**el bebé** baby
**beber** v drink
**la bebida** n drink
**beis** beige
**el béisbol** baseball
**besar** v kiss
**el biberón** baby bottle

**la biblioteca** library
**la bicicleta** bicycle;
 **~ de montaña** mountain bike
**bienvenido** welcome
**el billete** *n* bill (money)
**el biquini** bikini
**blanco** white
**la blusa** blouse
**la boca** mouth
**el bol** bowl
**el boleto** ~ ticket;
 **~ de autobús** bus ticket;
 **~ de ida** one-way (ticket);
 **~ de ida y vuelta** round trip
 [return BE]; **~ electrónico**
 e-ticket
**el bolígrafo** pen
**la bolsa de basura** garbage
 [rubbish BE] bag
**el bolsillo** pocket
**el bolso** purse [handbag BE]
**los bomberos** fire department
**la bombilla** lightbulb
**bonito** cute
**borrar** *v* clear (on an ATM);
 **~** *v* delete (computer)
**el bosque** forest; **~ pluvial**
 rainforest
**las botas** boots;
 **~ de montaña** hiking boots
**el bote** jar
**la botella** bottle
**el brazo** arm

**británico** British
**el broche** brooch
**bucear** to dive
**bueno** *adj* good
**buenas noches** good evening
**buenas tardes** good afternoon
**buenos días** good morning
**la bufanda** scarf
**el buzón de correo** mailbox
 [postbox BE]

**C**

**la cabaña** cabin (house)
**el cabaré** cabaret
**la cabeza** head (body part)
**la cafetería** cafe, coffee shop, snack
 bar
**la caja** case (amount);
 **~ fuerte** *n* safe
**el cajero** cashier;
 **~ automático** ATM
**el calcetín** sock
**la calefacción** heater [heating BE]
**calentar** *v* heat, warm
**la calidad** quality
**la calle de sentido único** one-way
 street
**calor** hot, warm (temperature)
**las calorías** calories
**los calzoncillos** briefs [underpants
 BE] (clothing)
**la cama** single bed; **~ de
 matrimonio** double bed

**la cámara** camera;
  **~ digital** digital camera
**la camarera** waitress
**el camarero** waiter
**el camarote** cabin (ship)
**cambiar** v change, exchange, transfer
**el cambio** n change (money);
  **~ de divisas** currency exchange
**caminar** v walk
**la caminata** n walk
**el camino** path
**la camisa** shirt
**la camiseta** T-shirt
**el cámping** campsite
**el campo** field (sports);
  **~ de batalla** battleground;
  **~ de golf** golf course
**Canadá** Canada
**canadiense** Canadian
**cancelar** v cancel
**cansado** tired
**el cañón** canyon
**la cara** face
**los caramelos** candy [sweets BE]
**la caravana** mobile home
**el carbón** charcoal
**el carnicero** butcher
**caro** expensive
**el carrete** film (camera)
**el carrito** cart [trolley BE] (grocery
  store); **~ de equipaje** luggage cart
**la carta** letter
**la carta** menu; **~ de**

**bebidas** drink menu; **~ para
niños** children's menu; **~ de
vinos** wine list
**la cartera** wallet
**el cartón** carton; **~ de tabaco**
  carton of cigarettes
**la casa** house; **~ de cambio**
  currency exchange office
**casado** married
**casarse** v marry
**la cascada** waterfall
**el casco** helmet
**el casillero** locker; **~** reservation desk
**el casino** casino
**el castillo** castle
**el catarro** cold (sickness)
**la catedral** cathedral
**el catre** cot
**causar daño** v damage
**el cazo** saucepan
**el CD** CD
**la cena** dinner
**el centímetro** centimeter
**el centro** downtown area;
  **~ comercial** shopping
  mall [centre BE]; **~ de
  negocios** business center;
  **~ de salud y belleza** spa
**el cepillo de pelo** hair brush
**la cerámica** pottery
**cerca** near; **~ de aquí** nearby
**la cerilla** n match
**cerrado** closed

**cerrar** v close, lock; **~ sesión** v log off (computer)

**el cerrojo** n lock

**el certificado** certificate; **~ de la policía** police report

**la cesta** basket (grocery store)

**el chaleco salvavidas** life jacket

**el champú** shampoo

**la chaqueta** jacket

**la charcutería** delicatessen

**el cheque** n check [cheque BE] (payment); **~ de viajero** traveler's check [cheque BE]

**el chicle** chewing gum

**chino** Chinese

**el chupete** pacifier [soother BE]

**el cibercafé** internet cafe

**el ciclismo** cycling

**el ciclomotor** moped

**la ciencia** science

**el cigarrillo** cigarette

**la cima** peak (of a mountain)

**el cine** movie theater

**la cinta transportadora** conveyor belt

**el cinturón** belt

**el circuito de carreras** racetrack

**la cita** appointment

**la ciudad** town

**la clase** class; **~ económica** economy class; **~ preferente** business class

**la clave** personal identification number (PIN)

**el club de jazz** jazz club

**cobrar** v bill (charge); **~** v cash; **~** v charge (credit card)

**el cobre** copper

**el coche** stroller [pushchair BE]

**la cocina** kitchen

**cocinar** v cook

**el código de país** country code

**el codo** elbow

**el colegio** school

**la colina** hill

**el collar** necklace

**la colonia** cologne

**el color** color

**la columna vertebral** spine (body part)

**el comedor** dining room

**comer** v eat

**la comida** food, lunch, meal; **~ rápida** fast food

**la comisaría** police station

**cómo** how

**el compañero de trabajo** colleague

**la compañía** company; **~ aérea** airline; **~ de seguros** insurance company

**comprar** v buy, shop

**la computadora** computer

**con** with; **~ plomo** leaded (gas)

**el concierto** concert

**conducir** v drive

**conectarse** *v* connect (internet)
**la conexión** connection (internet);
~ **de vuelo** connection (flight)
**la conferencia** conference
**confirmar** *v* confirm
**el congelador** freezer
**la congestión** congestion
**conocer** *v* meet (someone)
**la consigna automática** luggage
locker
**el consulado** Consulate
**el consultor** consultant
**contagioso** contagious
**la contraseña** password
**el control de pasaportes** passport
control
**el corazón** heart
**la corbata** tie (clothing)
**el correo** *n* mail [post BE]; ~ **aéreo**
airmail; ~ **certificado** registered
mail; ~ **electrónico** *n* e-mail
**cortar** *v* cut (hair); ~ **en**
**rodajas** to slice
**cortarse las puntas** v trim (hair cut)
**el corte** *n* cut (injury); ~ **de pelo**
haircut
**corto** short
**costar** *v* cost
**la costilla** rib (body part)
**la crema** cream; ~ **antiséptica**
antiseptic cream; ~ **de afeitar**
shaving cream; ~ **hidratante**
lotion

**el cristal** crystal
**el cruce** intersection
**cuándo** when (question)
**cuánto cuesta** how much
**el cubierto** utensil
**la cuchara** spoon;
~ **medidora** measuring spoon
**la cucharadita** teaspoon
**la cuchilla desechable** disposable
razor
**el cuchillo** knife
**el cuello** neck; ~ **en V** V-neck;
~ **redondo** crew neck
**la cuenta** account; ~ **de ahorros**
savings account; ~ **corriente**
checking [current BE] account
**cuero** leather
**la cueva** cave
**el cumpleaños** birthday
**la cuna** crib
**la curita** bandage

**D**

**dar** to give; ~ **de lactar** breastfeed
~ **fuego** light (cigarette); ~ **las**
**gracias a** v thank
**de** from, of; ~ **acuerdo** OK; ~ **la**
**mañana** a.m.; ~ **la tarde** p.m.;
~ **la zona** local
**declarar** *v* declare
**el dedo** finger; ~ **del pie** toe
**deletrear** *v* spell
**delicioso** delicious

**el denim** denim
**la dentadura** denture
**el dentista** dentist
**dentro** in
**la depilacion** wax;
  **~ de cejas** eyebrow wax;
  **~ de las ingles** bikini wax
**deportes** sports
**depositar** v deposit
**el depósito bancario** deposit
  (bank)
**la derecha** right (direction)
**desaparecido** missing
**el desatascador** plunger
**desatendido** unattended
**el desayuno** breakfast
**descansado** well-rested
**desconectar** v disconnect
  (computer)
**el descuento** discount
**desechable** disposable
**el desierto** desert
**el desodorante** deodorant
**despachar medicamentos** v fill
  [make up BE] a prescription
**el despacho de boletos** ticket
  office
**despacio** slowly
**despertarse** v wake
**después** after
**el detergente** detergent
**detrás de** behind (direction)
**devolver** v exchange, return

(goods)
**el día** day
**diabético** diabetic
**el diamante** diamond
**la diarrea** diarrhea
**el diente** tooth
**el diésel** diesel
**difícil** difficult
**digital** digital
**el dinero** money
**la dirección** direction
**la dirección** address; **~ de correo
  electrónico** e-mail address
**discapacitado** handicapped
  [disabled BE]
**la discoteca** club (dance, night);
  **~ gay** gay club
**disculparse** v excuse (to get
  attention)
**disfrutar** v enjoy
**disponible** available
**divorciar** v divorce
**doblada** dubbed
**doblando (la esquina)** around
  (the corner)
**la docena** dozen
**el documento de
  identidad** identification
**el dólar** dollar (U.S.)
**el dolor** pain;
  **~ de cabeza** headache;
  **~ de espalda** backache;
  **~ de estómago** stomachache;

**~ de oído** earache;
**~ de pecho** chest pain
**los dolores menstruales**
   menstrual cramps
**dónde** where (question)
**dormir** v sleep
**el dormitorio** dormitory
**la ducha** shower
**dulce** sweet (taste)
**durante** during
**el DVD** DVD

**E**

**la edad** age
**el edificio** building
**el efectivo** cash
**el efecto secundario** side effect
**el ejemplar** specimen
**embarazada** pregnant
**embarcar** v board
**la emergencia** emergency
**el empaste** filling (tooth)
**empezar** v begin, start
**empinado** steep
**empujar** v push (door sign)
**en la esquina** on the corner
**el encaje** lace
**el encendedor** lighter
**encender** v turn on
**el enchufe eléctrico** electric outlet
**encontrarse mal** v be ill
**la enfermedad de transmisión**
   **sexual** sexually transmitted
   disease (STD)
**el enfermero/la enfermera** nurse
**enfermo** sick
**enseñar** v show
**entender** v understand
**la entrada** admission/cover charge
   **~** entrance
**entrar** v enter
**el entretenimiento** entertainment
**enviar** v send, ship; **~ por correo**
   v mail; **~ un correo electrónico**
   v e-mail; **~ un fax** v fax ;
   **~ un mensaje de texto** v text
   (send a message)
**envolver** v wrap
**la época** period (of time)
**el equipaje** luggage [baggage BE];
   **~ de mano** carry-on (piece of
   hand luggage)
**el equipo** team
**el equipo** equipment; **~ de**
   **buceo** diving equipment; **~ de**
   **esnórquel** snorkeling equipment
**equis ele (XL)** extra large
**el error** mistake
**la erupción cutánea** rash
**las escaleras** stairs;
   **~** *mecánicas* escalators
**el escáner** scanner
**el escaparate** window case
**la escoba** broom
**el escozor** sting
**escribir** v write;

**~ a máquina** *v* type
**el escurridor** colander
**el esguince** sprain
**el esmalte** enamel (jewelry)
**eso** that
**la espalda** back
**España** Spain
**el español** Spanish
**la espátula** spatula
**la especialidad de la casa** special (food)
**el especialista** specialist (doctor)
**la espera** *n* wait
**esperar** *v* wait
**la espuma para el pelo** mousse (hair)
**el esquí** *n* ski
**esquiar** *v* ski
**los esquís acuáticos** water skis
**esta noche** tonight
**la estaca** tent peg
**la estación** station; **~ de autobuses** bus station; **~ de metro** subway [underground BE] station; **~ de tren** train [railway BE] station
**estacionar** *v* park
**el estadio** stadium
**el estado de salud** condition (medical)
**los Estados Unidos** United States (U.S.)
**estadounidense** American

**el estanco** tobacconist
**el estanque** pond
**estar** *v* be; **~ de paso** *v* pass through
**la estatua** statue
**el este** east
**el estilista** hairstylist
**esto** this
**el estómago** stomach
**estrellarse** *v* crash (car)
**estreñido** constipated
**estudiando** studying
**el estudiante** student
**estudiar** *v* study
**el euro** euro
**el exceso** excess; **~ de velocidad** speeding
**la excursión** excursion
**experto** expert (skill level)
**la extensión** extension (phone)
**extraer** *v* extract (tooth)
**extraño** strange

**F**
**fácil** easy
**la factura** bill [invoice BE]
**la facturación** check-in (airport)
**facturar** check (luggage)
**la falda** skirt
**la familia** family
**la farmacia** pharmacy [chemist BE]
**el fax** *n* fax
**la fecha** date (calendar)

**feliz** happy
**feo** ugly
**el ferry** ferry
**la fianza** deposit (to reserve a room)
**la fiebre** fever
**el film transparente** plastic wrap [cling film BE]
**el fin de semana** weekend
**firmar** *v* sign (name)
**la flor** flower
**la fórmula infantil** formula (baby)
**el formulario** form
**la foto** exposure (film); ~ photo;
~**copia** photocopy;
~**grafía** photography;
~ **digital** digital photo
**los frenos** brakes (car)
**frente a** opposite
**fresco** fresh
**frío** cold (temperature)
**las frutas y verduras** produce
**la frutería y verdulería** produce store
**el fuego** fire
**la fuente** fountain
**fuera** outside
**el fuerte** fort
**fumar** *v* smoke
**la funda para la cámara** camera case
**el fútbol** soccer [football BE]

## G

**las gafas** glasses;
~ **de sol** sunglasses
**el garaje** garage (parking)
**la garganta** throat
**el gas butano** cooking gas
**la gasolina** gas [petrol BE];
~ **sin plomo** unleaded gas
**la gasolinera** gas [petrol BE] station
**gay** gay
**el gerente** manager
**el gimnasio** gym
**el ginecólogo** gynecologist
**la gomina** gel (hair)
**la gota** drop (medicine)
**grabar** *v* burn (CD); ~ *v* **engrave**
**gracias** thank you
**los grados** degrees (temperature);
~ **centígrado** Celsius
**el gramo** gram
**grande** large
**los grandes almacenes** department store
**la granja** farm
**gratuito** free
**gris** gray
**la grúa** tow truck
**el grupo** group
**guapo** attractive
**guardar** *v* save (computer)
**la guarnición** side dish, order
**el guía** guide

**la guía**  guide book; **~ de tiendas**  store directory
**gustar**  *v* like; **me gusta** I like

## H

**ha sufrido daños**  damaged
**la habitación**  room;
  **~ individual**  single room;
  **~ libre**  vacancy
**hablar**  *v* speak
**hacer**  *v* do;
  **~ una apuesta**  *v* place (a bet);
  **~ un arreglo**  *v* alter;
  **~ una llamada**  *v* phone;
  **~ las maletas**  *v* pack;
  **~ turismo**  sightseeing
**hambriento**  hungry
**helado**  *adj.* frozen; *~n* ice cream
**la hermana**  sister
**el hermano**  brother
**el hielo**  ice
**el hígado**  liver (body part)
**la hinchazón**  swelling
**hipermétrope**  far-sighted [long-sighted BE]
**el hipódromo**  horsetrack
**el hockey**  hockey; **~ sobre hielo**  ice hockey
**la hoja de afeitar**  razor blade
**hola**  hello
**el hombre**  man
**el hombro**  shoulder
**hondo**  deeply

**la hora**  hour
**el horario**  *n* schedule [timetable BE]
**los horarios**  hours;
  **~ de atención al público**  business hours; **~ de oficina**  office hours; **~ de visita**  visiting hours
**las horas de consulta**  office hours (doctor's)
**la hornilla**  stove
**el hornillo**  camp stove
**el horno**  oven
**el hospital**  hospital
**el hotel**  hotel
**hoy**  today
**el hueso**  bone

## I

**el ibuprofeno**  ibuprofen
**la ida y vuelta**  round-trip [return BE]
**la iglesia**  church
**el impermeable**  raincoat
**impresionante**  stunning
**imprimir**  *v* print
**el impuesto**  duty (tax)
**incluir**  *v* include
**inconsciente**  unconscious
**increíble**  amazing
**la infección vaginal**  vaginal infection
**infectado**  infected

**el inglés** English
**iniciar sesión** v log on (computer)
**el inodoro químico** chemical
  toilet
**el insecto** bug
**la insolación** sunstroke
**el insomnio** insomnia
**la insulina** insulin
**interesante** interesting
**internacional** international
  (airport area)
**la internet** internet
**el/la intérprete** interpreter
**el intestino** intestine
**introducir** v insert
**ir a** v go (somewhere)
**ir de compras** v go shopping
**Irlanda** Ireland
**irlandés** Irish
**el IVA** sales tax [VAT BE]
**la izquierda** left (direction)

## J

**el jabón** soap
**el jardín botánico** botanical
  garden
**la jarra** carafe
**el jazz** jazz
**el jersey** sweater
**joven** young
**las joyas** jewelry
**la joyería** jeweler
**jubilado** retired

**jugar** v play
**el juguete** toy

## K

**el kilo** kilo; **~gramo** kilogram;
  **~metraje** mileage
**el kilómetro** kilometer;
  **~ cuadrado** square kilometer

## L

**el labio** lip
**la laca** hairspray
**el ladrón** thief
**el lago** lake
**la lana** wool
**la lancha motora** motor boat
**largo** long
**el lavabo** sink
**la lavadora** washing machine
**la lavandería** laundromat
  [launderette BE]
**lavar** v wash
**lavar la ropa** laundry
**el lavavajillas** dishwasher
**la lección** lesson
**lejos** far
**la lengua** tongue
**la lente** lens
**los lentes de contacto** contact
  lenses
**las letras** arts
**las libras esterlinas** pounds
  (British sterling)

**libre de impuestos** duty-free
**la librería** bookstore
**el libro** book
**la lima de uñas** nail file
**limpiar** *v* clean
**la limpieza de cutis** facial
**limpio** *adj* clean
**la línea** line (train)
**el lino** linen
**la linterna** flashlight
**el líquido** liquid; **~ de lentes de contacto** contact lens solution; **~ lavavajillas** dishwashing liquid
**listo** ready
**la litera** berth
**el litro** liter
**la llamada** *n* call; **~ de teléfono** phone call; **~ despertador** wake-up call
**llamar** *v* call
**la llave** key; **~ de habitación** room key; **~ electrónica** key card
**el llavero** key ring
**las llegadas** arrivals (airport)
**llegar** *v* arrive
**llenar** *v* fill
**llevar** *v* take; **~ en auto** lift (to give a ride)
**la lluvia** rain
**lluvioso** rainy
**lo siento** sorry
**localizar** *v* reach
**la loción para después de**

**afeitar** aftershave
**la luz** light (overhead)

## M

**la madre** mother
**magnífico** magnificent
**el malestar estomacal** upset stomach
**la maleta** bag, suitcase
**la mandíbula** jaw
**las mangas cortas** short sleeves
**las mangas largas** long sleeves
**la manicura** manicure
**la mano** hand
**la manta** blanket
**mañana** tomorrow; **la ~** morning
**el mapa** map; **~ de carreteras** road map; **~ de ciudad** town map; **~ de la pista** trail [piste BE] map
**el mar** sea
**marcar** *v* dial
**mareado** dizzy
**el mareo** motion [travel BE] sickness
**el marido** husband
**marrón** brown
**el martillo** hammer
**más** more; **~ alto** louder; **~ bajo** lower; **~ barato** cheaper; **~ despacio** slower; **~ grande** larger; **~ pequeño** smaller; **~ rápido** faster; **~ tarde** later; **~**

**temprano** earlier
**el masaje** massage;
~ **deportivo** sports massage
**el mástil** tent pole
**el mecánico** mechanic
**la media hora** half hour
**mediano** medium (size)
**la medianoche** midnight
**el medicamento** medicine
**el médico** doctor
**medio** half; ~ **kilo** half-kilo;
~**día** noon [midday BE]
**medir** v measure (someone)
**mejor** best
**menos** less
**el mensaje** message;
~ **instantáneo** instant message
**el mercado** market
**el mes** month
**la mesa** table
**el metro** subway [underground BE]
**el metro cuadrado** square meter
**la mezquita** mosque
**el microondas** microwave
**el minibar** mini-bar
**el minuto** minute
**el mirador** overlook [viewpoint BE]
(scenic place)
**mirar** v look
**la misa** mass (church service)
**mismo** same
**los mocasines** loafers
**la mochila** backpack

**molestar** v bother
**la moneda** coin, currency
**la montaña** mountain
**el monumento conmemorativo**
memorial (place)
**morado** purple
**el mostrador de información**
**information** desk
**mostrar** v display
**la moto acuática** jet ski
**la motocicleta** motorcycle
**movilidad** mobility
**la mujer** wife, woman
**la multa** fine (fee for breaking law)
**la municipalidad** town hall
**la muñeca** doll; ~ **wrist**
**el músculo** muscle
**el museo** museum
**la música** music; ~ **clásica**
classical music; ~ **folk** folk music;
~ **pop** pop music
**el muslo** thigh

# N

**nacional** domestic
**la nacionalidad** nationality
**nada** nothing
**nadar** v swim
**las nalgas** buttocks
**naranja** orange (color, fruit)
**la nariz** nose
**necesitar** v need
**los negocios** business

**negro** black
**nevado** snowy
**la nevera** refrigerator
**el nieto** grandchild
**la niña** girl
**la niñera** babysitter
**el niño** boy, child
**el nivel intermedio** intermediate
**no** no
**la noche** evening, night
**el nombre** name;
  **~ de usuario** username
**normal** regular
**las normas de vestuario** dress
  code
**el norte** north
**la novia** girlfriend
**el novio** boyfriend
**el número** number; **~ de fax**
  fax number; **~ de permiso**
  **de conducir** driver's license
  number; **~ de teléfono** phone
  number; **~ de teléfono de**
  **información** information (phone)

## O

**la obra de teatro** n play (theater)
**el oculista** optician
**el oeste** west
**la oficina** office; **~ de correos**
  post office; **~ de objetos**
  **perdidos** lost and found; **~ de**
  **turismo** tourist information office

**el ojo** eye
**la olla** pot
**la ópera** opera
**la oreja** ear
**la orlna** urine
**el oro** gold; **~ amarillo** yellow
  gold; **~ blanco** white gold
**la orquesta** orchestra
**oscuro** dark
**el otro camino** alternate route
**la oxígenoterapia** oxygen
  treatment

## P

**padecer del corazón** heart
  condition
**el padre** father
**pagar** v pay
**el pájaro** bird
**el palacio** palace; **~ de las**
  **cortes** parliament building
**los palillos chinos** chopsticks
**la panadería** bakery
**los pantalones** pants [trousers BE];
  **~ cortos** shorts
**las pantuflas** slippers
**el pañal** diaper [nappy BE]
**el pañuelo de papel** tissue
**el papel** paper; **~ de**
  **aluminio** aluminum [kitchen BE]
  foil; **~ de cocina** paper towel;
  **~ higiénico** toilet paper
**el paquete** package

**para** for; **~ llevar** to go [take away BE]; **~ no fumadores** non-smoking

**el paracetamol** acetaminophen [paracetamol BE]

**la parada** *n* stop; **~ de autobús** bus stop

**el paraguas** umbrella

**pararse** *v* stop

**el párking** parking garage

**el parque** playpen; **~** park; **~ de atracciones** amusement park

**el partido** game; **~ de fútbol** soccer [football BE]; **~ de voleibol** volleyball game

**el pasajero** passenger; **~ con billete** ticketed passenger

**el pasaporte** passport

**el pase de acceso a los remontes** lift pass

**el pasillo** aisle

**la pasta de dientes** toothpaste

**la pastelería** pastry shop

**el patio de recreo** playground

**el peatón** pedestrian

**el pecho** chest (body part)

**el pediatra** pediatrician

**la pedicura** pedicure

**pedir** *v* order

**el peinado** hairstyle

**el peine** comb

**la película** movie

**peligroso** dangerous

**el pelo** hair

**el peltre** pewter

**la peluquería de caballeros** barber

**la peluquería** hair salon

**los pendientes** earrings

**el pene** penis

**la penicilina** penicillin

**la pensión** bed and breakfast

**pequeño** small

**perder** *v* lose (something)

**perdido** lost

**el perfume** perfume

**el periódico** newspaper

**la perla** pearl

**permitir** *v* allow, permit

**el perro guía** guide dog

**la persona con discapacidad visual** visually impaired person

**la picadura de insecto** insect bite

**picante** spicy

**picar** *v* stamp (a ticket)

**el pie** foot

**la piel** skin

**la pierna** leg

**la pieza** part (for car)

**los pijamas** pajamas

**la pila** battery

**la píldora** pill (birth control)

**la piscina** pool; **~ cubierta** indoor pool; **~** exterior outdoor pool; **~ infantil** kiddie [paddling BE] pool

**la pista** trail [piste BE]

**la pizzería** pizzeria
**el placer** pleasure
**la plancha** *n* iron (clothes)
**planchar** *v* iron
**la planta** floor [storey BE];
  **~ baja** ground floor
**la plata** silver;
  **~ esterlina** sterling silver
**el platino** platinum
**el plato** dish (kitchen);
  **~ principal** main course
**la playa** beach
**la plaza** town square
**la policía** police
**la pomada** cream (ointment)
**ponerse en contacto con** *v*
  contact
**por** for; ~ per; **~ día** per day;
  **~ favor** please; **~ hora** per hour;
  **~ la noche** overnight; **~ noche**
  per night; **~ semana** per week
**el postre** dessert
**el precio** price
**precioso** beautiful
**el prefijo** area code
**la pregunta** question
**presentar** *v* introduce
**el preservativo** condom
**la primera clase** first class
**primero** first
**los principales sitios de interés**
  main attraction
**principiante** beginner, novice (skill

level)
**la prioridad de paso** right of way
**la prisa** rush
**el probador** fitting room
**probar** *v* taste
**el problema** problem
**el producto** good;
  **~ de limpieza** cleaning product
**programar** *v* schedule
**prohibir** *v* prohibit
**el pronóstico** forecast
**pronunciar** *v* pronounce
**el protector solar** sunscreen
**provisional** temporary
**próximo** next
**el público** public
**el pueblo** village
**el puente** bridge
**la puerta** gate (airport); ~ door;
  **~ de incendios** fire door
**el pulmón** lung
**la pulsera** bracelet
**el puro** cigar

## Q

**qué** what (question)
**quedar bien** *v* fit (clothing)
**quedarse** *v* stay
**la queja** complaint
**la quemadura solar** sunburn
**querer** *v* love (someone)
**quién** who (question)
**el quiosco** newsstand

# R

**la ración** portion; **~ para niños** children's portion
**la rampa para silla de ruedas** wheelchair ramp
**el rap** rap (music)
**rápido** express, fast
**la raqueta** racket (sports); **~ de nieve** snowshoe
**la reacción alérgica** allergic reaction
**recargar** v recharge
**la recepción** reception
**la receta** prescription
**recetar** v prescribe
**rechazar** v decline (credit card)
**recibir** v receive
**el recibo** receipt
**reciclar** recycle
**el reclamo de equipaje** baggage claim
**recoger** v pick up (something)
**la recomendación** recommendation
**recomendar** v recommend
**el recorrido** tour; **~ en autobús** bus tour; **~ turístico** sightseeing tour
**recto** straight
**el recuerdo** souvenir
**el regalo** gift
la región region
**el registro** check-in (hotel);

**~ del coche** vehicle registration
**la regla** period (menstrual)
**el Reino Unido** United Kingdom (U.K.)
**la relación** relationship
**rellenar** v fill out (form)
**el reloj** watch; **~ de pared** wall clock
**el remolque** trailer
**reparar** v fix (repair)
**el repelente de insectos** insect repellent
**repetir** v repeat
**la resaca** hangover
**la reserva** reservation; **~ natural** nature preserve
**reservar** v reserve
**el/la residente de la UE** EU resident
**respirar** v breathe
**el restaurante** restaurant
**retirar** v withdraw; **~ fondos** withdrawal (bank)
**retrasarse** v delay
**la reunión** meeting
**revelar** v develop (film)
**revisar** v check (on something)
**la revista** magazine
**el riñón** kidney (body part)
**el río** river
**robado** stolen
**robar** v steal
**el robo** theft

**la rodilla** knee
**rojo** red
**romántico** romantic
**romper** v break
**la ropa** clothing;
**~ interior** underwear
**rosa** pink
**roto** broken
**el rubgy** rugby
**la rueda** tire [tyre BE];
**~ pinchada** flat tire [tyre BE]
**las ruinas** ruins
**la ruta** route; **~ de
senderismo** walking route

**S**

**la sábana** sheet
**el sacacorchos** corkscrew
**el saco de dormir** sleeping bag
**la sala** room; **~ de conciertos**
concert hall; **~ de espera** waiting
room; **~ de reuniones** meeting
room
**la salida** check-out (hotel)
**la salida** n exit; **~ de
urgencia** emergency exit
**las salidas** departures (airport)
**salir** v exit, leave
**el salón** room; **~ de
congresos** convention hall;
**~ de juegos recreativos** arcade;
**~ de manicura** nail salon
**¡Salud!** Cheers!

**la salud** health
**las sandalias** sandals
**sangrar** v bleed
**la sangre** blood
**el santuario** shrine
**la sartén** frying pan
**la sauna** sauna
**el secador de pelo** hair dryer
**la secreción** discharge (bodily fluid)
**la seda** silk
**sediento** thirsty
**la seguridad** security
**el seguro** insurance
**seguro** safe (protected)
**el sello** n stamp (postage)
**el semáforo** traffic light
**la semana** week
**semanal** weekly
**el seminario** seminar
**el sendero** trail; **~ para
bicicletas** bike route
**el seno** breast
**sentarse** v sit
**separado** separated (marriage)
**ser** v be
**serio** serious
**el servicio** restroom [toilet BE];
**~** service (in a restaurant);
**~ completo** full-service;
**~ de habitaciones** room
service; **~ inalámbrico a
internet** wireless internet
service; **~ de internet** internet

service; ~ **de lavandería** laundry
service; ~ **de limpieza de**
**habitaciones** housekeeping
service
la **servilleta** napkin
**sí** yes
el **sida** AIDS
la **silla** chair; ~ **para niños** child
seat; ~ **de ruedas** wheelchair;
~ **alta** highchair
el **símbolo** symbol (keyboard)
**sin** without; ~ **alcohol** non-
alcoholic; ~ **grasa** fat free;
~ **receta** over the counter
(medication)
la **sinagoga** synagogue
el **sitio de interés** attraction
(place)
el **sobre** envelope
el **socorrista** lifeguard
el **sol** sun
**solamente** only
**soleado** sunny
**solo** alone
**soltero** single (marriage)
el **sombrero** hat
la **somnolencia** drowsiness
**sordo** deaf
**soso** bland
el **subtítulo** subtitle
**sucio** dirty
la **sudadera** sweatshirt
el **suelo** floor

el **sujetador** bra
**súper** super (fuel)
**superior** upper
el **supermercado** grocery store,
supermarket
la **supervisión** supervision
el **sur** south
el **surfista** windsurfer

**T**

la **tabla** board; ~ **de snowboard**
snowboard; ~ **de surf** surfboard
la **tableta** tablet (medicine)
la **talla** size; ~ **grande** plus size;
~ **pequeña** petite size
el **taller** garage (repair)
el **talón de equipaje** luggage
[baggage BE] ticket
el **tampón** tampon
**tarde** late (time)
la **tarde** afternoon
la **tarjeta** card; ~ **de cajero**
**automático** ATM card;
~ **de crédito** credit card;
~ **de débito** debit card;
~ **de embarque** boarding pass;
~ **internacional de estudiante**
international student card; ~ **de**
**memoria** memory card; ~ **de**
**negocios** business card; ~ **postal**
postcard; ~ **de seguro** insurance
card; ~ **de socio** membership
card; ~ **telefónica** phone card

**la tasa** fee
**el taxi** taxi
**la taza** cup; **~ medidora** measuring cup
el teatro theater; **~ de la ópera** opera house
**la tela impermeable** groundcloth [groundsheet BE]
**el teleférico** cable car
**el teléfono** telephone; **~ móvil** cell [mobile BE] phone; **~ público** pay phone
**la telesilla** chair lift
**el telesquí** ski/drag lift
**la televisión** TV
**el templo** temple (religious)
**temprano** early
**el tenedor** fork
**tener** v have; **~ dolor** v hurt (have pain); **~ náuseas** v be nauseous
**el tenis** tennis
**la tensión arterial** blood pressure
**la terminal** terminal (airport)
**terminar** v end
**la terracota** terracotta
**terrible** terrible
**el texto** n text (message)
**el tiempo** time; **~** weather
**la tienda** store; **~ de alimentos naturales** health food store; **~ de antigüedades** antique store; **~ de bebidas alcohólicas**

liquor store [off-licence BE]; **~ de campaña** tent; **~ de deportes** sporting goods store; **~ de fotografía** camera store; **~ de juguetes** toy store; **~ de música** music store; **~ de recuerdos** souvenir store; **~ de regalos** gift shop; **~ de ropa** clothing store
**las tijeras** scissors
**la tintorería** dry cleaner
**el tipo de cambio** exchange rate
**tirar** v pull (door sign)
**la toalla** towel
**la toalla higiénica** sanitary napkin [pad BE]
**la toallita** baby wipe
**el tobillo** ankle
**el torneo de golf** golf tournament
**la torre** tower
**la tos** n cough
**toser** v cough
**el total** total (amount)
**trabajar** v work
**tradicional** traditional
**traducir** v translate
**traer** v bring
**tragar** v swallow
**el traje** suit
**el traje de baño** swimsuit
**tranquilo** quiet
**el trapeador** mop

**el tren** train; **~ rápido** express train
**triste** sad
**el trozo** piece
**la tumbona** deck chair
**el turista** tourist

## U

**último** last
**la universidad** university
**uno** one
**la uña** nail; **~ del dedo** fingernail; **~ del pie** toenail
**urgente** urgent
**usar** v use

## V

**las vacaciones** vacation [holiday BE]
**vaciar** v empty
**la vacuna** vaccination
**la vagina** vagina
**la validez** validity
**valioso** valuable
**el valle** valley
**el valor** value
**los vaqueros** jeans
**el vaso** glass (drinking)
**vegetariano** vegetarian
**la vejiga** bladder
**vender** v sell
**el veneno** poison
**venir** v come

**la ventana** window
**el ventilador** fan (appliance)
**ver** v see
**verde** green
**el vestido** dress (piece of clothing)
**el viaje** trip
**el vidrio** glass (material)
**viejo** old
**el viñedo** vineyard
**la violación** n rape
**violar** v rape
**la visa** visa (passport document)
**visitar** v visit
**la vitamina** vitamin
**la vitrina** display case
**viudo** widowed
**vivir** v live
**vomitar** v vomit
**el vuelo** flight; **~ internacional** international flight; **~ nacional** domestic flight

## Z

**la zapatería** shoe store
**las zapatillas** sneakers
**los zapatos** shoes
**la zona** area; **~ de compras** shopping area; **~ de fumadores** smoking area; **~ para picnic** picnic area
**el zoológico** zoo
**zurcir** v mend